TRUE

ALSO BY **KOSTYA KENNEDY**

Lasting Impact: One Team, One Season.
 What Happens When Our Sons Play Football

Pete Rose: An American Dilemma

56: Joe DiMaggio and the Last Magic Number in Sports

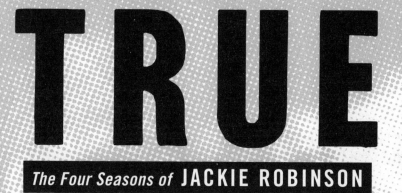

TRUE

The Four Seasons of JACKIE ROBINSON

KOSTYA KENNEDY

ST. MARTIN'S PRESS ≋ NEW YORK

First published in the United States by St. Martin's Press, an imprint of St. Martin's Publishing Group

www.stmartins.com

Designed by Jonathan Bennett

Interior Photographs: Spring (Courtesy of William J. Fitzpatrick); Summer (AP Photo/stf); Autumn (George Silk, The LIFE Picture Collection/Shutterstock .com); Winter (GRANGER—Historical Picture Archive); Afterlife (Courtesy of Kostya Kennedy)

A portion of "Foundation" appeared in *Sports Illustrated*.

Library of Congress Cataloging-in-Publication Data

Names: Kennedy, Kostya, author.
Title: True : the four seasons of Jackie Robinson / Kostya Kennedy.
Description: First edition. | New York : St. Martin's Press, 2022. |
    Includes bibliographical references and index.
Identifiers: LCCN 2021057160 | ISBN 9781250274045 (hardcover) |
    ISBN 9781250274052 (ebook)
Subjects: LCSH: Robinson, Jackie, 1919–1972. | Baseball players—United
    States—Biography. | African American baseball players—Biography. |
    African Americans—Social conditions—20th century. | African
    Americans—Civil rights—History—20th century. | United States—Race
    relations—History—20th century.
Classification: LCC GV865.R6 K46 2022 | DDC 796.357092
    [B]—dc23/eng/20211222
LC record available at https://lccn.loc.gov/2021057160

Our books may be purchased in bulk for promotional, educational, or business use. Please contact your local bookseller or the Macmillan Corporate and Premium Sales Department at 1-800-221-7945, extension 5442, or by email at MacmillanSpecialMarkets@macmillan.com.

First Edition: 2022

10   9   8   7   6   5   4   3   2   1

Amy. Sonya. Maya.

CONTENTS

Whatever the context and circumstances,
Jackie Robinson remained true—true to the effort and the mission,
true to his convictions and his contradictions.

PART ONE

SPRING

—

1946

STANCE

Back then, over the years of his career and after he retired, certain attention was paid to the way Jackie Robinson stood at the plate. His stance. He held his hands high, though not extravagantly so, and he gripped his bat all the way down at the end of its handle, his left pinkie wrapped loosely around the knob. He would wag the bat—34 inches, 35 ounces, of blond ash turned by hand in Louisville, Kentucky—straight up and down, a short range of motion on either side of a 45-degree angle to the earth. Robinson kept his arms back and away from his body, as if, perhaps, he were about to squeeze something waterlogged that might drip on him. He did not waggle his fingers or work his palms on the wood. His grip was firm and constant. He was a right-handed batter, and extremely dangerous.

Robinson kept his hips and backside taut and motionless when he was up at the plate, his left side turned just outward toward third base. He did not bend his knees, at least not to any measure perceptible to those watching him, nor did he crouch forward above the belt. He stood straight, and from instep to shoulder there emerged, as he settled in, a strong feeling of the implacable. Robinson was not quite rigid at the plate—there was too much warm flesh, too much life coursing through him for that. But he was solid standing there, exceptionally solid, and not likely to be moved. A sculpted pillar. Even in his first years of professional ball, at ages twenty-seven, twenty-eight, Robinson was thicker than you might have thought, a football player's cruel, purposeful body draped now in the thick, loose-fitting

3

flannel of his Dodger grays. He tended toward the back of the batter's box, duckfooted, his legs more than shoulder width apart and the whole of him ever so slightly crowding the plate. There was an intensity to every element of that stance, an energy—or what opposing pitchers might correctly have observed as a kind of directed menace.

It was a unique batting stance, of course, as all batting stances are. But it was not excessive in any of its particulars. Nor was it unusual in the way of some other batting stances. Stan Musial, for example, stood hunched over at the top of his back, his red Cardinals cap like the bloom of a rare narcissus. Ted Williams, despite his almost clinical manner in the box, proved curiously coiled. Joe DiMaggio stood quiet, poetic even. Willie Mays seemed to be scrambling around when he was up there, all anticipation, while the way that Yogi Berra rested his bat on his shoulder leant a languidness to it all. These were a few of the other great hitters in Robinson's time.

Yet Robinson's batting stance may have been the most notable and influential of them all. Throughout his career—early on, certainly, as well as later, even beyond his retirement—it became the most imitated baseball batting stance in the world. In those crucial years in the middle of the twentieth century, America—relieved, proud, posttraumatized—was moving headlong past World War II and at the same time trying to lurch forward, out of the grips of its worst and grimmest sin, to find a way to bend the arc of its own moral history toward justice. The experience of the war was material both to the appetite for change and the resistance to it.

And if the struggle for justice, for sanity, was centuries old in America—beginning with the unheeded cries of the earliest abolitionists and coursing through the Civil War—this was now a new movement, a new soon-to-be definable era. The purpose and intent with which Jackie Robinson played, and with which he and his wife, Rachel, lived, were inevitably, inextricably, and manifestly entwined with the fact that he was the *first*. The first in baseball, America's class-blurring milieu. He and Rachel began their journey before the modern civil rights movement found its full-throated voice. On the day that Robinson broke into the major leagues, Martin Luther King Jr. was eighteen years old and had yet to deliver his first sermon.

Robinson gave people, young people and children crucially among them, something physical to regard and emulate. God, he looked good up there. Confident, at ease. They mimicked his batting stance in Florida and Alabama and Georgia, and in California on the campus of UCLA, where Robinson had played college football, and they mimicked him on the streets of the boroughs of New York. Some had seen him in Brooklyn or in Daytona Beach or, as time went on, in any of the towns where Jackie and the Dodgers appeared on the road. Others did their best to co-opt the batting stance despite having only seen Robinson on a snippet of film or in a photograph—or not having seen him at all, but simply copying another child's rendition. It was one thing to emulate DiMaggio or Williams or later Mays, and another still to be up there, standing just so on a sandlot or stickball court, waiting for a schoolmate's pitch, and thinking, *Oh, what it would be like to be Jackie Robinson up at bat!*

There is one other aspect of Jackie's batting stance to consider, and for all the other elements, this is perhaps most important: the way that he looked out, from his squared, handsome, unyielding face, with its solid cheekbones and solid chin, and a jaw you couldn't miss. His left ear was prominent and unprotected in that time before baseball adopted the batting helmet and the earflap—both of which Robinson could have used. His cap, and his alone among the hundreds of players in the game, was fortified by a lining of thick cloth and fiberglass, a minimal defense against the pitches that came toward his head, thrown with intent.

Robinson's lips tended to purse as he awaited a pitch, his nose showed a crease in its bridge, and his eyes stared straight out with an uncompromising focus on the mound. His brows thick, his forehead furrowed. It was this very gaze—"the look that meant he was ready and all business," as his teammate Ralph Branca would say many years later—that Robinson fixed on a six-foot-four-inch left-handed minor leaguer, the Jersey City Giants' hard-throwing and square-jawed Warren Sandel, in the top of the first inning of an early afternoon game on April 18, 1946, the day Robinson, a rookie with the visiting Montreal Royals, officially began his soul-shifting, nation-bending baseball career.

MONTREAL

The land reaches northward off the base of the great continent and leans east into the North Atlantic, its shores protected here and again by outer islands, its modern shipyards secure, the whale-rich waters of the open ocean calming in the Gulf of St. Lawrence, and then once more in the inner bay, where the waves finally come up against the rocky, thick thumb of risen land—the Gaspé Peninsula.

The peninsula points toward the island of Newfoundland, on the far side of the gulf, and then beyond, many, many leagues away, in a direct line to the harbors of western France. It was on the Gaspé Peninsula, in the summer of 1534, that the explorer Jacques Cartier, having set sail weeks before from the port at Saint-Malo, came ashore with his men and planted a tall cross, staking a claim literally and figuratively to the land. They called the land the Country of Canadas, deriving this from the Iroquois name.

The earliest settlers—and those who came later, in the 1600s with Samuel de Champlain, and then those who came after that—built a new life over many decades. They fished for salmon and cod, hunted game, and grew barley and beans and squash. They baked white bread and planted kitchen gardens outside their wooden homes. They traveled the Saint Lawrence River and put up trading posts

along its banks. They weathered the bitter cold and the long winter nights and built canoes that traveled on ice, and they sought to
deliver their Christian god to the natives. By and large, the settlers
communed and coexisted—far more peaceably than did other settlers
of the New World—with the Aboriginal peoples who had lived there
for so many years.

In the 1700s the British arrived in earnest, and the French and the
British did urgent and bloody battle for property and solvency, particularly in the Seven Years' War and spectacularly in the battle of the
Plains of Abraham, at which the British prevailed. Eventually Britain
took all of Canada but, as a way to preserve some harmony for the life
ahead, carved out a region where much of the French way of law and
life and language and worship would continue, its heritage secure in
what was then, as now, known as the Province of Quebec.

The beating heart of this province, its most populous and dynamic
city, its cultural bellwether and economic pulse through the nine-
teenth century and into the twentieth, was first known as Hochelaga,
then renamed Ville-Marie, and finally—in accordance with the big
bountiful hill in its midst—Mont Royal. Montreal. The waterfronts
of the city thrived and expanded, and workers arrived, from Ireland
and Scotland especially, to build new bridges. It was here, in Montreal, that Quebec's first railway track was laid and the first tall buildings raised. The population swelled in the years before the Great War
and swelled again afterward, and in the 1920s visitors came north
to Montreal from the United States, briefly escaping Prohibition and
creating a suddenly fervent nightlife where the lonely found love, and
the misfits their kin, and the lights stayed on until dawn.

The Great Depression wounded and tempered the city, as it did all
North American cities, until the start of World War II. Long lines of
men queued for hours outside the Montreal armories, eager to enlist
with the Allies, even while others abstained. Overnight the city's fac-
tories began humming and churning and reconfiguring themselves,

employing thousands of workers to build rifles, tanks, and airplanes. Civilian pilots flew arms across the Atlantic to Britain. Montreal became Canada's arsenal, helping in great measure to aid the effort that would win the war.

The history of new people coming to Montreal, building new lives, and wanting to stay had by then created a varied and polyglot place. Immigrants had continued to arrive (and were arriving) from Britain and France, surely, but also from Hungary and Greece and Poland, and, in great numbers, from Italy. There were Catholic churches on these Montreal streets and Protestant churches on those, and synagogues here and there, and Black churches like the United Union Church, a pillar of prayer and togetherness. The people of Montreal spoke French primarily but English too (especially in matters of business and commerce), and what emerged was a world of living alongside one another. The mix of ethnicities and the distinct languages created divisions among the people even as they fostered shared perspectives as well.

It was into this city—specifically, the neighborhood of Villeray, solidly French but just a streetcar stop from the coalescing blocks of Little Italy, north of downtown and nearer to the narrow Prairies River than to the great Saint Lawrence, to a home on the Avenue de Gaspé—that in the springtime of 1946 Jackie Robinson and his buoyant, beautiful bride, Rachel, came to live.

Jackie had his baseball gloves with him (his bats were with the team) and a few pairs of good new shoes, and Rachel counted among her tasteful wardrobe the long ermine coat that Jackie had saved up for all through their engagement and given to her as a wedding gift two months before. The air was still cool when the Robinsons arrived in Montreal that early spring, cold at night, and thin ice clung to the edges of the rivers. Yellow-billed gulls wheeling above the water could be heard in the inner streets, and on the porches and side streets of Villeray, the plantings of bunchberry and trillium had not yet begun to bloom. For the Robinsons, there was something sweet and welcome about Montreal. The city imparted a freshness and warmth despite the first seasonal chill—and it offered the promise of a respite.

Their wedding in Los Angeles seemed so long ago, even if the fact of their marriage, their grounded new love and their extraordinary new circumstances, felt deliciously young and urgent. They'd been married on a late Sunday afternoon at a great and significant Black church, the People's Independent Church of Christ, just south of downtown Los Angeles, not far from where Rachel was raised and attended high school. As they stood at the altar, they were a dozen miles west of Pasadena, where Jackie had grown up on Pepper Street and gone to Pasadena Junior College. He did the long jump and played basketball, baseball, and football and in 1938 was named Junior College Player of the Year.

After that, Jackie attended UCLA, where he lettered in four sports—unheard of—reeling off kick returns on the football field that left defenders sprawled on the turf and earned him national headlines. On the basketball court, Jackie scored, winning Conference MVP, and in his Bruins singlet he soared, leading the NCAA with a 25-foot long jump. He would have been Olympic material (like his big brother Mack), if only the Olympics were being held. In Robinson's day, the UCLA athletics department scheduled track meets carefully, so that Jackie could have time to finish his leaps and then swiftly slip into his baseball cleats, pull on his cap, and make his bones on the ball field as a middle infielder with uncommon speed.

Rachel was a freshman on that Westwood campus in the fall of 1940 and Jackie a senior. She knew his name, as everyone did, and she formed her preconceptions, as anyone might. They met for the first time in the student union and began the tentative forays of courtship, walking side by side and then stopping together to talk in the parking lot, the bright California sun on the spires of Kerckhoff Hall behind them. He wore crisp white shirts, and he smiled without hesitation, and she recognized in him a surety and an edge—and a decorum besides. *She is lovely*, he thought each time they met, and he noticed with satisfaction how quickly her shyness fell away. Rachel looked right at Jack when they spoke, and she cocked her head when she disagreed. She projected directness and honesty and, most lastingly, a warmth that Jackie knew, even in that first year, he never wanted to be without.

The guys from the old Pepper Street Gang put on suits for the wedding, and they whooped Jackie's name as he came down the aisle. He wore a vest beneath his fitted jacket, and on his left breast a pocket square and a boutonnière. Rachel stood aglow in her old-satin ivory gown. A laced headdress. A long, sweeping train. Her photograph ran in the sports pages—a fetching close-up with her bouquet and the caption "Jackie's Choice"—and nearby a photograph of Jackie signing their marriage license. "A 'til death do us part contract," as one reporter put it. That picture, of Robinson on his wedding day with a pen in hand, echoed for all who saw it the photograph that had gone out a few months before, in late October of 1945, when Jackie signed up to play baseball for the Montreal Royals in the Brooklyn Dodgers farm system—an astonishing piece of history taking place, with the Royals president, Hector Racine, and the Dodgers' general manager, Branch Rickey, looking on. Five hundred newspapers must have run that picture, and hundreds of others reported on the news.

The wedding day, adorned with a traditional white cake and many stems of white gladioli, and then a reception back at Rachel's childhood home on Thirty-sixth Street—all under her mother's joyful watch—took place more than five years after their first, gentle small talk by the hood of Rachel's Ford. Theirs was a long unofficial and then official engagement. Jackie had left UCLA early, without graduating, while Rachel stayed on and earned her nursing degree. They'd stayed committed while Jackie served in the army, first at Fort Riley and then at Fort Hood. There, on an intrabase bus far from home, he had made a righteous stand, refusing to yield his seat—drawing not only ire and indignation but also a spurious court-martial before being clearly acquitted.[1] Along the way, Jackie and Rachel had weathered their own fears and mixed feelings—Rachel once returned her engagement ring to Jackie by mail—but found their way back to each other and to a renewal of their commitment. Throughout that time, the couple felt a continuing sense of anticipation and possibility. These were the years of World War II, and Jackie and Rachel were in their twenties.

After the army, Robinson played some Negro league ball for Kansas City, lighting up the ball field and riding those old backbreaking buses. That's where the Dodgers and Branch Rickey found him, and the momentous contract was signed. Jackie then went on to ride even older, more backbreaking buses, barnstorming in the winter months with a baseball team in Venezuela, honing his unpolished skills for the challenge before him. Rachel spent her own time far from home that winter, going to New York to work as a nurse at a hospital and as a hostess at a restaurant. By then she was peering into shop windows and saving money for her trousseau.

For years, the couple had been leading such active lives, taut against

---

1. On July 6, 1944, Robinson, knowing his rights by military law, ignored a bus driver's demand and stayed in his seat near the front of an army bus. Coincidentally, just ten days later, on July 16, Irene Morgan, a twenty-seven-year-old woman from Baltimore traveling on a Greyhound bus in Virginia, also refused an order to leave her seat. Morgan was arrested under state segregation law, but appealed her case, and eventually—with the legal help of the NAACP and cocounsel Thurgood Marshall—took it to the US Supreme Court. Two years later, on June 3, 1946, the court overturned Morgan's conviction and ruled Virginia's law unconstitutional. Segregation was now illegal on interstate travel. Yet it would be years before that law was properly enforced. In April of 1947 (the same month in which Robinson made his Brooklyn Dodgers debut), as an outgrowth of the Irene Morgan decision and part of a concerted two-week effort known as the Journey of Reconciliation, protesters sat in interracial pairs near the front of buses and traveled into the South. This direct action led to arrests and to protesters' being sentenced to chain gangs. The Journey of Reconciliation is viewed as a sharp precursor to the nation-changing Freedom Rides of 1961.

the pressures and opportunities in the worlds they were entering. But now, in their brief stretch as a married couple, the sharp reality of their circumstances and of Jackie's venture had come rushing in, taking them to places—physically, mentally, emotionally, spiritually—neither of them had ever imagined. In two months, they had already experienced so much together, even more than the distance of 2,900 miles between an altar in a familiar Los Angeles church and their new life with a professional baseball team in downtown Montreal would suggest.

They lived at number 8232 Avenue de Gaspé, occupying the second-floor apartment, a few steps up from the street. There was a short steel stairway railing painted black and a small concrete landing and an attractive outer wall built of mortared stone. Many houses on their block looked like this. The Robinsons had found the apartment on a list provided by the team, and Rachel first went to see it on her own. "I can handle this, Jack," she said that morning. They were staying in a rooming house downtown during that early time in Montreal, and Jackie had to get to practice that day.

How will I be welcomed? Rachel thought now, as she stood alone on the landing, about to press the bell. She prepared for the reaction: the door opening and the first momentary double take followed by a startled look, or a despairing look. The signs, as Rachel recognized them, of someone preparing to reject her for some reason other than the one it was. But the woman who came to the door showed Rachel around with this big smile on her face, proud of the place. *It's so well organized, so neatly kept*, Rachel thought, then said aloud. And when they sat down to tea, the landlady said that, if Rachel didn't mind, she'd like to leave her linens, glassware, and china for the Robinsons to use. Rachel went back to the apartment with Jackie after practice that very day, and they signed the lease.

It was a quiet street, lined with low trees, and as the weeks and months went on, children from other neighborhoods—Verdun, maybe, LaSalle—would walk up de Gaspé from Jarry Park, hoping to catch sight of Jackie or at least point to the house and say to one another: "There's where he lives." On game days, Jackie took the streetcar to the corner of Ontario and Delorimier, to Delorimier Stadium, or Delorimier Downs, as it was also called. Later Rachel would do the same and go sit in the stands, invariably teeming stands, full of high energy and general delight. The streetcars were crowded and, after all the heavy use they'd gotten during the war, often out for repairs, so sometimes Jackie or Rachel rode the bus instead.

The crowds at the stadium that season were large from the start, the fans alight with anticipation. The Royals had won the pennant in 1945 for the first time in ten years, and the team was again rich with promise. The International League operated the highest level of minor league ball, a last stop before Brooklyn, and Branch Rickey had spent the war years stocking talent throughout the Dodgers system. Now the war was over. There was money on the streets, and the Royals home opener was set for the first day of May.

The front office felt bullish, expecting seven thousand fans or more—which would have been very strong for a weekday and above average for Opening Day. There had been professional baseball in Montreal since the 1890s, more or less, so the Royals' budget setters had plenty of history to go on. Still, when predicting the crowd for this home opener against the Jersey City Giants, they made a gross miscalculation.

Sixteen thousand one hundred forty-four fans came into Delorimier Stadium that Wednesday afternoon. It was the largest Opening Day crowd since the day the park had opened, in 1928. The stands were full through the box seats near the infield and through much of the bench seating farther out as well. There were gamblers taking bets, and vendors selling pop, and people trading stories of the excuses they'd made for getting out of work—a funeral to attend or a fever to nurse. The mayor of Montreal, Camillien Houde, arrived to throw out the ceremonial first pitch, just as he had at that 1928 debut. Hundreds of servicemen sat among the crowd, and before the game, a military band struck up on the field. It must have been sixty degrees, with little more than an occasional breeze, when the Royals right-hander Bob Fontaine, himself just back in baseball after a long turn in the US Army Air Forces, stepped up onto the pitcher's mound to get the game under way. It was unusual—very, very unusual, the old-timers said that day—to see this kind of excitement at Delorimier Downs. Robinson was in the lineup, batting second and playing second base.

The crowd rose when he came to bat in the first inning and stayed standing as he drew a walk, and then a few batters later came round on a single by the big Montreal first baseman, Les Burge. It was the first Royals run of the season at the stadium. They rose again in the sixth, when Robinson pulled a single into left field. Between innings, Mayor Houde sought out Robinson, and they posed for a photograph. The happy fans saw Robinson start two double plays on that cloudless afternoon—Robinson to shortstop Stan Breard to Burge—and the Royals rolled out ahead and stayed there, winning 12–9.

The team was home for two straight weeks, and Robinson, it seemed, was in the middle of almost everything. A double and a stolen base to help beat the Giants again a couple of days later. Two hits in a game against the Newark Bears. Two more hits, a stolen base, and a run knocked in to lead a win over the Orioles. Robinson was hardly the only star. The center fielder Marvin "Rabbit" Rackley might have been the fastest player in the league; the left fielder Tommy Tatum kept driving in the runs that won the game; Les Burge clouted home runs over the right field fence; the third baseman Al Campanis won a game with a grand slam. And yet, "Robinson was the player we were there to see," recalls Mitzi Melnick. She was fifteen years old in 1946, and lived over by Mont Royal, maybe a half hour's travel to

Delorimier Downs. It was part of Melnick's general approach to life that spring that, whenever she could, she was going to find ways to slip out of Baron Byng High School a little early and take the streetcar to the game. On Ladies' Days, Mitzi and her friends got in free. "He got a standing ovation every time he got a hit," Melnick says. "He just brought such excitement, the way that he played. You would be watching him, and you would also be looking around and connecting with the other people there with you, like, 'Isn't this great.'"

Robinson was not so seasoned as his teammates, who had, to a man, played many more games of professional ball than he. Apart from college, Robinson had experienced only the freewheeling half season in the Negro American League and a stint in Venezuela. In the field, he would thrill the Montreal fans one day—a lunge to one side, a running catch into short right field—but would muff a simple ground ball or make a wild throw the next. He was at times out of position, or forgot to go into the outfield and take the relay throw for a play at home plate. Up at bat he could be out-crafted by a pitcher with a plan, and he often swung at pitches he wished he had not swung at. That season in Montreal, Robinson, at twenty-seven years old, was a marvelous young player, crash-learning the professional game.

Robinson was also raw as a base runner—although on this front, his skill was without peer in the league. He sent opposing teams "into fits of frenzy," a reporter noted of the way Robinson worked his leads off every base. "He can stop and start with unbelievable suddenness." On tag plays, Robinson eluded fielders in ways that took even umpires by surprise. During those opening weeks of the season, Lew Hayman, a founder of Montreal's new Big Four football club, the Alouettes, let it be known that come autumn, he'd like to hire Robinson to play for his team too.[2]

---

2. Robinson did not go on to play for the Alouettes, but Hayman and his cofounders, responding to Robinson's success and resonance in Montreal, were bent on bringing in a Black player. That player was Herb Trawick, a former lineman at Kentucky

By the end of that first home stand in Montreal, the Royals had won 9 of 10 games. They were leading the International League with a record of 16–8. Robinson, playing every day, was batting .326. He had stolen 13 bases and scored 26 runs, better than a run a game. He was, as he would later confide, still finding his way in the glare, in the day-after-day of it all, but he now knew without question that he could put on his glove and knot his cleats and really play with these guys. This league would not, on any merits of his ability, contain him.

Quickly there developed a new respect for Robinson from those within the game, and from those perhaps less predisposed to have it. Early on in this unprecedented athletic life, Robinson got glimpses of his power to impact thought through the manner in which, and the level at which, he played baseball. The Royals manager Clay Hopper had been born in 1902 in Porterville, Mississippi, by the border with Alabama, and in the off-season he sold cotton out of Greenwood, near the center of the state. He had been in professional baseball for twenty years, and during Royals spring training of 1946, Hopper said some things aloud that made his personal perspective clear. Surveying Robinson in the field early on, Hopper expressed surprise that Branch Rickey considered a Black person (although Hopper used a very different, abhorrent term) to be a human being. On another day, as a Black child scampered near a spring training field, Robinson overheard Hopper suggesting that the child would "make a nice mouthful for an alligator."

There's no telling what true changes might have then, or ever, occurred in Clay Hopper's breast, but as the season moved along and the fiber and caliber of Robinson as a ballplayer and a man swiftly became clear, Hopper began saying and doing other things. He told people that Robinson was the most effective base runner he had ever

---

State. Trawick would play 12 seasons for the Alouettes, including his rookie year of 1946, when Trawick was named an All-Star and the Alouettes, beginning in late September, played their home games at Delorimier Downs.

seen, and that he could drive the energy on the field as few players could. Hopper witnessed qualities in Robinson that he could not deny. In early April, in an exhibition game against Indianapolis, Paul Derringer, the old and contentious right-hander from Springfield, Kentucky, had thrown at Robinson not once but twice. After a pitch toward Robinson's head forced him, as Hopper would tell it, "to put his chin right in the dirt," Robinson stood up; assumed his batting stance; hung in there on a biting, inside curve; and ripped the ball on a blur past third base for a hit. A few innings later, Derringer again knocked down Robinson. He got up and tripled to deep left field.

Almost overnight Hopper became an ally. He complimented Robinson without prompting to peers and to opposing players. From the Montreal dugout, he called out encouragement to Robinson just as he did to the other Royals. And Hopper could be protective. At times when throngs of exhilirated well-meaning fans swarmed around Robinson after a game, confining him, Hopper would push through the crowd and escort Jackie away. Robinson was thankful for this. Whatever the motivations of Hopper's alliance, the alliance was firm. It had not taken the manager or any member of the Royals long to see what Robinson could do for the team.

By the middle of May, the tenor of Robinson's life as a Montreal Royal had been set. There were many months still to go, and little was certain—and each day brought new situations to meet and appreciate. There would, in the months ahead, be unforeseen challenges and delights. The season—and by extension the future, Jackie and Rachel felt—was full of promise.

Anticipation for Robinson's arrival had been bubbling since the day he signed, six months before the 1946 season started. Racine, the Royals president, had called on local newspaper and radio reporters to come to his office at Delorimier Downs for what he termed "the biggest baseball story to ever hit this town." And if the news had indeed been

wholly unexpected—the gathering of twenty-five pressmen expected
to hear that Montreal was getting a major league team, or perhaps
that Babe Ruth was coming to manage the Royals—the surprise was
embraced and Robinson immediately became a figure to follow. As a
headline in the local weekly, *Le Petit Journal*, put it (in translation): A
BASEBALL BOMBSHELL—ROYALS' SIGNING OF A BLACK PLAYER SPURS OVER-
WHELMING INTEREST THROUGHOUT NORTH AMERICA.

The article, and the many others in Canadian newspapers during
those days and weeks sifted the news through a particular sieve: *This
Black-and-white business is a big deal down in the United States. Here?
Not so much.* Racine, with Branch Rickey and Robinson beside him,
declared Montreal a bastion without racial prejudice, and Robinson
said that the Montreal club was "likely the only club where I might
have been given this chance." Yes, local observers agreed, the signing
of Robinson was daring and radical in the larger picture, and certainly
there was great excitement, even pride, that an athlete of high ped-
igree was coming to do something so historic under these northern
lights. But the core of the issue, the details of which troubled small
minds in so many regions of the United States—that Black men and
white men would locker beside one another, and shower in the same
showers and take the field together, all within the scope of the sport
that more than any other represented America's vision of itself—
these kinds of details were not by and large troubling in the Province
of Quebec. There was little patience or purchase for such concerns. In
its essence, Robinson's signing raised in Montreal an earnest shrug, a
sense of moral satisfaction layered through the predominantly white
citizenry. *We don't care about that. We're good people here. We'll show
that to the world.*

Yet on the ground, there was a clear marginalization of Black
Montrealers, the small-in-numbers populace who lived for the most
part in particular areas of town, who stayed only in particular hotels or rooming houses, who found jobs in labor and service—porters

on the Canadian railways, red caps, bellhops, Sunday shoeshiners—who were excluded from the white-collar world. For Black people in Montreal, as the historian Dorothy Williams wrote, "issues of race and racism weighed heavily in the day-to-day reality."

You could clip a brand-new newspaper ad for a bookkeeper's job and go to the address in the listing the very same day and be told upon arrival that the job had suddenly been filled. You could answer a different notice the next morning and find upon arrival that *that* bookkeeper's job was also no longer available. Again and again and again, those doors would be closed.

"Aspiring to something higher, let alone to become a doctor or a lawyer or a professor at a college, required that you have an extraordinary vision for yourself, and an extraordinary drive," says Ivan Livingstone, who grew up in Verdun and was sixteen years old in 1946, and would go on to play professional football before becoming a chemistry teacher. In the 1940s, his father worked on the railroad. "Having a career much beyond the menial could seem unthinkable to many of us in the Black community," says Livingstone. "Barely an option."

And yet there were no back-of-the-bus mandates in Canada, no "us 'n' them" water fountains, no violent mobs. Next to the more divisive issues cleaving Montreal—specifically the at-times unhappy fault lines around language and religion—the Black-white divide was softer, not at all the fundamental rift found in America. The province was removed from its own swim in the swamp of slavery by nearly a century and a half, and was free from any statutory segregation. You could find Black folks and white folks shopping side by side in the cigar stores of Westmount, or hanging around outside the cafés along Saint Antoine, or greeting one another on evening walks just inland from the banks of the Lachine Canal. Racism existed, says another historian, Jack Jedwab, but "it wasn't quite activated in the same way."

Excitement and anticipation surrounded Robinson's arrival, and after he signed on to become a Royal, Montreal fans read and heard the objections that came from certain quarters of the United States—most particularly during the Royals preseason exhibition games in March of 1946. As the Montreal locals saw reports of the hate Robinson endured as a Black ballplayer in the American Deep South, many of them were beginning to learn about injustices they had not grasped with such immediacy or intimacy before.

BEFORE MONTREAL, FLORIDA

Those weeks in the South in early 1946 proved to be an education for the Robinsons as well. They left California at the end of February, newlyweds bound for an unfamiliar part of the world and into a context that had no precedent. Rachel was nervous, Jackie too. From the sharp unease of his white neighbors when he was a child in Pasadena to his teenage run-ins with police to the flat stares and hard refusals he was met with as a private and second lieutenant in the US Army, not to mention his experiences as a barnstorming athlete, Jackie more than Rachel had been acquainted with the indignities that America and the South could inflict. Still, neither was prepared for what would reveal itself in Florida that spring.

Jackie—born in the South, to the rich crops and hard, unfair labor that drove the way of life on the loamy soil of Grady County, Georgia, fifteen miles up from the Florida line—was the grandson of an enslaved man and the son of a sharecropper. His father left the family soon after Jackie was born. Jackie departed Georgia for good at sixteen months old, on a cross-country westbound train, with his elder siblings beside him, held in his mother's arms.

More than a quarter century later, Jackie and Rachel set out on a West–South journey to join the Royals at spring training in Daytona

Beach, Florida—a pilgrimage of a kind and a true tale that in later chronicling would take on the aura of legend.

In New Orleans, they were bumped from a connecting flight and then bumped again in Pensacola. In the Pensacola airport, for the first time in her life, Rachel saw a whites-only bathroom. She walked in and used it. Then she drank from a whites-only water fountain. When the next flight was ready to board, Jackie and Rachel were told there was no longer room for them on the plane. White passengers had been allowed on board to take the Robinsons' seats. Jackie, boiling inside, kept his outer cool.

The Robinsons spent the night in a squalid, segregated hotel with newspaper covering the bed. They ate the fried chicken that Jackie's mother, Mallie, had packed for them in a shoebox. *Prescient*, Rachel thought. *Mallie had an idea*. Rachel was wearing the ermine coat and a hat she'd bought in Harlem. Jackie had on a sport coat and, for much of the journey, a loosely knotted tie.

Jackie gathered their suitcases, and Rachel her leather handbag, and they boarded a bus for the final legs to Daytona Beach, a long ride over from Pensacola and then down from Jacksonville, along narrow roads, through potato fields and cotton fields and past the Twelve Mile Swamp and citrus groves. Rachel had never been ordered to the back of a bus before, as she and Jackie now were. The seats back there were hard benches and did not recline like the soft seats at the front of the bus. The benches and the area around them grew increasingly crowded as the bus ride went on. Black farm laborers came in from the fields and filled the aisle. Many had to stand.

And over the long hours, a process developed, organically and without specific direction, whereby bags and tools were corralled into corners, and bottoms scooched over to make space for others to squeeze in. Then folks who were sitting would stand for a while so that those who were standing could sit. On the back benches of that Greyhound bus, there emerged a coordinated, cooperative spirit, which allowed the Robinsons, in the words of Rachel, to recover and to stabilize. They would deal with stress by finding similar signs of hope. "That business on the bus made me feel good," Rachel would say. "I made a whole thing out of it."

Jackie slept when he could along the way. He had gone to watch organized baseball just a few times in his life, and only occasionally had he played in exhibition games against ballplayers from those leagues. He couldn't stop wondering how good the other guys who were trying to make the Royals would be, or what kind of stuff the pitchers would throw when he came to bat. He felt anxious about the limited baseball coaching and mentorship he had to draw on. Rachel, riding the southbound bus through the small towns and the long flat fields, would see Jackie twitch and jerk, and reach up toward his collarbone, rubbing his chest in his sleep. She herself stayed awake for nearly the entire trip.

They lived that month in the Daytona Beach home of Joe and Duff Harris (a local couple who had volunteered as hosts) in a tiny bedroom at the top of the stairs. They had been scheduled to spend a week in Sanford, Jackie training with the Royals on diamonds near the US naval air station, but after hardly a day, the team left Sanford suddenly, under threat that a white mob was fixing to drive Robinson away. Later in March, Dodger games in DeLand and in Jacksonville (where the stadium gates were padlocked) were canceled rather than allowed to proceed with Robinson on the team. On another day, a policeman escorted Robinson from the field. Some folks really didn't want Robinson there; others said they didn't want to cause any trouble. "I don't want to embarrass any team," said a Miami city official about the Royals potentially playing there. "But if they do come they can't play and that's flat."

In Miami, where the Giants sometimes played, Black fans were not allowed into the ballpark; in many Florida parks, they were permitted only to sit in Jim Crow stands far from home plate. Rachel attended games and scrimmages sometimes, at Kelly Field, where the Royals practiced, and at City Island Park, downtown, for games against the Dodgers, and at some of the other ballfields too. She was the only one of the ballplayers' wives who had been permitted (in her case, expressly invited) to join on the trip. The other players were not sleeping in a small bedroom in a local family's home, but rather lived in the Riviera Hotel, up along the Halifax River in Holly Hill. The hotel had a piano lounge and a golf course, and a boat dock that spanned more than three hundred feet.

At one Florida ballpark, on a weekend afternoon, Rachel arrived and saw so many Black families gathered outside to see the game, to see Jackie. Men wore soft-brimmed hats, thick ties, and overlarge suits. Women had on nice shoes and long dresses; children were held by the hand. *It's such an outing for them*, Rachel thought, *a lovely outing*. These fans were not allowed into the front entrance of the ballpark, could not go through the turnstiles as other fans did. Instead, they had to bend and squirm through a hole cut into the fence at the back of the diamond. And when the designated seating area filled to capacity, these fans sat on the ground, in the deepest parts of the outfield, to watch the game, prepared to scramble when a long ball came near. All of that while wearing their churchgoing clothes. Rachel could not bring herself to go into that particular ballpark to watch Jackie play that day. She stayed out in the parking lot and tried to get the play-by-play on the radio, and waited for the game to end so that she and Jackie could go on home.

In that little room at the Harrises', Jackie and Rachel played gin rummy and made love, and took refuge from the heat of the outside world. She massaged his sore right arm, which was badly strained by all the infield work and his own extra efforts to impress, and then wrapped it gently in cold compresses. They lay together and breathed in unison and called this their honeymoon, and when they talked about what was happening around them and what might happen next, they found their optimism steady and undiminished. At the breakfast table, Joe and Duff smiled and called them lovebirds.

In Daytona Beach, the games took place before big crowds. The segregated stands off right field were long bench rows made of wood and shaded by roofing from the afternoon sun. On arriving to the ballpark for the first workouts, Jackie sensed displeasure in some of the other ballplayers. *It's like they're suspicious*, he'd thought. The other players, like him, were vying for jobs among a field of contenders greatly swollen in number by the talent now back from the war. Never had Jackie been around so many white players, nor had he been among so many ballplayers competing against one another. "I have to make the Royals first," he said when reporters asked if he had his mind set on taking Pee Wee Reese's job on the Dodgers. So they asked next if it was Royals infielder Stan Breard, Montreal's most popular player, whom Robinson hoped to unseat. Reese had been a National League All-Star in 1942, his last season before the navy, and Breard, soft glove and major league arm, was the next-best shortstop in the Dodgers system. Jackie had played shortstop in the Negro leagues. "I mean to do the best I can," Robinson said to the reporters.

Soon, as the days of fielding drills and batting practice and shagging fly balls unfolded, Jackie felt the displeasure and suspicion begin to wane and felt instead a mood of warmth and good-naturedness. He and a few other Royals played pepper on the apron of grass behind home plate at Kelly Field. "So far it has been a real pleasure playing here with the fellows," Jackie wrote to a friend from back home, Ralph Norton, in the middle of March. Daylight came into the little bedroom through a narrow window, and there was a single chair and a small wooden table for letter writing. "I did not expect any trouble, but I also did not expect to be welcomed as I have." He had known Ralph Norton at Pasadena Junior College, and in his let-

ter Robinson recalled names of other old friends as well: "Glick, Van-
derweer, Shatford." He wrote how nice it might be to know what
those guys were up to, and he recalled happy memories of running
the football so powerfully out of the PJC backfield. There was a bit of
wistfulness in the way Robinson wrote, recalling a world and a time
that seemed almost weightless, that seemed safe. When Jackie was
not with Rachel that spring, he felt a keen sense of being out there all
alone. "I would appreciate hearing more from you," Jackie wrote to
Ralph Norton.

He did not hit much in the early days, fooled by the breaking stuff,
and he was troubled by the sore arm. He never threw that well anyway. The early notion that he might play shortstop was scrapped in
favor of second base and the shorter throw to first. A Royals infielder,
Lou Rochelli, worked with Robinson on judging the angle of the ball
off the bat and making the pivot on a double play. Robinson could
really dart and turn, and he had a way of spearing with his glove
those balls that were nearly out of reach. He stayed right with it when
a ground ball kicked hard off the dry and patchy grass of the infield.
"You okay?" asked Stan Breard after Robinson took a bad hop off
his cheek one day, and Jackie said he was fine. Not ready for the major leagues yet, Branch Rickey told reporters of Robinson. But just
you wait. Photos of Jackie on the basepaths, rounding a bag in stride,
made it into the New York papers.

From the first game at City Island Park, Black fans who had not
gone to see the Royals or Dodgers in previous years were in attendance before, during, and after every game, the Jim Crow stands
filled to capacity and beyond, the spectators highly tuned to what was
happening on the field. One Black reporter—and the Black reporters, too, were made to sit in the distant stands, away from the main—
wrote that each time a ground ball went toward Robinson, and each
time that Robinson dug in at the plate, the reporter would feel his
own heart in his throat. After Robinson did begin to hit that spring,

the faculty from Bethune-Cookman College, including the great social driver Mary McLeod Bethune herself, came over to the Harrises' house to celebrate.

The notion that there was a lot more at stake than his own career was becoming clearer to Robinson by the day. People were invested in him. When a scout from the Mexican League appeared at Kelly Field and offered Robinson $6,000 to abandon his barrier-breaking path and go instead to Mexico and play, Robinson declined. Mexican League scouts were all over Florida that year, trying to lure players in a failed gambit to stand up a world-class league. Rumors were that Ted Williams had been offered $300,000. "Even if you offered me that much, I would not come," Robinson told the scout from the Mexican League.

Standing inside the chalk on deck circle, swinging two bats, and preparing to stride toward the plate, Robinson could see and hear the many Black fans out in right field beginning to stir. There was shouting as he took his place at bat—"Come on, Robbie, sock a home run!"—and Jackie could feel himself become tense and overanxious. The old right-hander Curt Davis might be looking in at him from the mound, or the young, taller right-hander Hal Gregg. *Let's get a hit now, let's do something*, Robinson thought. *Some folks out here are really pulling for me.* And then after the at bat, especially if he had struck out or popped one weakly into the air, but even if he got on base, the physical effort lingered within him. *I must be swinging hard enough to break my back*, he thought.

He heard the voices of the fans and felt the way the Bethune-Cookman professors gripped his hand in the Harrises' front room and saw how the Black writers such as Wendell Smith and Sam Lacy wrote even his small moments large, and it was all a constant reminder to Robinson that something was expected of him, some act of leadership, some newsworthy achievement. At times, Robinson was torn between resenting people for having those expectations and loving them for the hope and possibility that they kept alive.

"If we make the club, it will be on our own merit," Robinson wrote in his letter to Ralph Norton. "If not it will be due to the fact that the many ballplayers Montreal has are better." Often when Jackie used the term *we* in letters and conversation, he meant himself and Rachel. But sometimes that spring, he meant himself and Johnny Wright, another Black baseball player whom the Dodgers had signed. The official announcement came four weeks before spring training began and did not generate anything close to the excitement and response that Robinson's signing had generated. The Dodgers, and Branch Rickey, expressed hope that bringing in Wright might provide comradeship for Robinson, another soul in the cauldron.

While it was true that Wright and Robinson at times endured similar heat—the potential presence of *both* of them is what led to some of the games being canceled and the city elders to wring their bigoted hands—and while they were sometimes paired together in headlines and newspaper stories, and while both were, of course, Black men and baseball players, and while each supported the other at every public turn, they were not at all alike in a human sense. Robinson did not think that Johnny Wright had the temperament to make it as a ballplayer under the circumstances and pressures they were facing. At times Wright seemed cowed by the insults that came from the dugout of the opposing team.

He stood just under six feet tall and weighed a wet sock north of 170 pounds, and his right arm was longer than his left. "Willowy" is the way that one writer characterized Johnny Wright. His fastball, some said, was as fast as Satchel Paige's, and he had a curveball that broke off a ledge. He was also working on a changeup, a pitch he had not needed to throw very often to achieve his success in baseball thus far, but one, it soon became apparent, that he was going to need now.

Wright was born in New Orleans, and he had lived there all his life. "I am a Southerner . . . so I know what is coming," he said before the start of spring training. When he left New Orleans for Daytona

Beach, his wife of nine years, Mildred, stayed behind with their daughter and son. They lived in the low, redbrick buildings of the Lafitte Housing Project, a mile off the Mississippi, and attended church at St. John the Baptist. The kids were at the elementary school, and Wright's parents lived over by Hollygrove. Before Johnny set out for Florida, the whole family posed together for photographs. Although Wright was twenty-nine, he and the Dodgers told everyone he was twenty-seven, just like Robinson.

Wright, compared with Robinson, was more practiced in the rhythms of the game. He had been playing baseball in earnest for many years, since the early 1930s, including for a cruelly comic novelty team called the Zulus, which played on stereotypes of tribal African men. He pitched for the Newark Eagles in the Negro National League, and then for the great Homestead Grays, alongside Cool Papa Bell and Josh Gibson and Buck Leonard. It was said that in 1943, Johnny Wright went 31–5 for the Grays, and then pitched two shutouts to help them win the Negro World Series. He also pitched very well during his time in the navy, and he held his own against a team of major leaguers in an exhibition game at Ebbets Field.

Like Robinson, Wright was not permitted to stay with the other ballplayers at the Riviera Hotel in Daytona Beach. He lived instead with another volunteer host, in a house not far from the Harrises'. In the mornings, Robinson and Wright would sometimes walk together in their flannel uniforms over to Kelly Field, which was, like their hosts' homes, in the Black part of town. The other Royals and the Dodgers came down by car or in a team bus. Occasionally the two men, shunted outside the social circles of the team, would take a meal together where they could, in a Black-run diner not far from the park. Another time, late in spring training, Robinson and Wright drove together to a Negro league game in Jacksonville, where in the locker room, both teams celebrated them for what they were trying to do in organized ball. But although they had in common the blunt pain of exclusion, for the most part, Robinson and Wright did not spend many hours together away from the park. After their time as teammates on the Royals in 1946, they did not continue a relationship or go on to see one another in later years.

Another thing that Johnny Wright was known for was having pretty good control. The statistics from that time are uncertain, but he was known for it, along with the speed and the curveball. At spring training with the Royals, though, Wright did *not* have good control. In one game, he walked four batters and hit another in a single inning. During a scrimmage against the Dodgers, he gave up 10 hits and 8 runs. Everyone knew that Happy Chandler, the commissioner of Major League Baseball, was in the stands watching Wright pitch in that game. "I just didn't have it," Wright said with a sigh. On days he wasn't pitching, Wright jogged the circumference of Kelly Field to try to get into better shape and take his mind off everything.

Mainly, as the Dodgers acknowledged, Johnny Wright had been signed and invited to spring training as a means of refracting even a few rays of the spotlight focused so directly on Jackie Robinson. It was understood—by Robinson and the reporters and Branch Rickey and Clay Hopper and the scout, Clyde Sukeforth, who was Rickey's lead on Robinson and other Black players—that this was Robinson's adventure, his case to crack and his journey into history, and that Johnny Wright, for all his talent and his record of success, was an auxiliary figure. He was, at best, a Robin to Jackie's Batman.

And yet—perhaps because of Wright's previous impressive accomplishments or because his failures in the spring were attributable in part to nervousness, which some believed would fade—some around the game advanced the idea that it might be Wright, and not Robinson, who had a better path toward sticking with Montreal and making it to the Dodgers. Robinson, too, had struggled in the early spring games, and the Brooklyn lineup was thick with infield talent ahead of him: along with Pee Wee Reese at shortstop, Eddie Stanky was a productive player and highly dependable at second base. Brooklyn's pitching staff, however, was not so highly regarded; one could more easily foresee an opening there.

In early April, after the Royals announced that both Robinson and Wright had made the team, and would travel north to start the season, there was similar talk. "Wright will do all right if he can get his control. He is a good pitcher and he knows how to pitch," said Jim Semler, the owner of the New York Black Yankees. "I don't know what to say about Robinson. I doubt that he will be able to hit the kind of pitching they'll be dishing up to him."

Semler made those observations during the last few days in Florida, a week to the day before the Royals were to open their International League season on a Thursday afternoon in New Jersey, against the Jersey City Giants.

From the batter's box at Roosevelt Stadium, looking east with the bright sun straight overhead, Robinson could see the clean, green outfield grass where, just a short while before, he had stood along with the rest of the Royals, and directly beside Johnny Wright, holding his cap to his chest for the playing of the national anthem. Beyond the outfield fence were empty fields and old lots, a few low warehouses and then the outline of taller buildings, the edges of downtown Jersey City. Behind the stadium, behind home plate, lay Newark Bay. You sometimes got a touch of salt in the air, and the pennants atop the bleachers moved lazily, whimsically, in what little wind there was. Sun soaked, yes, but the day was not quite warm, and the men in the stands wore topcoats over their jackets and ties. Tickets to the game had been heavily oversold, and the crowd swelled well beyond the stadium's capacity, to twenty-five thousand or more. People stood in the aisles and in the no-man's-land behind the seats and blew on their hands and flagged down the coffee vendors as they passed. The atmosphere was that of a major league game, not of the minors. Reporters crowded into the press seats, and photographers stood on the field, and bunting hung from the railings in honor of Opening Day.

It was the Thursday before Easter, Maundy Thursday, and Passover had begun two evenings before, and many schools in the area were closed for the week. "Wild-eyed fans of all hues and races and creeds" is how a writer from the *Pittsburgh Courier* described the crowd. This was an extraordinary moment at Roosevelt Stadium, as it would have been anywhere in the nation on that day. Black people and white people, Jews and Gentiles, craning forward to see, calling out now to the player at bat. Rachel had left her seat to walk through the crowd, a kind of nervous pacing. Robinson cut a figure at the plate, solid and fierce. There was one out in the bottom of the first inning, and there was nobody on base. "The hopes of 14 million Negroes" rested on him, said the writer from the *Courier*.

Robinson recognized the Jersey City pitcher, Warren Sandel— *From a pass-the-hat game in California, maybe?*—and, from his stance, he watched Sandel's angular face. Handsome. Amused. Sandel was known as a wiseacre, given to a laxity in temperament that, along with irregular command, may have kept him from making the big club. But he could throw. He was taller than Robinson by five inches, and nearly as broad, and his fastball popped. Sandel was born in St. Louis in 1921, and for the better part of the last five seasons, he had played ball out West, in the minors first and then in the Coast Guard. When, as Robinson prepared to hit, it was suggested to Sandel that he might take this opportunity to throw at him intentionally, as pitchers had done in the spring, Sandel wouldn't have it. "Not how I do things," Sandel said. "I'm going to try to get him out." The fans whistled and hollered. Sandel wound up and threw, and Jackie let the pitch go by. Ball one.

Robinson did not have great success his first time up, that historic first at bat. He was conscious of a fluttering in his stomach and a tightness in his throat. His knees had a rubbery quality, less than steady, and he felt more aware of the crowd than he would have liked. For five pitches, Robinson did not swing at all, and the count ran full. On the sixth pitch, he grounded the ball to shortstop, sharply enough that he was thrown out easily, with strides to spare. Sigh, clap, back to the dugout. The crowd cheered the moment, and Jackie looked for Rachel in the stands. *The ice is broken*, he thought, *whatever happens next*.

Later in the game, Robinson did have success, success at a level bordering on the absurd, success that he attributed most of all to luck and perhaps, he said, to a spiritual intervention. He had prayed particular prayers that morning before going out to the field.

For Robinson's second time at bat, in the third inning, there were two runners on base and nobody out, and Sandel was anticipating a bunt. Clay Hopper gave Robinson the sign to swing away. Sandel came with the hard one, letter high and not enough wrinkle, and Robinson swung and lined it on a long buzzing blur, 335 feet into the left field stands. Three-run homer. The crowd roared Jackie's whole way around the bases, and Hopper grinned widely and clapped Robinson's back as he rounded third, and George Shuba, who was next in the batting order, gripped Robinson's hand as he arrived at home plate.

The next time up, in the fourth inning, Robinson, seeing how the Jersey City third basemen was playing him so deep, did indeed bunt, leaving one right down the line and easily beating the throw. Later he came to bat again and lined a hard single into right field. And he came up for a final time and saw that the same third baseman, a very young player named Larry Miggins, was again playing too deep. So Robinson bunted for a hit once more. Twice that day, Robinson stole a base. And twice that day, upon reaching third base, he engaged in the kind of pitcher torment for which he would be renowned, showing the skill and the inclination that for Branch Rickey were central to Robinson's allure. In his very first professional game in a formerly whites-only league, Robinson took his long lead off third base, raced suddenly toward home plate, then stopped and darted back. The crowd was up and shouting. And the fluttering in Robinson's stomach had long since gone away.

Look at him! Look what he's doing! Voices called out of the stands. This was something entirely new. Robinson stutter-stepped and feinted and broke forward again as the pitcher went into his windup. And both times, the pitcher—first the right-hander Phillip Oates and then the right-hander Hub Andrews—saw Robinson's movement, stopped in mid-windup, and were called by the umpire for a balk, so that Robinson jogged home. He scored four times in the game, and Branch Rickey was delivered reports by phone at his Ebbets Field office. The Royals won 14–1.

The people poured out of the stands and surrounded Robinson before he could leave the field, all those children off from school swarming thickly around him, tugging on his shirt and his pants legs, hoping for an autograph or just to keep him in their midst. When at last he made it through the crowd, his jersey and cap askew, his face beaded with sweat, things weren't much calmer in the locker room. The press and the glad-handers were all about, and when Robinson entered the room, his teammates—George Shuba and Stan Breard and Herman Franks and redheaded Red Durrett and Tommy Tatum and Rabbit Rackley and Johnny Wright, still in the big blue warm-up jacket he had worn all day—congratulated him lustily and grasped his hand and brought him near. "That was the day the dam burst between me and my teammates," Robinson would say. "Northerners and southerners alike . . . they appreciated the way I had come through."

The reporters in the clubhouse pushed in around Robinson and shot questions at him as he undressed, and they followed him to the shower and called out questions even then, so that it took quite some time for Robinson to get his dress clothes on and his tie properly knotted. When he finally stepped out of Roosevelt Stadium, into the parking lot near the boats bobbing in Newark Bay, Rachel was there to greet him.

"You've had quite a day, little man," she said, and took hold of his arm. The streetlights had come on around them, and the sun was nearly down.

"The most significant sports story of the century" is how one reporter described that game in Jersey City. By this reckoning, Robinson and baseball had on that afternoon taken up "the cudgel of democracy." Newspapers across the nation, as well as in Canada, of course, in Montreal, carried the news and details of Robinson's debut. A photo of George Shuba shaking Robinson's hand as Robinson crossed home plate—a simple act drenched in symbolism—appeared on front pages and in sports sections everywhere. Shuba was twenty-one years old, out of Youngstown, Ohio, the youngest of ten children born to a mother badly beset with arthritis. He went to Holy Name from the age of six, and then to Youngstown's Chaney High. He hadn't really thought he was doing something worth remarking on by greeting Robinson at the plate in Jersey City. When a guy hit a home run, you put out your arm and shook his hand.

Shuba was quiet and gentle and solitary, afraid to fly in planes. He would go on to stick with the Dodgers for a few seasons in the 1950s, and then he turned back home to the Youngstown suburbs and took a job as a postal clerk, raising with his wife a boy and two girls. The family said a prayer from the old country before every evening meal. In that time, and all through the long later years of his life—up until the day he died, in 2014, at the age of eighty-nine—Shuba kept a framed print of the 1946 photograph of him shaking Jackie Robinson's hand on his living room wall.

News reports cheered Robinson's debut, some of them dissecting his performance as well as its significance. They discussed his muscle-bound shoulders and his extraordinary baserunning. A paper in

Hudson County, New York, put together a sequence of photographs showing how Robinson—all speed and derring-do—got on base and then came around to score, all without the ball ever leaving the infield. (Because of a printing mistake or ill-timed negligence—or the hand of a prankster, who is to say?—those photos were published upside down.) Stories in various sections of the newspaper called the day in Jersey City "historic," and the *Courier* ran this front-page headline: AMERICAN WAY TRIUMPHS IN ROBINSON EXPERIMENT. An aspirational thought delivered in all earnestness despite the fact that for sixteen score and seven years—since the August day in 1619 when the *White Lion* anchored with its human cargo at Point Comfort, in the Colony of Virginia, and right through to that current day in 1946—the American way was decidedly not defined by the sort of racial unity suggested by Robinson's debut.[3]

On Easter Sunday, for a doubleheader in Newark, twenty-five thousand people again turned out to see Robinson and the Royals (and, yes, the hometown Bears), a gathering that included some six thousand Black fans, fifteen times the number that might typically have attended. They arrived early, some straight from first sermons at church, and were milling outside by 10:00 a.m. Between games, they gathered again, beneath the stands and with white fans among them, and hollered for Jackie to come out from the Royals locker room until he did, signing autographs as the crowd pressed close. Someone had brought him a rabbit—an Easter bunny, as it were—for good luck.

---

3. Neither was more recent history quite conducive to the image of a nation aspiring to inclusivity. An enduring sports fable of the era just before and during World War II—that is, the time leading to Robinson's debut—revolves around the embarrassment, some said fury, that Adolf Hitler felt at the success of the Black US track star Jesse Owens, who won four gold medals at the 1936 Olympics in Berlin. (In one of Owens's events, the 200 meters, Robinson's older brother Mack took silver.) It has been pointed out, and with eloquence some years ago by Russell Baker of the *New York Times*, that in 1936, such embarrassment could not have been felt by the owners and officials of America's baseball establishment. That year, just as in the decades before and for a decade to come, they simply didn't let Black ballplayers play.

The crowds were smaller in Syracuse, the smallest city in the league, though there, too, a cadre of Black fans arrived, in a group organized and led by the Elks Lodge. They saw the Chiefs win two games, and they saw Robinson get hit on the hand by a pitch and then look out at the pitcher, Earl Harrist. There were words from the Syracuse dugout then, calls for Jackie to "Stop trying to hit the ball with your hand!" a tongue-in-cheek needling that drew a smile from Robinson himself and changed the tone from some of the other, much less congenial things that Syracuse players had been shouting. *Guys are getting on me pretty good*, said Robinson to himself before he'd settled into the box for that at bat. He held his chin high and gazed impassively into the noisy Syracuse dugout.

"I don't feel sorry for you," said the Chiefs catcher, Dick West, through his mask. "You can go to hell." West was born in Louisville, Kentucky, and Harrist came out of Dubach, Louisiana, a tiny country town, and both of them had spent time in the major leagues. Syracuse was an affiliate of the Cincinnati Reds. As far as intentionally hitting Robinson with a pitch, who knows? Harrist was a knuckleballer and had trouble with his control as a rule.

The fans stamped their feet in the stands as the game went on and clapped their gloved hands. The ground in the vast outfield at MacArthur Stadium was winter hard, and frost touched the railings and the tops of the dugouts. In Syracuse, Robinson and Johnny Wright stayed in the Onandaga Hotel, along with the rest of the Royals, out of the unseasonable cold and the sharp wind that blew in off the crizzled shores of Onandaga Lake and right through the center of town, conditions that canceled the last of the three scheduled games. We sure aren't in Florida anymore, the guys on the team agreed.

In Baltimore, the crowds were thick again, another twenty-five thousand out for a Sunday doubleheader, among them Frank "Shag" Shaughnessy, the president of the International League. Shag was afraid of what might happen in Baltimore, afraid that a riot of some kind might occur. He had called Branch Rickey beforehand and asked him to keep Robinson out of the lineup, leave him up north for a few days. It was not a request that Branch Rickey would honor. In the first of the two games in Baltimore that Sunday afternoon, Robinson scored the game-winner in the ninth inning.

There were men and women alive in Baltimore who'd heard eyewitness accounts of the bloodshed at the start of the Civil War, who could remember knowing people in Maryland who had kept slaves. For Robinson in the spring of 1946, there would be no sharing a hotel with the team in Baltimore—he's "staying with relatives" is how the papers put it—and from the stands there, he heard the worst of the words and felt the heat of real anger. The seating was segregated but you could hear the loudest chirps and threats from one section to the next. Rachel, for all her poise and stoicism even then at twenty-three, felt a shiver of fear. Tears came to her eyes, and she had the fleeting thought, *Maybe we should just quit.*

In the final game against the Orioles, Jackie was again hit by a pitch, and he trotted straight down to first base. He had a double and two singles in the game, a 10–0 win for Montreal. He stole a base and scored four runs. The Royals on that two-week season opener had won some games and lost some games, winding up at 6–6 overall, and Jackie batted .362. He had felt happiness at times and accomplishment and relief, though never did the sense of moment and uncertainty subside. The newness of the experiment surrounded Jackie and Rachel, and with it came the understanding and reality of Jackie's baseball life.

Earlier that year, on February 12, two days after Rachel and Jackie were married in Los Angeles, US Army Sergeant Isaac Woodard, a Black man newly discharged from military service, was beaten to the point of permanent blindness by white police officers in the town of Batesville, South Carolina. Two weeks later, around the time Rachel and Jackie were beginning their baseball journey in Florida, an incident involving a Black navy veteran and a white store clerk set off an extended riot in Columbia, Tennessee. Homes in the Black part of town were looted and fired into by white patrolmen, and scores of Black people were arrested; after an altercation, two of them were killed.

By April, news of the attack on Isaac Woodard had not yet emerged in the way it would be documented and take hold later that year. But you could read about the Columbia riots pretty much from the start. The executive secretary of the National Association for the Advancement of Colored People (NAACP), Walter White, was working on the case, as was the head of the association's Legal Defense Fund, Thurgood Marshall.

It was becoming clear that Black soldiers who had served in World War II—much like those who served in World War I—were being expressly targeted for violence and abuse. It may be, particularly in states riven by segregation, that bigots feared the implicit respect, a rise in status, being conferred on Black soldiers who had risked their lives in service.[4] The hypocrisy of the United States trumpeting a military victory over Nazism even while subjugating and committing violence against its own citizens was plain. "They fought by our side during the war and they merit the same opportunity to play baseball with us like they do all other sports," the Montreal Royals president Hector Racine had said upon the signing of Jackie Robinson.

The team left Baltimore in two cargo planes bound five hundred miles north for Montreal, twenty-two passengers each. They had awakened early for the morning flights, and on the plane, players dozed and read newspapers and played cards. Jackie and Rachel sat

---

4. The social justice pioneer Bryan Stevenson has said, "Historically, it was a provocation for Black men to wear the uniform, to claim that role." Stevenson is the founder of the Equal Justice Initiative and the author of the book *Just Mercy*. EJI's powerful and sobering 2017 report, "Lynching in America: Targeting Black Veterans," traces such murders back to the Civil War.

beside each other and spoke in quiet voices. The hostility of the Baltimore crowd and the hardness of the weeks down south still clung to Rachel.

Everyone held their breaths as the plane prepared to land, and applauded when it did. They passed through customs as a bloc, and got into buses that took them into the town. Johnny Wright thought he might put to use a little of the French he had picked up at home in New Orleans, Creole country. The trunks of equipment were delivered to Delorimier Downs, and Jackie and Rachel found a rooming house in the part of town deemed appropriate for them to stay. There were some issues with finding housing in the city just then, a by-product of the end of the war. But Jackie and Rachel would not be boarders for long. Soon they would be settling in to their apartment on a quiet, sunlit street, their home in Montreal on the Avenue de Gaspé.

MONTREAL, MIDSUMMER

It was 341 feet down the left field line and 440 to straightaway center field, and the wooden outfield fence was given over to ads for the Parc Belmont amusement park and British Consols cigarettes and Coca-Cola (sold in the stadium) and now, with postwar rationing still in effect but beginning to wind down, a lavish sales pitch for tins of Tendersweet Ham. The right field corner was just 293 feet from home—a plaything for the Royals' lefty sluggers. The old scoreboard rose above the fence, and then beyond the scoreboard stood the Knit to Fit factory, onto whose flat roof those lefty hitters like Les Burge and Red Durrett and George Shuba (before he got sent to Mobile) liked to try to hit the ball. It was summer now, and the weather better for hitting and the nights warm enough that the last of the tuques had been put away for the season. Most of the fans at Delorimier Downs spoke French as their first language, and the vendors swallowed their aitches as they worked the crowd: "'Ot dog! 'Ot dog! Get your 'ot dogs!" they shouted. And by the middle innings, "Ice cream! *Glacée!* Ice cream!"

Or you could eat before the game, hamburgers and extra-thin chips, perhaps, or scrambled eggs and a plate of poutine to share, right across Ontario Street at the Montreal Royals Restaurant, a diner of a kind. There was always a crowd there leading up to game time, a lot of activity by the restaurant's entranceway and a wait to order. But if you went earlier in the day, or on days when there was no game, the place was quieter. You might see a ballplayer inside at the counter with his coffee cup and the *Gazette*. This was a big, broad intersection, and on a corner opposite the stadium was a drugstore, where you could buy a liniment for your pitching shoulder that everyone said made your arm feel like new.

There weren't many cars on the road then, not for a few years yet. The streetcar cost seven cents and the bus a nickel, or you might find a live transfer on the ground somewhere and ride free. Bleacher seats for a Sunday doubleheader could be had for a quarter. "As soon as you got onto the streetcar going in that general direction, it felt like everyone was on their way to the stadium," says Mitzi Melnick. "Everybody was happy, and it was always noisy. A lot of talk, a lot of laughter. It was that time, you know? And if we were talking about the players, we were talking about Jackie Robinson."

They would step off in front of the stadium's brick façade and line up for tickets, and sometimes, if the sky was overcast, the floodlights on the stanchions around the park would already be on, the bright lights a sign of prosperity. The stadium had a tavern attached to it, as well as a roller-skating rink. A lot of the young people had good feelings about the place from going there with their skates and skate keys, on weekend nights, to hear the music and drink pop—or something stiffer—with a date. Sometimes a group of French boys and a group of Anglo boys circled each other, shouting, and took things outside.

On Royals game days, people arrived from all across the city, from the Plateau and Outremont, from Verdun and Little Burgundy. Griffintown. Mile End. Villeray. Westmount. They came from just off the island over the Cartier Bridge and from farther out, suburbs like Saint-Jean-sur-Richelieu. They traveled in family bunches sometimes, on an outing from Ottawa or Toronto, northern New York or Nashua, New Hampshire—a town where another minor league team, the Nashua Dodgers, was tearing it up in Class B with Roy Campanella at catcher and Don Newcombe on the hill. Yes, even from Nashua, nearly three hundred miles away, they descended on Delorimier Stadium. ("*Allez!* Let's make a trip of it to Montreal!") People drove in from Concord, Maine, and Montpelier, Vermont, and from any number of towns all over that upper band of New England, for a chance to see the Royals and Jackie Robinson. To that street corner and that stadium, that summer.

"For us that year, it was different. It *felt* different," says Ivan Livingstone, who was as good a high school athlete as Montreal had in those years. "As soon as you got near the park, you got the energy. There were not a lot of Black people in the stands, but we gained a level of respect. I remember people smiling at us, as if we were associated with Jackie, as if we had something to do with it! And the truth is, we kind of felt like we did have something to do with it. Like we were on the inside." The Royals were winning that summer, and never in their history had the team drawn so many fans.

On any given day, Robinson might steal home or hit a line drive that rolled to the center field wall—*he's off!* "People headed out to the park, expecting him to do something magnificent," says Chuck Este. "And we would wait for them to come back and tell us if he did. He was like our version of Maurice Richard. I was six years old that summer, and I remember it well. My father would come home off the railroad after working a trip to Western Canada. First thing, he'd take off that company hat and the clothes. Sometimes he'd have fresh sockeye salmon in a bag, and we'd have big gatherings with our neighbors. Folks were all still talking about the war. And I remember learning about Jackie Robinson that summer. He's the reason that I started playing baseball. He initiated the idea in me."

Years afterward, Este himself played at Delorimier Downs, as a teenage prospect. Once, with scouts in the house, he hit a ball off the face of the Knit to Fit factory. He would later sign a minor league contract with the Giants, and in 1959 was invited, along with other prospects, to spring training in Casa Grande, where he met Willie Mays. He and Mays spoke on the outfield grass. "Black ballplayers found each other," Este says. "Mays saw me and came over." And then, just like that, Este hurt his arm and saw that professional baseball was too big a hill to climb and went back home to live in Montreal.

After games sometimes, Jackie and Rachel ate dinner at home with Sam Maltin and his wife, Belle. Now and then, Rachel and Belle might meet downtown of an afternoon, go to Ogilvy and Eaton's, pick up a pair of pantyhose or cotton gloves, maybe have a sandwich in the restaurant. There was a fresh postwar energy downtown, more stock and variety on the shelves—not just in the department stores but also in the smaller shops. Everything seemed to be springing to life: the bookstores and the bakeries (for the first time in years of sugar rationing, icing was allowed on cakes), the boutiques and the sporting goods shops. At McNiece's by Central Station, the good golf clubs had come back in, and all kinds of baseball equipment, and newly sewn leather footballs like the ones the pros used in the Big Four. In the shoe stores, salesmen worked the window displays. At the newsstands, the comic books sold out.

Rachel loved to browse the downtown shops and then take the streetcar home, to the stop by Jarry Park. Construction sites rumbled in the neighborhood, and the smell of meat sauce came from the big pots in so many kitchens. She turned off Jarry and onto de Gaspé, and when the kids on the stoops saw Rachel coming, they ran up and took her shopping bags and walked beside her the rest of the way home, up the few stone steps, and delivered the bags inside. She was always happy to embrace this kindness and, after all the walking she'd done, happy as well to be relieved of her bags. Rachel was pregnant.

The women in the neighborhood offered her extra ration tickets for meat and stopped by with fresh-baked sugar pie and generally watched out for her. She was showing by the end of June, and as the season went on, Rachel was much less likely to go on the road with Jackie. By late in the season, she didn't go at all. The neighbors invited her to sit out on the back porches with them on warm summer evenings. (She only wished she knew more French!) Rachel, in turn, put out fruit in a bowl she set on a table at the back of the apartment, leaving the door open wide, with just the screen closed. When the kids who lived upstairs came down the outside staircase, they would see the bowl, Rachel's signal for them to come inside and take from the fruit that Rachel had bought and they had helped her carry home. There were six children or more in the upstairs apartment and not a lot of money in the family for extras. Rachel always believed that kindness should be reciprocated.

The locals felt an excitement with the Robinsons living among them, this handsome, unusual young couple from America. ("The *couple noir*," as Rachel picked up.) They had never known anyone like them. Some of the children asked, for reasons unclear, if the Robinsons were Dutch. It didn't matter if folks on the block were baseball fans or not; they knew they were part of something, a foot forward in progress. If it so happened that this man, Jackie Robinson, was an athlete who lifted the hometown baseball team to victory, who did wondrous things on the field and inspired headlines in *La Presse*, then *tant mieux*—so much the better. This was a special time.

For all the warmth and solicitude of the neighbors, the companion-ship of Sam and Belle, and the guidance of Wendell Smith, the Rob-insons were ultimately—in the deepest, most reflective sense—alone. The two of them. Jackie and Rachel were not privy to the flavor of the banter, the offhand intimacy, of their French-speaking neighbors. Nor were they ever fully sure that the nuances of their own words would be understood.

Johnny Wright was no longer with the team. His control problems, along with his unease, had persisted. The Royals sent him to the Class C team in Trois-Rivières, one hundred miles away, and upon doing so, announced the addition of Roy Partlow, a left-handed pitcher whom Branch Rickey had signed from the Negro leagues. Partlow had been the ace of the Philadelphia Stars in 1945, had pitched con-vincingly for the Homestead Grays before that, and, from the years of barnstorming, had filled his own ledger with major leaguers he had struck out. Partlow must have been thirty-four years old when he came to Montreal, maybe thirty-five.

If Jackie had found, in his association with Johnny Wright, moments of respite—the shared look or nod of understanding in the locker room after another one of those days—he did not connect even in this way with Partlow. Silent Roy, the writers called him. He seemed disen-gaged at times and given to sulk. Partlow was not nearly so deferential to the game and its institutions as Jackie was. By Jackie's lights, he did not seem to honor or embrace the daily mission. Partlow pitched well at times, but very badly at others, and soon—like Wright—he was sent up the river to Trois-Rivières. The Royals did not bring in anyone else from the Negro leagues that season. Jackie, the only Black player on the team, and in all the International League, was on his own.

"He was a competitor to his core, so the players were obliged to accept him," is what the Royals pitcher Jean-Pierre Roy would say of Jackie many years later. "In 1946 he made us win."

Teammates rallied around the way Jackie played and cheered him when he came in to score. They glared back or shouted fiercely in his defense when hateful words issued from other dugouts. Yet when Robinson was plainly spiked at second base, his calf or lower thigh gouged and bleeding, or when a pitcher came at Robinson with a straight fastball inexplicably far inside, that was Robinson's burden to bear alone. His recourse was invariably the same. One night, for example, Buffalo Bisons right-hander Art Houtteman hit Robinson with a pitch. In a later game against the Bisons, Robinson pointedly rattled pitcher Ted Gray with his movements on the basepaths and ultimately stole home plate.

On the road, even in the cities where Robinson stayed in the same hotel as his teammates, dining rooms could be problematic, the proprietors not quite refusing service but clearly dismayed. It was not uncommon for Robinson to take dinner in his room. "We all lived together once we got to the ball field," said the shortstop Al Campanis of that season's Royals. "But then we went apart."

Jackie and Rachel attended the United Union Church on Sunday mornings when they could. They went in through the wooden door by the pulpit, and the parishioners would catch sight of them—Jackie so fit, his upper arms taut beneath the sleeves of his suit; Rachel with her handbag held at the waist, a ruffle on her hat—and murmur to one another and follow them with their eyes. Occasionally during the service, Rev. Dr. Charles Este would allude to the Robinsons or mention Jackie by name.

"When they came, they would sit to the left of the Reverend Este," says Ivan Livingstone, who sang in the choir. "We knew that's where they would be. You looked over at them." The church was cool inside and contained within it the Negro Community Center, which had become more active and crowded since the end of the war. You could study French at the center or take a sewing class or see a film. There were dental appointments on the weekdays and a health clinic available for all ages. Kids went to kindergarten. The Boys' Club held meetings. Teenagers threw around a ball out back. The adult mixers on Saturday nights started at eight o'clock. The Sunday morning sermons began at eleven. "As a community, we wanted to be together," says Livingstone. "We found strength in one another."

In June, Jackie missed some games with a leg injury—a charley horse of some kind, a strain. Rumors resurfaced that his ankles were not sound, damaged during his football days, or that his pigeon-toed gait was beating on his feet. ("His only weakness is his dogs," said a scout.) Never before had Robinson played so many baseball games in such a compressed period as he did that spring and summer. Never had so much depended on his performance. A large drawing of Robinson finishing his swing appeared in the *Gazette*, with text all around it, hailing his high batting average and his style of play. THE COLORED COMET read the headline above.

The team trainer, Ernie Cook, worked ointment into Jackie's legs, and when Robinson joined the Montreal Canadiens (yes, the Rocket Richard–Toe Blake Montreal Canadiens, defending Stanley Cup champions), to visit the military hospital and sign autographs for wounded veterans, the great hockey players advised Jackie on how to help himself heal. The stiffness and pain did, with rest, soon begin to subside. Hopper expressed open relief when X-rays came back negative. After a little more than a week, Robinson was back in the Royals lineup.

Droves of Black fans continued to attend Royals games, in Buffalo and Rochester, and in Toronto, where a large group arrived in a caravan from Detroit. Jackie sent letters to Rachel from the road. "Don't worry," he wrote in one of them, "I'll give Jr. something to read about later in his life." At home, at Delorimier Downs, the noise rose from the stands the moment Jackie stepped out of the dugout and began to swing his bats on deck.

Rabbit Rackley, who batted in front of Jackie, said he liked to think the cheering was for him. In one game, the public address announcer

said that a fan had pledged to give twenty-five dollars to any Royals player who hit a home run. A few moments later, the announcer
added that if Robinson were the one to hit it, the fan would give fifty
dollars. All through the season, Jackie found comfort and relief in
the French-speaking announcer pronouncing his name: "I imagined
I wasn't Jackie Robinson at all," he said. "I wasn't the player of whom
so much was expected. I was Yakee Rob-een-sen, the new second
baseman of the Montreal Royals."

Later in the summer, with the Royals well out in front of the rest of
the league, Jackie missed time again. He was slumping a bit, and he
felt tired at the park. He often slept fitfully and did not always have
his typical appetite. "I think you have a nervous condition," Rachel
said to him. She said he should see a doctor, and Hopper agreed.

The doctor looked Jackie over and ran some simple tests. "Too
much tension," he said, and suggested that Robinson might be close
to a breakdown. "Take ten days off," the doctor said. "Play golf, relax.
Eat lunch. No baseball."

Rachel imagined they would use the time off to heal and recuper-
ate, as they had on certain afternoons and evenings at the Harrises'
in Daytona Beach. They could go on picnics and take gentle walks,
maybe over by Mont Royal. One could even ride an open streetcar
there, the Golden Chariot, looking out at the park, with its heavy-
limbed maples and tree-planted slopes, and rolling past the large old
houses and smaller brick residences along the street.

The Golden Chariot's route went up beyond Fletcher's Field, at the
foot of the mountain, where games and outings were held and where
Mitzi Melnick watched her older brother play soccer that summer, a
novelty then in Montreal. Fletcher's Field would come to be known
as Refugee Boulevard for all the Jewish immigrants who settled in
the surrounding streets after the war. A sizable gathering had come
for the soccer.

"And then we heard screaming out of the crowd, not far from

where we were," Melnick remembers. "A woman was pointing across to the other side. She started running right across the field and toward this man and screaming in her language. It was not English or French. I don't know what it was. Someone told us that she was screaming that the man was a Nazi guard she recognized from the concentration camp. The crowd understood her, and you had to see what happened to that guy—they just went after him, hard and angry. They were *on* him. I don't even know what could have happened to that guy that day." Though immigrating legally was not easy in that time, Canada was one of the places that people—Nazi soldiers as well as refugees—came to after the war.

Jackie did not last long in his doctor-prescribed hiatus. "He made it exactly one day," Rachel recalled. There were no picnics, no Golden Chariot rides. He tried to rest, but that first morning at home, he read about the Royals in the newspaper and he missed his teammates. He missed the game. He told Rachel that he wanted to be out there, protecting his lead in the race for the batting title so that no one could say he'd taken an easy way out. Jackie felt so relieved that the doctor had not diagnosed something worse than nerves. He had really been feeling lousy. So after the one day off, Robinson returned to the second spot in the batting order and continued to enliven the summertime crowds, among them Mitzi Melnick, who arrived one sunlit afternoon carrying a little Brownie black box camera she had gotten for her birthday. Before the game, she called out to Robinson, asking to take his photograph.

"Sure, come down here," he said, and motioned with his hand. Mitzi slipped out of the stands and onto the field, into the curve of grass behind home plate, and moved toward the dugout, where Jackie stood, one foot out, one foot in. Young boys leaned over the dugout roof, becapped and gleeful, and Robinson, the sun bright on his face, looked straight into Mitzi's camera as she took the picture. That day and the day of the soccer game at Fletcher's Field were for Mitzi Melnick indelible moments from the summer of 1946.

Melnick kept that photograph of Jackie Robinson for years and years and years, in a special place for herself, until she had her own family and her own baseball-gripped child, Mitch. On the day he moved out and left home for a place of his own, at the age of twenty-one, she gave him that picture of Jackie Robinson at the dugout at Delorimier Downs. In his mother Mitzi's words, Mitch "flipped, when he saw it, loved it more than I could have imagined."

Robinson would indeed win the International League batting title in 1946. He stole 40 bases, more than any Royal save Marvin Rackley, and scored more runs than any player on any team in the league. Robinson hit 25 doubles and 8 triples. He walked 92 times and struck out only 27, and he finished with 155 hits in 124 games. The Royals won the International League pennant by nearly 20 games.

By the time the playoffs began in the second week of September—first up, a series against fourth-place Newark—the baseball people in Montreal had a feeling that these would be the last games in which they would have a chance to watch Robinson play. That if there were justice in the world, and if there were the courage and motivation that had already been implied, then the fans in Montreal would not, once these playoffs ended, see Jackie Robinson in the International League ever again.

HAD ROBINSON GONE EARLY TO BROOKLYN

Conjecture and speculation that Robinson might be called up from the Royals to the Dodgers at some point in 1946 began early in the season. Other prominent Royals also emerged as candidates for a call-up, but discussions of a promotion to the big leagues mainly revolved around Jackie Robinson. The manager of the Dodgers, Leo Durocher, for one, made it clear he would like to have him. Newspapers brought up the idea every week or two as the 1946 season progressed. The suggestions, however, were always flatly dismissed by Branch Rickey as well as by Mel Jones, the Royals general manager. "We're not going to pull anyone up off of your team," Branch Rickey told Clay Hopper during a visit to Montreal in June, and he stuck to his word even though Robinson was playing so spectacularly and Brooklyn could have used a little help.

The Dodgers and Cardinals were in a tight race for the National League pennant, Brooklyn leading for much of the season until, in late August, St. Louis edged in front. The teams would ultimately tie for first place, necessitating a best-of-three playoff, which the Cardinals won. The Dodgers at that time had appeared in only one World Series in twenty-seven years, so the opportunity that presented itself that summer of 1946, the highly attended first season after the war, was not an opportunity to take lightly.

Branch Rickey understood that integrating the major leagues by promoting Robinson would have been an even greater risk during the heat of a pennant race. If Robinson, still so unfinished as a ball-player, so new to the sport, went 0 for 4 in a crucial game or made an ill-timed error or struck out at a pivotal moment, that failure would be magnified. Further, the Dodgers, who were scoring on average four and a half runs per game, did not appear to have a pressing need for the offense Robinson could potentially provide. What if Robinson joined the Brooklyn lineup, and for whatever reason, the team went into a slump for a week or two? Robinson might be blamed by fans and teammates. Bringing Robinson into a late summer pennant race, Branch Rickey knew, could have ratcheted up the intensity and discourse around Robinson's National League debut even beyond what it was already destined to be: the most anticipated, talked-about, and heavily freighted debut in the history of professional sports.

Robinson, like any player with ambition, naturally would not have minded going to the major leagues in 1946. For one thing, it would have meant a higher salary for the soon-to-be father. He was a highly competitive player who believed he was good enough to play at that top level. It was also true that even the best of the minor leagues—that is to say, the International League—was touched by a share of uneven characters and hinky men. The Mexican League bird dogs who'd hovered in Daytona Beach lurked around International League stadiums for much of the season. And the gambling in those grandstands was obvious. When Robinson was asked directly about a potential call-up to the Dodgers, however, he demurred. He remarked on how much he appreciated his Royals teammates, and how much he and Rachel liked living in Montreal, and he said he was happy to play wherever in the organization the Dodgers wanted him to play.

So, while several big league teams brought up minor leaguers that season (including the Cardinals, whose addition from Rochester, the infielder Vernal "Nippy" Jones, had a couple of hits and a key RBI during the final days of September), the Dodgers did not. Given what would go on to unfold in 1947—when Robinson was the major league's Rookie of the Year and led the National League in stolen bases, and engendered with his play the favorable response and general acceptance that proved critical to societal advancement—it seems clear that keeping Robinson in the minor leagues for the 1946 season was the right decision.

And yet, what of another, less significant aspect of Robinson's presence: namely his extraordinary impact on the performance and success of the Dodgers, who would reach six World Series in ten seasons during Robinson's career? Robinson, by the statistical measure of wins above replacement (WAR), was a four-win player in his rookie year of 1947. (The number suggests that having Robinson in the lineup, rather than a "replacement level" or minimum-salaried player, was worth four wins to the Dodgers.) He was, on average, a seven-win player over his first seven major league seasons. What if he had come up for, say, the final six to eight weeks of the 1946 season? Might he have helped the Dodgers win even one more game to outlast the Cardinals in the pennant race?

Imagine Robinson had gotten some time at second base to spell Brooklyn's Eddie Stanky, who over the last six weeks of 1946 batted just .207 in 140 at bats at the top of the lineup. With an occasional spot start, might not Robinson have improved the team? Or what if Robinson had seen a few games at third base, a position at which he had begun to experiment and at which Brooklyn engaged a hodge-podge of players in 1946? Cookie Lavagetto, the Dodgers' primary late-season third baseman, batted a damaging .198 from mid-July on, with a similarly damaging .267 slugging percentage. Robinson could have done better than that.

When he did come up, in 1947, Robinson played first base for the Dodgers. Imagine if in 1946, some of the late-season at bats that went to right-handed-hitting first baseman Howie Schultz (.237 batting average with a poor .640 OPS[5] in August and September) or left-handed-hitting first baseman Ed Stevens (a brutal .180, .565) had gone instead to Robinson. In those final months of the 1946 season, the Dodgers entrusted utility infielders such as Eddie Miksis (5 for 47 from August 1 on) and Bob Ramazzotti (3 for 22) with important at bats and pinch-hitting assignments. None of the players mentioned in these paragraphs were at all disruptive or dangerous on the basepaths.

During August and September, the Dodgers lost eight games by one run. They lost six games by two runs. With an opportunity to play—even as a backup, a pinch-runner and once-a-week starter, even while adjusting to the better pitching and the higher stakes—might Robinson not have turned even one of those narrow losses into a win, thus delivering to Brooklyn the pennant? During a two-week stretch with the Royals that August, Robinson batted, no misprint, .509 over 55 at bats.

And if, with Robinson on the roster, the Dodgers had indeed won

---

5. OPS stands for "on-base plus slugging percentage," perhaps the best simple measure of a batter's overall effectiveness. In 1946, the average OPS for a Dodger batter, includ-ing pitchers, was .709.

the 1946 National League pennant, might the team have gone on to achieve what the Cardinals did that year—that is, beating the Red Sox in the World Series? It would have been the first championship in the team's then sixty-three-year history. And if Brooklyn had won, how might that have changed the complexion of what was to come? How might the rare experience of playing in and winning a World Series have impacted the Dodgers' performance the following year, in the 1947 World Series against the Yankees? Would the presumably seasoned team have played better as a whole? Even a small improvement would have made the difference. Might Robinson himself, who admitted to a feeling of awe under the bright scrutiny of that first major league World Series in 1947, been slightly more at ease and in his element? Maybe he would have produced better than his disappointing .310 on-base percentage. Maybe he would not have made the baserunning mistake that led to his being thrown out at third base in Game One. Maybe, instead of losing the tight Series in seven games, the Dodgers would have beaten the Yankees in 1947 for the title.

And if the Dodgers had won the World Series in either 1946 or 1947, or both, what would that have then meant to the ambience and character of Ebbets Field and New York baseball in those historic "Wait Till Next Year!" seasons of the late 1940s and 1950s? Would the Dodgers and their fans still have carried that bittersweet aura of noble also-rans, that scarlet mark of being snakebit in the big game, a rationalized, heartbreak-in-October-builds-love-and-fortitude pride that has shaped so many ruminations and reminisces and Weltanschauungen in the decades since? Would it still have been a defining characteristic of that Brooklyn era, which spawned a cottage industry of movies, books, mementos? And what of 1955? Would the team's extraordinary, omigod-it-finally-happened World Series victory that autumn—the first and only championship in Brooklyn Dodgers history—have lifted the borough with its magical, impossible-dream quality had it been preceded by a World Series win, or two, in the late 1940s?

It is no stretch to imagine Robinson competing in the major leagues in 1946, and not at all far-fetched to surmise that his presence could have made the Dodgers one crucial win better that season. What butterfly effect might have ensued, we can never know. What we know is that Robinson did not come up to play for Brooklyn that year. The Dodgers lost the National League pennant, while Robinson stayed in Montreal right through to the end, into October, with the Royals.

A LETTER IN ATLANTA

On August 6, 1946, a letter to the editor appeared in the *Atlanta Constitution*, addressing the deeply disturbing racial tenor of the time. The *Constitution* had recently reported on murders committed by white mobs: Maceo Snipes, who in late July had become the first Black person to cast a vote in a Democratic primary in Taylor County, Georgia, was subsequently shot in the back by members of the Ku Klux Klan. A few days later, two Black couples were surrounded and murdered by a group of fifteen to twenty white men on a dirt road near Watkinsville, about sixty miles east of Atlanta. (And about 240 miles north of Jackie Robinson's birthplace in Cairo, Georgia.) The murdered couples were George W. and Mae Murray Dorsey, and Roger and Dorothy Malcom. George was a veteran of World War II who had spent five years in the Pacific. Dorothy was pregnant.

The murders were very much on people's minds at the time, but the letter to the editor of the *Constitution* did not discuss them directly. Rather, it set out to make a wider point. "I often find when decent treatment for the Negro is urged, a certain class of people hurry to raise the scarecrow of social mingling and intermarriage," the letter began. "These questions have nothing to do with the case . . . it is simple dust to obscure the real question of rights and opportunities."

Black people, the letter emphasized, simply wanted the "basic rights and opportunities of American citizens."

Jackie Robinson was two thousand miles from Atlanta at Delorimier Stadium on the day that letter was published, playing second base and getting five hits in six at bats against the Syracuse Chiefs in the otherwise all-white International League. But the letter's reference to "the scarecrow of social mingling and intermarriage" was one that Robinson, like so many Black men, could painfully relate to. It also presaged a particularly grotesque line of insult that the Philadelphia Phillies manager, Ben Chapman, would level at Robinson as part of a racist campaign of verbal attacks early in the 1947 season: the suggestion that Robinson was having sex with, or angling to have sex with, the wives of his teammates. Rather than turn the Dodgers against him, this hateful line—along with Chapman's other invectives—helped to unite the Brooklyn team in support of Robinson.

There was something else noteworthy about that letter in the *Atlanta Constitution* and its place in the arc of the movement toward racial justice that Robinson, with his ballplaying and his demeanor, was helping to forge. The letter—which touched specifically on the right to "equal opportunities" in education and public services and, in words that called to mind those recent murders, the need for "equality before the law"—was written by a seventeen-year-old sociology major and rising junior at Morehouse College. It was the first piece of writing that the student had ever published with so large a readership, and at the end of the letter he signed his name: *M. L. King, Jr.*

THE LAST OF ROBINSON'S BEGINNING

They had beaten the Newark Bears in six games and then dispatched Syracuse in five—Robinson standing out in various ways—and now the Royals were in Louisville, Kentucky, playing the Louisville Colonels, champions of the American Association, in the Junior World Series. Montreal had reached this World Series only once before, in 1941. In Louisville, Robinson stayed in a Black-run hotel, isolated from the rest of the team, and at the Colonels' Parkway Field, the stands were firmly segregated, with only a small section for Black fans. For each of the Royals' three Junior World Series games in Louisville that late September, the Black section was filled to capacity, and thousands of other Black fans— many having traveled for hours—were turned away. Some of them found their way onto the rooftop of a building in back of the left field wall and peered in to watch the game, and Jackie Robinson, as best they could.

Altogether, Parkway Field seated a little more than thirteen thousand people and there Robinson was a target of the harshest verbal treatment he had yet to receive on a baseball field. The language he heard, with its edge of loathing and fear, was full-on. *I expected it to be bad, but it is worse than I expected*, thought Robinson in the dugout. His hands had become unusually damp, and he was aware of a persistent, low-boiling nausea. Fans booed and shouted the worst racial slurs at him, and made open threats each time his name was announced or he touched the ball in the field. Robinson kept his eyes strictly on the game around him and did not look into the crowd. "He took it most gracefully and conducted himself in his every move as a gentleman," the Louisville *Courier-Journal* reported.

Robinson, however, went 1 for 10 with only a single in those three games, and the Royals lost two of the three. There were times during that season, the Louisville games among them, when Robinson would, in spite of himself, feel doubt creeping in. Doubt about everything. He felt what the hate had the power to do to him, and he had seen what it could do to Rachel. "Sometimes I wonder if it is worth it," Robinson said to Royals general manager Mel Jones in Jones's office at the stadium.

"Sit in the boat," Jones suggested to Robinson. It was a Branch

Rickey metaphor for how best to ride out a storm in the figurative sea. "Let's sit in the boat," Jones said. Robinson always did.

Later, after the Junior World Series had ended, numerous letters would come to the Louisville *Courier-Journal* expressing dismay at how poorly the Colonels had treated the Black fans by turning them away from the gate, and at how odiously the Louisville fans had berated Robinson. Some letter writers identified themselves as war veterans and others as ballpark regulars, and along with the professed moral indignation, a further objection to the poor behavior of the team and the fans was that it amounted to bad strategy—that it was, in the words of one reader from Indianapolis, "a fatal mistake that gave Montreal the inspiration and determination to win."

The Junior World Series was best of seven, and when the teams got up to Montreal for the fourth game, snow blanketed the ground. The leaves were all but down, and the soil was already hardening, and the air was wet and cold. Temperatures fell to the low forties by game time, and at Delorimier Stadium the fans wore overcoats. Some of the older men, *habitants* for generations, had bound their coats with the *ceinture fléchée*, the arrow sash, in a show of tradition and pride. And in Game Four, the first of that year's Junior World Series game to be played in Montreal, each time a Louisville player came to bat— first the speedy outfielder Johnny Welaj, then scrappy little Chick Genovese, and right on down the lineup—and each time a Louisville player made a play in the field or did anything in any conspicuous way, the fans in Montreal booed and snarled as they never before had booed or snarled at opposing players. They had heard about the treatment given to Robinson in Louisville, and they didn't like it one bit.

He scored the game-tying run in the ninth inning of Game Four, and then lashed the game-winning hit in the tenth—a line drive that whistled over the shortstop's head. The Series now was tied at two games apiece. The next day, Game Five, Robinson lined a double down the left field line in the first inning and tripled to the base of the light tower in left center in the seventh, and then, with two outs and the bases loaded in the eighth inning, he set down a surprise squeeze bunt for Montreal's fifth run in a 5–3 game. The Royals were one win away from the title, and the next day, they got it. The final score of Game Six was 2–0, Montreal, and Robinson again had two hits, and again made critical plays in the field. In the sixth inning, he started a double play to kill a Louisville rally: Robinson to Campanis to Burge, 4-6-3. And in the ninth, he turned another double play, getting to a ground ball up the middle, stepping on second base, and throwing to Burge to end the Colonels' final hopes. Rachel, more than seven months along, had flown back home to Los Angeles by then, ahead of the birth.

Jackie said that what moved him about the fans in Montreal was the sincerity of their loyalty and jubilation. In the cold of the late day, the fans on the field at Delorimier Downs (excepting, surely, the seventy-nine who had traveled nine hundred miles from Louisville to cheer the Colonels) celebrated the Junior World Series win with the fervor of the long deprived. They lifted up the fine veteran pitcher Curt Davis, who was forty-three years old and had thirteen big league seasons behind him, and carried him around the field. They lifted up the manager, Clay Hopper, and carried him all around too. But it was Robinson they wanted and Robinson they waited for and Robinson they finally raised. They hoisted him higher and longer than the others, breaking into chants and into song—"La Marseillaise," for one— and shouted his name again and again: "Jackie, Jackie!" and "Robby, Robby!" They yelled, "Jackie Robinson!" and "Yakee Rob-een-sen!"

Even when the people set him back on to the ground, they continued to serenade and besiege him, touch him and kiss him, as Robinson—his face wet with tears of joy and relief—tried to break free. They followed him into the streets en masse and saw him break into a run, away from the happy ruckus, and disappear into a car bound for the airport. Jackie left Montreal that very night, headed to play more baseball—a slate of games in various cities with the barn-storming Jackie Robinson All-Stars.

"It was wonderful, playing up there in Canada where people are so fair and so considerate," Robinson said not long afterward. "There were times, however, that I felt pretty bad. I got down in the dumps a number of times and began to wonder if I could keep going. It was during such times that my wife came through like a champion. She was always able to pull me up and keep me going. I don't know what I would have done without her. She deserves just as much credit for my success as anyone else."

News of the Royals winning the Junior World Series—and of the great and affectionate tribute the fans had given as they mobbed Robinson—was celebrated on the front page of the national edition of the *Pittsburgh Courier*, under the headline A LESSON OF GOODWILL AMONG MEN. Also on that front page, practically cheek by jowl with the sports news: coverage of the aftermath of those late-July murders in Georgia by a mob of white men. The FBI investigation into the killings of the Black couples, the *Courier* reported, had produced no witnesses, no substantive evidence, and not a single arrest. The case—today known and commemorated as the Moore's Ford Lynchings—would proceed throughout the fall and inspire protests near the Capitol in Washington, DC. It also led to the formation of the President's Committee on Civil Rights, under Harry Truman. A grand jury heard testimony, but that testimony was sealed by the court. By the end of 1946, despite the general agreement that the murders had occurred and were perpetrated by members of that mob, the case was effectively closed without prosecution.[6]

---

6. Many decades later, after a purported witness emerged and new attention focused on the unsolved case, both the Georgia Bureau of Investigation and the FBI began new investigations into the Moore's Ford Lynchings, though neither produced any finding. In 2014, the writer and historian Anthony Pitch sued to have the grand jury testimony unsealed. The suit spent years in the courts. Pitch died in 2019, and on March 27, 2020, nearly seventy-four years after the murders were committed, an appeals court ruled

For the final months of 1946, the Robinsons were together again in Los Angeles, in the warmth of the western sun, with Jackie's and Rachel's families all around them. On November 18, Jackie Robinson Jr. was born at the Good Samaritan Hospital on Wilshire Boulevard. He had a head of hair and his mother's forehead and lashes thick and sweet as a butterfly's wings. Jackie was with Rachel in the room for the birth, and afterward the new family lived in Rachel's girlhood home, where Jackie Jr. became known to all as Sugar Plum. Jackie sent a telegram to the neighbors at 8234 Avenue de Gaspé, announcing the birth.

To earn extra money, Robinson played basketball on a local semipro team. He knew by then that the Dodgers planned to open their next spring training in Cuba, deliberately away from the American South. "I think I am going to get a chance with the Dodgers," he allowed to a reporter. He was aware, as anyone was, that he was better than the league he'd left behind. But still he had not heard from Branch Rickey about any plans for 1947. Robinson did not know what would be coming next.

Jackie and Rachel would always recall—throughout their time in baseball, and then into their riper years together, and then, for Rachel, through the many years of her life without him—how precious and important was that season as a young couple in Montreal. They would recall the fruit sellers and the gentle smell of wood outside the apartment on de Gaspé, and the big exultant crowds at Delorimier Stadium cheering Robinson in Franglais, and the narrow looks and hard words from the players in Syracuse, and Jackie being spiked at second base by Rochester's Johnny Bucha, and being nearly hit in the head and then hit in the elbow by the Orioles' left-hander Sid West,

that the testimony remain permanently sealed. This was two months before the death of George Floyd, a Black man who was murdered by a white police officer, Derek Chauvin, in Minneapolis, sparking outrage and protests in thousands of cities in the United States and around the world.

and all the people in Montreal who would approach them—both of them—sweetly and shyly for autographs when they were out for a meal downtown.

They would recall the men in soft hats on the corner of Ontario Street scalping tickets, and the taste of just-baked sugar pie, and the night after those first frightening games in Baltimore in April, when Rachel had cried in their room. They would recall Jackie's warm hand on Rachel's bare, beautiful, late-summer belly, and how this had been a period of time when their own new and great love, as well as the warmth of so many fans, had come up side by side with hate, and how it had been this time in 1946 that gave the two of them a framework and an outlook—a sustenance and a strength and a level of crucial new learning in their young, widening lives—that they would carry with them into the next season and the next and the next, and all throughout the long, wonderful, demanding, extraordinary years ahead.

PART TWO

SUMMER
—
1949

BASEPATHS

Of all the attributes that attended Jackie Robinson's play on the base-ball diamond—and there were many—none stood out so magnifi-cently, at the time or in memory, in legend and in fact, as the way that he ran the bases. Nothing else he did as a ballplayer quite so profoundly impacted both the games that he played and, it must be said, the lives of those who saw him play. Robinson could change a game with a feint.

He had raw speed, to be sure, an asset conspicuous from his earliest time as an athlete, and in his college years of extraordinary feats, and certainly in the flower of his baseball career. You saw the speed in his bursts down the first base line when he set down a bunt, and also in his straight sprints around the bases when he'd lined one deep into the gap. At times, Robinson seemed to hit the ball on a dead run.

Still, other players of Robinson's era possessed pure speed of this order. The Dodgers' mystical hero Pete Reiser, during his gorgeous 1940s heyday of breaking bones (his) and swelling hearts (his fans'), chased fly balls through the Ebbets Field outfield with the flush of an Olympic sprinter; in his fleeting peak, Reiser stole bases at will. Even the part-time Dodgers outfielder Marvin Rackley, his speed his sin-gular virtue, might have put Robinson to the test in a forty-yard dash. And this is to say nothing of the great Cool Papa Bell, whose career of memory-making touched, at its tail end, the start of Robinson's. "If he bunts and it bounces twice, put it in your pocket," said Double Duty Radcliffe about Cool Papa Bell.

Robinson, though, was defined not simply by his flat-out speed but by his attitude and approach besides. His quickness. His ingenuity. None of Robinson's contemporaries displayed his ability to start and stop and start and stop and start again, to jink his way past fielders and potential tags, to rattle and embarrass and elude. He would hover at times and then explode. For Robinson, each time on base promised an essay into new possibilities. "Daring," he said. "That's half my game."

He brought to the National League a dazzle and pluck sometimes seen in the Negro leagues, and he delivered this supremely and uniquely, applying the skills of a football player: a running back who could with a shake and a rustle be free of the pack and off into the open field, bound for the end zone. And Robinson, it is to be remembered, was a highly intelligent baseball player. "His most obvious stock in trade is his noodle. I don't think there is a smarter ball player in the International League," observed a scout during Robinson's season as a Montreal Royal. The intelligence enabled Robinson to make up ground on players who had far more in-game experience than he, and it augmented his magnificent physical skills. Nowhere was this intelligence more apparent, or more useful, than when he was on the basepaths. You were never sure what Jackie was going to do.

He would knock a single into the outfield and make the hard, often overlong turn at first base—testing the outfielder's attention, trying to provoke. He would go back to the bag and put his hands on his hips, akimbo, but only for a moment, just touching them there, until his hands were off his body again, first held taut and outward about waist high, and then dropped down to dangle, his fingers twitching perhaps, and then not, his arms and his hands, like the rest of him, signifying that he was ready to run. For a pitcher, in particular—although for a catcher, too—this could be a disconcerting sight. Anticipation surged through the crowd, and discomfort nagged at the defense.

He led the National League in stolen bases as a rookie in 1947, and led all of baseball in '49, and he remained among the league's leaders right through the end of his career. He would steal second or third or, most dramatically, home. He studied pitchers for their tells. Nor was he adverse to calculated risk. No one in the league got thrown out more than Robinson did. "Don't worry if you get caught," Branch Rickey said. And Jackie did not worry. High volume was part of the strategy. Sometimes, Robinson knew, the threat of a steal could be as effective as the steal itself.[7]

He tended to take the extra base. In his rookie year, 1947, Robinson once made it to second base on a walk. Another time he scored from second base on a sacrifice fly. Over the course of his ten-season career—including the later years, when his straight speed was not what it once had been—Robinson took an extra base 385 times, the third-most in all of baseball during that time. The impact of Robinson's baserunning is in some ways measurable by statistics, but in many ways it is not. Early in 1949, for example, during a series of preseason exhibition games in Georgia—the first integrated baseball games the state had ever hosted—Robinson twice set off to steal home. Both times, Carl Furillo, at the bat, was hit by the pitch. Robinson returned to third base. The Dodgers had another runner on.

Robinson's baserunning affected almost every game he played in, in various ways. You could select games at random and see this at work. Let's take these: three games in four days played at Ebbets Field in early June of 1949. This was about one month before the

---

7. Robinson, like Pee Wee Reese, the Dodgers' other exceptional base runner, was empowered to make his own decisions about when to try to steal and when not. He was smart about it. During the 1949 season, for example, he was caught stealing a league-high 16 times—but 12 of those failed attempts came with two outs, diminishing the chance that the out on the basepaths actually foiled a Dodgers scoring opportunity. And on only two occasions in all of 1949 was Robinson caught stealing when the Dodgers were trailing in a game.

All-Star Game in Brooklyn, when the Dodgers were thick in the pennant race, and Robinson was the best player in the major leagues.

On Wednesday, June 1, in the bottom of the third inning against St. Louis, Robinson was on first base, with Pee Wee Reese on third and Mike McCormick on second. There were two outs, and the Cardinals led 1–0. Gil Hodges hit a line drive single to center field. Reese scored, and so did McCormick. When the throw in from the outfield got away from the cutoff man, first baseman Nippy Jones, Robinson rounded third base aggressively, getting way past the bag and goading the St. Louis catcher Del Rice, who, having backed up Jones, now held the ball between first and home. Rice threw hard to the third baseman, Eddie Kazak, to try to nab Robinson diving back to the bag.

Instead, Robinson broke for home, to where Kazak threw the ball to Jones, who'd come in to cover the plate. (The Cardinals pitcher Al Brazle was near the plate as well, lending at least moral support.) Jones tried to swipe-tag Robinson, but Robinson slid away from Jones's glove and knocked over the umpire, Scotty Robb, who ruled Robinson safe as he fell. This infuriated not only the stunned Cardinals fielders who'd failed to contain Robinson but also several of their teammates, who came out of the dugout to argue the call with Robb. Del Rice was thrown out of the game and later suspended. The Dodgers had a 3–1 lead.

The very next night, before a crowd of nearly thirty-three thousand fans, the Dodgers led the Cardinals 3–1, with two outs in the bottom of the sixth inning. Robinson was on third base, and the Cardinals pitcher was Harry Brecheen, a thirty-four-year-old left-hander with a good screwball and excellent control. The count went to two balls and no strikes on the Dodgers batter, Roy Campanella, and it appeared that Brecheen may have been working around Campanella to instead face light-hitting Eddie Miksis. So Robinson took off to steal home. Brecheen's reaction was described as suddenly "befuddled," and his pitch to home plate was well inside, leading Campanella to jump back and roll to the ground out of the way, and forcing the catcher, Joe Garagiola, to one knee to corral the ball. Robinson arrived hard to the far side of the plate, his right hand up and clenched, the dry earth kicked up all around him. Garagiola applied the tag too late, and umpire Babe Pinelli, no question about it this time, called Robinson safe.

Two nights later, on Saturday, June 4, the Pirates were in Brooklyn. It was a high-scoring game, and in the fourth inning, Robinson hit a triple, a ground ball down the right field line. Now the score was tied 6–6 in the eighth, and Robinson was on first base with no outs. Gil Hodges set down a routine sacrifice bunt that was fielded by the pitcher Bob Muncrief, who threw to first, where the second baseman Danny Murtaugh was covering. As Robinson rounded second, he saw that the Pirates third baseman, Pete Castiglione, had strayed a bit far from third base. So Robinson kept running, and aimed his slide to the outfield edge of the third base bag. Castiglione, having frantically returned to the vicinity of the base, took the throw from Murtaugh, but was a hair too late with the tag. Two bases for Robinson on a sacrifice bunt. With one out and the winning run now on third, the Pirates infielders were forced to play in. So when the following batter, Furillo, hit a two-strike ground ball toward the middle of the diamond, it got through to center field and Robinson scored the decisive run.

These three examples—two against the Cardinals, one against the Pirates, in a span of four days—were not at all unusual. These were the kinds of things Robinson did all the time during his peak years, too often to count. Players talked about Robinson's disposition as a base runner, and many agreed that seeing him on the bases could invoke a sickened feeling among members of the opposing team. Along with being very fast, Robinson was also powerfully built—thick and broad—an unusual combination in baseball then. The Dodgers' Pee Wee Reese could also scamper disruptively on the bases, but Reese was a small man of 160 pounds. As the *Brooklyn Eagle* noted after Robinson exploited Harry Brecheen to steal that run on June 2: "When Robinson sets out to steal home, it doesn't pay to get in his way." Robinson, in a collision, would punish you.

An adage in baseball that has stretched across centuries, from Sam Crawford to Carl Crawford and beyond, holds that the sport's most exciting play is the triple. Suddenly the batted ball is bounding, unusually loose, and the runner is in full, dedicated flight, and the fielders are in frantic motion. And then the throw is coming in to third from the outfield, sometimes just as the runner does, the play resolving itself in a spray of dirt. Here's Ty Cobb with his lean strides and elegant, vicious slides in the 1910s and '20s. Here's Roberto Clemente, early 1970s, rounding the bases in full and earnest beauty. Here's a graying Pete Rose, 1980s, ending a roguish, three-base gallop by hurtling himself headfirst two feet off the ground. Here's José Reyes, vibrant in the late aughts, his legs like pistons on the basepaths, his arrival at third base the brightest ampere of joy.

But for baseball fans who found themselves in Ebbets Field or perhaps in another National League (or, in April or October, Yankee) stadium during the late 1940s and early 1950s, the most exciting play in baseball was not a triple. The most exciting play in baseball—and this is not introduced as hyperbole, but rather to honor a sentiment expressed by multiple fans and former players—was Jackie Robinson caught between fielders, in a rundown. "I've never seen anything like it on a baseball diamond, before or since," says the pitcher Carl Erskine, a Dodger from 1948 to 1959. "When Jackie got hung up, we'd all come forward in the dugout to watch. It was fascinating. To me it looked like a twelve-year-old playing with six-year-olds."

"We were playing in Daytona Beach in an exhibition game and they caught Robinson between first and second," Clay Hopper, the manager of the Montreal Royals, said a couple of months after the fact. "The whole ball club got in on the play and tried to run him down. Jackie would run right up to a guy at full speed, then stop dead in his tracks just before reaching him. None of us were surprised when Robinson reached second base safely. We'd have been surprised if they'd gotten him out."

On the streets of Brooklyn where the kids would imitate not only Robinson's batting stance but also his distinctive pigeon-toed run (just as young Yankee fans would, in later years, limp around the sandlot in imitation of Mickey Mantle; as young Giants fans would toss off their caps as they ran, to look like Willie Mays), Jackie's performance in a rundown had a particularly powerful influence. "Because we knew how hard it was," says Ronald Glassman. Ronny was eleven years old in 1949, and he lived in East Flatbush. "We would play running bases all the time. All you needed was three kids, two gloves, and a ball. Or not even the gloves." Running bases, for the deprived, is a game with two bases set a long throw apart, a fielder covering each base and a runner in between, trying to make it safely to one base or the other without being tagged. It's being in a rundown. "If you were the runner," Glassman goes on, "unless someone dropped the ball, it was really, really hard. It was like there was no place to go. You almost always got tagged. But Jackie would get out of it! He did it a lot. He could stop and reverse and shake around and keep it going until something happened. That really stayed with me."

As a general rule in baseball, the moment a runner is trapped in a rundown, the defense begins to mentally count on recording the out. It's like a lazy flyball to center field. For the vast majority of base runners, even the speedsters and the chance-takers among them, being in a rundown engenders a sense of disappointment and resignation. For Robinson, being in a rundown was an opportunity. A vehicle. His ability to escape the seemingly inescapable—not always, of course, not even usually, but more than often enough to elicit gasps and cheers and memories—was just the stuff to entrance a baseball fan.[8]

Robinson's peak came at a time when the mocking and mimicking of Black people remained a disturbingly common genre in American entertainment. On a Sunday night in 1949, you might have seen a blackface homage to minstrelsy on *The Fred Waring Show*, right after Ed Sullivan on CBS. There was blackface and damning stereotypes in animated film shorts: Universal's *Scrub Me Mama with a Boogie Beat*, for one; *Goldilocks and the Jivin' Bears*, for another. There were caricatures in newspapers, and exaggerated accents onstage and on-screen. All of it dismissive and exploitative, a category of base, cruel humor that played across so much of white society.

People could eat at a Coon Chicken Inn restaurant out West until 1957. Aunt Jemima grinned on your box of pancake mix.[9] And at New York's Waldorf-Astoria, two months before the start of Robinson's first season, the New York baseball writers' annual dinner included the tropes—a skit, within the night's revue, of a character portraying Robinson as a household servant and calling the Branch Rickey character "Massa." The character of baseball commissioner

---

8. One representative Robinson-in-a-rundown play retains a particular sheen because it was partially captured in a photograph. On May 31, 1951, in the eighth inning of a night game at Ebbets Field, Robinson got hung up between third and home after Carl Furillo missed a squeeze bunt attempt. Phillies catcher Andy Seminick, third baseman Willie Jones, and shortstop Granny Hamner all got involved in the play and began throwing the baseball back and forth to one another as Robinson scurried up and down the third base line. After five throws, the Phillies still had not tagged out Robinson, and he had succeeded in moving closer to the plate. The Philadelphia left fielder, Dick Sisler, and first baseman Jimmy Bloodworth had by now also joined the play to provide backup. So had the pitcher, Russ Meyer, and it was Meyer who, as Robinson came hurtling toward him, bobbled the sixth throw. The ball dropped and Robinson knocked into Meyer as he scored the fourth and deciding run of Brooklyn's 4–3 win. The surviving photograph shows five of the Phillies defenders (all save Sisler) converging on Robinson, who appears to have no perceivable path to safe passage. "There was just no way to get out of that," says Carl Erskine, who pitched for Brooklyn in the game. "But Jackie did." Erskine keeps his copy of the photograph framed on a wall—a reminder, he says, "that anything is possible."

9. Quaker Oats continued to use the Aunt Jemima character until June of 2020. Seriously.

Happy Chandler addressed the Jackie Robinson character as a "wooly headed rascal." And the Jackie Robinson character addressed the Happy Chandler character as "colonel" and "suh." There were a thousand people in attendance at the dinner, and the actors were themselves members of the Baseball Writers Association. "It was all such lampoonery, that no one's feelings were really hurt," wrote Arthur Daley, flashing myopia in the sports pages of the *New York Times*. What Wendell Smith wrote in the *Pittsburgh Courier* after the event was more telling: "When you start classifying fair-minded organizations in the world of sports, be sure to cross off the New York Chapter of the Baseball Writers Association."

Robinson on the basepaths looked different from the players trying to get him out—alight and undaunted. In control. The way the fielders might flail and reach awkwardly, and then, when Robinson's final dodge got him safely to the base, simply shake their heads—*Now, how did* that *happen?*—had in it an element of high slapstick. Practically Chaplinesque, even Three Stooges–like. So that for some, the thrill of Jackie's improbable jukes and wags and high steps yielded an added pleasure: There was something richly satisfying, even triumphant, in seeing the one Black man on the field work his craft so that the fielders all around him played the fools. All in all, to see Robinson turn the ordinary into the extraordinary that summer, to see him do things that he alone among his peers could do, might have led anyone to admire him. As a baseball fan, you loved him.

BROOKLYN

Robinson adored it when Ebbets Field looked and felt this way: full to its every reach, the big crowd buzzing and calling out, the people on top of everything, it seemed. You could hear, now, still nearly an hour before game time, the peanut vendors bellowing "Peanuts here!" and the fans laughing and clapping and shouting out the names of players. ("Teddy! Robby! DiMag! Preach!") On more ordinary days, when the crowds had not arrived so early, or during games when some quiet had settled over the action, the fans could hear the things the players shouted too. "Here we go, Ralphie! One, two, three!" or a strikeout crowned with a batter's cuss.

The grass had been freshly cut and the infield earth freshly groomed and the outfield fence, with its new Reiser-proof padding installed over the concrete, scrubbed clean. Photographers milled around, and so did unfamiliar men in suits, and the television cameras had CBS painted on their sides. Bunting hung off the railings as if for the World Series or Opening Day. You could smell the possibility of rain, and above the light towers the sky lay low in layers of gray and white. Eddie Joost and Vic Wertz tossed a ball back and forth, and Vern Stephens was standing by the side, fiddling with his Boston cap. Here and there, guys worked dirt out of their spikes. Robinson stood on the field near the dugout, holding a bat. It was the kind of moment where you want to pause and take in everything, save it for later.

This was baseball's 16th All-Star Game, and the first to be held in Brooklyn. Close to thirty-three thousand people were filling in the stands, a complete sellout on a Tuesday afternoon in mid-July. The game was meant to give fans a chance to see some of the great American League players they never (or rarely) had a chance to see in Brooklyn—DiMaggio, Williams, Doby, Kell—and a chance, too, for their Dodgers to be showcased. Not only Robinson but also six of his teammates were on the National League team: Pee Wee Reese, Ralph Branca, Roy Campanella, Gil Hodges, Don Newcombe, Preacher Roe. In a pinch, they could have manned the whole field. Robinson had drawn more All-Star votes than any other player in the National League. He was batting .362 and had driven in 65 runs in 78 games. "Attaboy, Jack!" came the cries from the stands. "Go get 'em, Jackie!" All-Star Game or any day, he always heard it from the crowd at Ebbets Field.

As an All-Star, Robinson was making history again, another first, and the photographers kept pulling him aside. He posed beside Stan Musial and Ralph Kiner, and then with Hodges and Reese, and then with all his Brooklyn teammates, and then, finally, in the image that would run the next day nationwide, alongside Campy and Newk and the Indians' Larry Doby: the four All-Star barrier breakers. Everyone wanted Jackie in a photo. *The player of most interest is Robinson*, thought Dominic DiMaggio, watching from the American League dugout. Usually in a situation like this, the player of most interest was Dom's brother Joe. Dom laughed. *The truth is, Robinson is of interest to me as well.* The word across baseball that year, even in the American League, was that a change had come over Robinson, a change plain in his countenance and in his manner, in his responses to the pressure points of the game. A new level up now, is what Dom DiMaggio had heard.

For all his success and dazzle his first two seasons in the majors—Rookie of the Year in 1947, another first-rate season in '48—there had been, as those who played with or against Robinson in earlier days knew, a softening to his edge, a cooling of the extracurricular intensity for which he was known. "Robinson got hotter than a General Electric burner when he was with the Kansas City Monarchs," said Othello Renfroe, who'd been the Kansas City catcher in '45. "And he had a truly copious supply of sizzling nouns, verbs and adjectives that went awfully well with that temper. When Robinson played with us, he was always up to his neck in every game."

That same hustle he displayed in Kansas City—had displayed everywhere he ever played—remained intact, an indispensable part of Robinson's game. He kept the same fire on the bases, but lost, for a time, the brimstone that went with it. When, in those first two seasons with the Dodgers, Robinson had been pelted with vile taunts, when he'd been slapped with an unnecessarily hard tag or intentionally hit with a pitch—and in those years, no one in baseball was hit

more often than Robinson—or when he was called out on a play despite clearly being safe, he might have shown a quick flash of anger,
a reflexive jerk of his torso and arms, but his fury would be just as
quickly contained, smothered in conscious restraint. That was the negotiated response, what Robinson had promised Branch Rickey, and
what Robinson himself recognized as the best, necessary choice. *Here,
fellas—here's my other cheek*.

In those years, first literally and then essentially, there was only Robinson as a bellwether. He realized that his demeanor and actions—as
the Black press cautioned and the white press noted, and as Branch
Rickey had understood from the start—might be interpreted as the
way *all* Black ballplayers would behave in such a context. As if he
were representing a general Black temperament and conduct. Had
Robinson reared up in anger, even with the clearest justification,
the consequences might have delivered the harder blow to progress.
Now, two years in the National League, three years in pro ball, he
was a known commodity: An individual more than a symbol. A ballplayer.

Robinson had made the leap, been the pioneer who set baseball on
a path that (fraught as it would be) led to Mays and Aaron and Gibson, to Reggie and Rickey and Betts. Robinson illuminated a way that
would then be lit by a collective lamp. By 1949, Robinson's mission
had evolved. "He had a passion about him, and a real sense of things,"
says Dodgers pitcher Carl Erskine. "And it was not just for baseball.
It was also for what he could *do* in baseball, in a game. For the bigger
things he was achieving through baseball."

"I'm not keeping myself under these wraps anymore," Robinson
said to Branch Rickey before the 1949 season began. "It's time." Rickey
agreed. The point was for Robinson to be the best player he could be.
He was thirty years old, and from spring training onward, he was
seriously locked in.

"They'd better be rough on me this year, because I am going to be rough on them," Robinson said to a reporter in March. The approach would yield, as Rachel observed with gentle diplomacy, "a freer style of play." Robinson undaunted. Unleashed to thrive. Up to his neck in every game.

You could see it. The new, dialed-up aggressiveness. A willingness to taunt a pitcher verbally from the basepaths, to bristle at an umpire on a tight play, to hurl an expletive toward the mound after yet again being hit by a pitch. Just a week before the All-Star Game, against the Phillies at Ebbets Field, there'd been a clash with Schoolboy Rowe.

It was a night game, Tuesday, July 5, and Ken Heintzelman was pitching for Philadelphia. The Phillies led 7–2, and Heintzelman had not allowed a run since the first inning by the time that Robinson came up to lead off the ninth. Schoolboy Rowe was in the Phillies dugout. He had moved to the front step, so he could be heard. "Knock him down!" Schoolboy Rowe yelled out to Heintzelman. "Stick it right in his fucking ear." The Phillies had never been kind to Robinson. Since he came into the league, they'd pretty much been the worst.

Rowe was a thirty-nine-year-old right-hander at the end of a dynamite career. He was born in Waco, Texas, and later lived in El Dorado, Arkansas, and had been called Schoolboy since the age of fourteen. He'd married his high school sweetheart, Edna, and he built his major league career as a horse at the head of the Tigers rotation during Detroit's best years of the 1930s. Once, while being interviewed on a popular radio program, Schoolboy said into the microphone: "How'm I doin', Edna?" and people loved his folksy charm. On the mound, he talked to the baseball from time to time—he called the ball Edna as well—and during his best years, he threw a big fastball and a drop-down overhand curve. Now, on the other side of arm injuries and the passage of time, Schoolboy Rowe relied on screwballs and knuckleballs and other crafty stuff. Big shoulders, broad across the forehead, solid jaw, eyebrows galore. There was some history between Schoolboy Rowe and Jackie Robinson as well.

The summer before, during an August 1948 game in Philadelphia, Robinson had gotten on base against Rowe. Robinson stole second, and then, with two outs, he made it to third and started bluffing down the line toward home, messing with Schoolboy's concentration. Rowe walked Duke Snider on four pitches. The next batter, Pee Wee Reese, hit the ball into the seats, and that was it for Schoolboy Rowe and the Phillies that day. Brooklyn wins. The very next time School-boy Rowe pitched against the Dodgers, a week later, he had Robinson in an 0–2 count in the first inning when he threw a fastball that struck Jackie in the hip. Robinson didn't say anything, just tossed aside his bat and went down to first base and filed it away. That was then. In the summer of 1949, things were different. When Robinson heard Rowe yelling out those things to Heintzelman—"In his damn ear, Kenny!"—he looked down at the Phillies catcher, Stan Lopata, and remarked on what a gutless thorn Schoolboy Rowe was. "Tell him yourself if you want to tell him," said Stan Lopata.

So Robinson did. He turned toward the Philadelphia dugout as he never had in 1948 or in 1947, when the Phillies, with their low and lousy manager Ben Chapman leading the way, bore a streak of hate that few teams bore. Now Jackie yelled straight toward the dugout, straight at Rowe, using language of the kind you would never hear Robinson use off the field or in a public setting but which you heard him use plenty on the field in 1949 and in the seasons that followed.

And then Schoolboy Rowe—who, to be clear, stood six foot four and was up near 220 pounds—came out of the dugout and began walking in a calm, even march toward home plate. Robinson put his eyes right back on Rowe's and started walking to meet him. It looked for a moment as though things might really blow—the players on both teams were on the balls of their feet, ready—before home plate umpire Artie Gore ran over and got up against Schoolboy Rowe and told him to shut it down and get back inside. Gore was in his early forties then and a little more than two years into his career as a major league umpire. He'd made his debut in the Braves vs. Dodgers game of April 15, 1947, at Ebbets Field, the game in which Robinson himself had made his debut. Gore was one of those good umpires who knew exactly what time it was. After a last bit of staring and glaring, Rowe turned back to the dugout and Robinson got back in the box against Heintzelman to finish his turn at bat.

The National League manager, the Braves' Billy Southworth, had Robinson batting second in the All-Star lineup, after Reese and ahead of Musial. The best middle infield in baseball was intact: Reese at shortstop, Robinson at second base. Those guys could turn the double play like nobody else. Southworth had chosen Dodgers manager Burt Shotton as one of his coaches for the game, so Shotton paced around the familiar dugout in his home park, wearing his customary street clothes as well as a pale fedora, looking like a real Connie Mack out there. The other National League coach was Bucky Walters, manager of the Cincinnati Reds. Walters had a little joke routine he liked to pull out whenever the Reds played the Dodgers that season. Tony Cuccinello, a Reds coach, would suggest a strategy for winning the game. Cuccinello: "Bucky, we've got to keep Robinson off the bases!" Walters: "Yeah, but how are you going to do it, Tony—kidnap him before the game?" By the time the All-Star Game rolled around, Brooklyn had a hold on first place.

There were still hardly any Black ballplayers in the major leagues then, absurdly few. Campy and Newk and Robinson in Brooklyn. Larry Doby and Minnie Miñoso and marvelous ol' Satchel Paige in Cleveland, and, just now, as of July 8, four days before the All-Star Game, Hank Thompson and Monte Irvin with the Giants. Robinson could have run off that list of names in a snap, of course. Any former Negro leaguer could have.

Irvin and Thompson, summoned from the Giants minor league team in Jersey City, debuted against the Dodgers at Ebbets Field.

Thompson had played some games in the American League with the St. Louis Browns back in '47, but now he was twenty-three, and it looked like he might be ready to stick. Irvin was another level of talent altogether—even though he was by now thirty years old and, as he could not help reminding himself, had left his greatest years behind him. His statistics from the Negro National League and Mexico were nuts—season batting averages of .397, .394, that sort of thing— and over the first few months of the 1949 season in Jersey City, he'd batted .373. Lots of power, lots of speed. Irvin could throw a ball from the outfield fence to home plate on a straight line five feet off the ground. "Most of the Black ballplayers thought Monte Irvin should have been the first Black player in the major leagues," Cool Papa Bell said some years after. "Monte was our best young ballplayer at that time. He could hit that long ball; he had a great arm; he could field; he could run. Yes, he could do everything." There were some terrific all-around ballplayers in the 1940s—major leaguers, Negro leaguers, both—but some baseball people back then would have told you that Monte Irvin was the best of the lot. According to Horace Stoneham, the owner of the Giants, one scout who saw Irvin play at age nineteen said simply: "The next DiMaggio."

Irvin was born in Haleburg, Alabama, in 1919, a few weeks after Jackie Robinson was born in Cairo, Georgia, eighty miles east. Irvin's family moved to New Jersey and he played high school baseball before catching on with the Newark Eagles in the Negro National League in 1938, the same time that Robinson was a four-sport star at junior college in Pasadena. So for Irvin, it had been a long eleven years of baseball— seasons before his time in the army, and seasons afterward—by the time he got the chance to break in with the New York Giants. When he lay down at night, Irvin could still feel the way the noisy old Negro league buses rattled them around as they traveled from game to game and town to town. He was six feet three inches and 195 pounds, and he could feel those bus rides in every one of his bones.

The Dodgers had signed Irvin first, in early 1949, but there was a kerfuffle over Branch Rickey signing Negro league players (Newark's Don Newcombe, for one) without paying a proper bonus to the Negro league team. The co-owner of the Eagles, the great and dynamic Effa Manley, said she might go ahead and sue Branch Rickey if he tried to take Irvin. So the Dodgers let Irvin out of his contract, and the Giants came in and signed him and paid a bonus to Manley and the Eagles. This was when Negro league baseball was onto hard times—in its final throes.

In the locker room before Irvin's first game in the majors, the Giants manager Leo Durocher said to the team: "I don't care what color you are. If you can play baseball, you can play on this club." It was exactly what Durocher had said back when he was managing the Dodgers and Robinson was breaking in. Irvin got into the game late, as a pinch hitter in the eighth inning. He came up with a runner on first base and nobody out, and he worked the count full and then drew a walk from Rex Barney. Hank Thompson played the whole nine innings at second base for the Giants, going 0 for 3. Robinson was in there for the Dodgers, playing second base and batting fourth, and even though you didn't talk to guys on the other team in those days—no kibitzing, especially not between a Giant and a Dodger— Robinson made a point of wishing Thompson and Irvin good luck on the field. Up until that day, July 8, 1949, two years and three months since he had broken in, Robinson had never played against a Black player in an official major league game.

As the years went on, Irvin would always say how happy he was for the chance that Jackie Robinson got, and he always emphasized that Robinson was a wonderful, well-suited choice to be the first, and he always allowed that Robinson had it toughest of all when it came to getting through the hard muck he had to cross to establish himself in the major leagues. But Irvin would also admit that for him and for some of the other great Negro league players, men like Satchel

Paige and Josh Gibson, there was jealousy toward Robinson too. Any number of Black players could have starred in the majors from the get-go, and everyone knew it. Paige had been striking out big leaguers in exhibition games since the early 1930s. In the '10s, Connie Mack and Babe Ruth were saying how John Henry Lloyd was the best ballplayer alive. A decade before that, Andrew Foster got nicknamed Rube after he beat Rube Waddell and the Philadelphia A's on a Sunday afternoon. That sort of thing happened plenty of times over the years.

The Giants debuts of Irvin and Thompson were noticed and commented on. "The unprecedented spectacle of two Negroes in Giant uniforms," read a story in the *New York Times*, and after the game, photos went around of the two guys smiling and touching the brims of their caps. But it wasn't much fanfare at all, really. Nothing, naturally, compared with the excitement that had attended Robinson's early games in organized baseball or what continued to attend Robinson years later and for the rest of his life.[10]

GEORGIA

The Dodgers had come up from Vero Beach to Brooklyn through the South in the spring of 1949, through Texas and Oklahoma, Georgia and the Carolinas, playing minor league clubs along the way. Thirteen exhibition games in two weeks, a Brooklyn barnstorming of Dixie. There was always an appetite for big league baseball in places that didn't have it. The Pirates swung through towns in Texas that year and left with tales of Ralph Kiner having hit baseballs out of the stadium and into the grocery store across the way, knocking cans of food off the shelves. Not once, but twice. *Literally, I tell you*, the locals said. (And listeners expressed no doubt. Kiner swung a 40-ounce

---

10. Monte Irvin : Jackie Robinson :: Charles Duke : Neil Armstrong

bat.) For the Dodgers, a big part of their trip was so that folks could get a chance to see Jackie Robinson. Branch Rickey did not mind the gate, that's for certain. Record attendance all along the way, more customers than the ballparks could contain, and racially mixed at every stop. Black fans sometimes climbed neighboring trees and sat on the branches to gander in. "They don't care to see the game," Robinson said. "All they want is to be able to say that they were there." You could hear it in the peach orchards a half mile off when Robinson stepped up to the plate.

The team had flown first from Florida to Beaumont, Texas. At least Beaumont would have been the landing place if not for the heavy fog that forced the plane farther west, buffeted in its flight by big winds and changing air pressure, the swerves and drops greening the gills of everyone on board. Robinson, Hodges, Hermanski, Branca, Barney, all of them sick at their seats. A hellish flight. The plane finally got down in Houston, hours from the ballpark by bus. Robinson and Roy Campanella had to find a place to stay that night. At no point during those weeks in the South were they permitted to sleep in the same hotels or eat at the same public tables as the rest of the team.

Robinson was in the lineup every day; Campanella only sometimes. Measures of both love and rancor stoked the southern crowds. Hissing alongside the applause in Beaumont. Growls amid the cheers in Fort Worth. And yet the games in Texas and Oklahoma unfolded in a kind of small-scale glory, the Dodgers playing beautiful baseball, Robinson among the stars on the field, no signs of physical unrest. Georgia, they all knew, would be the test. Never in that state had a Black man played professional baseball with white players. There was a game scheduled in Macon and then three more in Atlanta, against an old Southern Association team nicknamed the Crackers. The Ku Klux Klan's Grand Dragon of the realm, Samuel Green, fishing the murky eddies of public sentiment, had stirred a swirl of protest against Robinson and Campanella. In the first years after the war,

Green, a doctor in Atlanta, had consolidated his power in the Klan through some aggressive recruiting, appealing in part to fears of immigration, and by burning enormous crosses while leading cloaked ceremonies on the top of Stone Mountain. Green vowed a boycott or worse should the Crackers host the games. "The Atlanta club is slitting its own throat," was the metaphor Green used. Anonymous threats came in, against the Dodgers and the Crackers and against Robinson specifically. Burt Shotton read one in particular aloud to the team: a warning that Robinson would be shot if he took the field in Atlanta. The team went silent. Later, legend would attribute a version of the great response line to Pee Wee Reese, and place him on the field in Cincinnati, but it was in fact Gene Hermanski—"Yes, Gene, I can hear him still, with his perfect timing," said Carl Erskine—who broke the ice in the locker room: "Why don't we all wear number *42?*" Hermanski said. "Then the nut won't know who to shoot at."

The Dodgers laughed, Robinson especially—Gene, quick with the quip—and then they paused and let it get quiet again, and then they all picked up their gloves. The team was in the locker room at Ponce de Leon Park, and it was a couple of hours before game time, an 8:15 first pitch on a Friday night. Outside the stadium, picketers with Ku Klux Klan signs paced at the entranceways. But things had gone all right for the Dodgers in Macon the night before. And Branch Rickey had said from the outset that he believed the prospect of danger in Georgia was overstated, and the players had all along been doing their best to brush it off. When they went out to take pregame infield, Ponce de Leon Park was already nearly full. "Jackie, you mind moving over a few feet," Pee Wee said, his face bright with humor and kindness. "This guy might be a bad shot." Reese was maybe Robinson's best friend on the team that year.

Close to fifty thousand fans turned out for the three exhibition games in Atlanta, more than twenty-five thousand on Sunday, nearly double what the ballpark was meant to hold. So that's what a call for a boycott got Samuel Green.[11] Not a shot was heard, nor a fight reported. Most of the Black fans had to sit out in the bleachers, and on Sunday, they were ten rows deep in the outfield. White fans were allowed to take the better seats. The stands were Jim Crow, but there was some overlap at the edges of the sections.

The Atlanta police chief had assigned Black officers to the mainly Black seating areas, and white officers to the mainly white seating areas, and the crowd must have been about fifty-fifty in its racial makeup. After the games, when the rest of the Dodgers (save Campanella, of course) left to go back to the Hotel Ansley, with its en suite bathrooms and a dining room buffet you'd tell your wife about, Jackie was still at the ballpark signing his name for fans. He had a Boy Scout troop nestled around him on Saturday. A couple of days earlier, when the team first landed in Georgia, two white fans had gone over and greeted Robinson at the airport.

Robinson was 3 for 3 in Macon. He had a couple of hits in each of the three games in Atlanta and in front of that huge Sunday crowd, he doubled and singled and stole home. He had his hand bandaged up after getting spiked at third base, and then went back out. Overall on that trip through the South, Robinson batted better than .550. For his gate appeal and for his elevated level of play, Robinson was now drawing comparisons to Babe Ruth. Wrote Sam Lacy of Robinson and Campanella in the *Baltimore Afro-American*: "White fans came out early to see them, booed while watching them, but stayed after the game to get their autographs."

When the Crackers series with the Dodgers was done, folks went back home to the world of whites-only restrooms and segregated water fountains and segregated schools and segregated doctors' offices and whites-only lunch counters and Blacks sitting on the back of the

---

11. Nonetheless, Green was promoted to Grand Wizard of the Ku Klux Klan later that year, on August 4. Two weeks after that, he died of a heart attack.

bus. But they had all seen Jackie Robinson play for the Dodgers, that much was true. There was a restlessness in Atlanta then. That same week in April, Thurgood Marshall and the NAACP and the president of Morehouse College backed a petition to the Atlanta Board of Education, seeking that Black public schools get the equal treatment and support that was their right. This was five years before the *Brown v. Board of Education* Supreme Court decision that guaranteed equal access to public education.

Later in 1949, the Crackers' parent club, the Boston Braves, signed their first Black player, Sam Jethroe, who would in 1950 be named National League Rookie of the Year. And it was in a ballpark in Atlanta, specifically at Fulton County Stadium, that on April 8, 1974, exactly twenty-five years to the day after Robinson ignored the death threats and took the field at Ponce de Leon Park, that the Atlanta Braves' Hank Aaron turned on a belt-high fastball, lashing it deep into the night and over the left field fence for the 715th home run of his career.

BROOKLYN, THE STREETS

The Ebbets Field gates had opened at 11:00 a.m., at which time the last three thousand seats went on sale—in the bleachers, at a dollar apiece. Boston's Warren Spahn, an All-Star once again, would start for the National League, slated to go into his big lefty's windmill, raise his right leg, and deliver the first pitch at 1:30 p.m. Robinson was just as happy to have Spahn on his own side for once. Over two and a half seasons and four dozen at bats, Spahn had been a misery for Jackie. Before the game, Robinson and Joe DiMaggio were summoned together on the apron of the field, back of home plate, where they both autographed the same baseball and then gave it to a five-year-old girl, Kathleen Dugan, who had been cured of polio. Baseball commissioner Happy Chandler stood out there with DiMaggio and

Robinson, and so did someone representing the Sister Kenny Institute, which was just then beginning a fundraising drive.

DiMaggio was one of six Yankee All-Stars, including pitchers Vic Raschi and Allie Reynolds, who were acutely aware of the distress that Robinson could visit upon an opponent. Just before the 1949 season, the Yankees and Dodgers played three exhibition games at Ebbets Field, and the Dodgers had won all three. Robinson singled, scampered, and scored against Raschi in a 6–1 win in the first game. In the final game, with Reynolds pitching, Robinson went first to third, exploiting the briefest outfield lapse, then goaded Reynolds into wildness as he danced off third base and then finally stole home. "When you get into the locker room I want you to check your lockers," Yankees manager Casey Stengel snapped as the team came off the field. "He stole everything out there he wanted today so he might have stolen your jocks as well."

The All-Stars lined up along the foul lines to be introduced, organ chords dramatizing the announcement of each name and the voices from the stands crying out in Brooklynese, approving or disapproving of each player in turn. Robinson stood between Hodges to his right and Kiner to his left, and even between the two taller men, he was imposing. He was carrying about two hundred pounds then—in taut, midseason shape, injury-free—and he wore a size 13 shoe. A little while after the introductions, the United States attorney general, Tom C. Clark, a Harry Truman appointee then one month shy of beginning his tenure on the Supreme Court, threw out the ceremonial first ball.

Just off the corner of East Ninety-Fifth Street and Church Avenue, in East Flatbush, Brooklyn—call it four and a half miles from home plate at Ebbets Field—a small crowd had gathered on the sidewalk in front of the television shop to watch the All-Star Game. Within five years, half the households in America would have a television set in their home; within twelve years, that number would be nine out of ten. But in 1949, a television in Brooklyn was as rare as a hummingbird's nest. In a storefront like this, a TV might be on, facing the street, all afternoon and into the night, beckoning as choice cakes beckon from a baker's window. There was still an air of mystery and special science about televisions then, a giddy promise: See what magic can be yours, right in your own home! On Tuesday nights, eight o'clock, a group gathered there on East Ninety-Fifth Street to watch Milton Berle. On a Thursday, for *Winner Take All*. And on this particular afternoon, for the 16th Major League All-Star Game, chock-full of Dodgers and Yanks, described by Red Barber, the local voice who announced the Dodgers games.

Ira Glasser was eleven years old that summer, and he lived just a few doors down from the television shop, with his parents and younger sister, in a two-bedroom apartment—nine hundred square feet if it was that, one of four apartments in a two-story building. To Ira and his friends, the Brooklyn Dodgers were everything that summer. Jackie Robinson was everything and more. "If I thought about Jackie Robinson five minutes after I woke up, that was already late in the day," says Ira. "The reason was that he was the most exciting player. Period. On a team full of heroes—Snider, Reese, Furillo—Robinson was the one you emulated."

For Ira, the draw of Robinson was fierce—"the daring, the sheer skill, the relentless competitiveness, all strategically deployed," as he framed it seven decades later—and the scenes of Jackie that animated Barber's audio narrations quickened their hearts as well as their paces. Yet even for that, Ira didn't then know, couldn't possibly have known, how Robinson's play and his place on the Dodgers team (along in part with Barber's telling of it) would shape and drive Ira's own enormously impactful adult life. Many years later, though now many years ago, Ira came across the faded Dodgers cap he got at Ebbets Field in 1949. He has kept the cap close ever since.

Next to the TV store was a butcher's shop, and across the way stood Wagman's, where you went to get the smoked whitefish (and the bagels and the pickles and the cheese) on lucky Sunday mornings at home. Katz's grocery store, run by the brisk and wiry Mr. Katz, had a narrow façade but was the deepest store on the block. Often the adults who'd paused before that sidewalk TV would be holding a brown paper bag inscribed with a series of prices in Mr. Katz's blocky print, the sack filled with bottles of milk or a half dozen eggs for the following day.

Ira's grandmother lived two blocks down, on Ninety-third Street, also between Church and Willmohr. She sometimes took Ira with her to the poultry market, a brutish, cacophonous place where the chickens were killed in the back, then handed heartily over, warm and pulsing. Back in her kitchen, Grandma would pull out the feathers herself and cook the chicken whole for Friday night dinner. There was a comic book shop called Sonny's and a place to get an egg cream at a counter, and George and Sid's for the real pastrami, and Harry's Barbershop at fifteen cents a cut. Through the doorway next to George and Sid's, a bearish dentist, Elias Strugatz, would see you and administer his evil drill, one flight up.

This was the world. And all the guys who really mattered to Ira— Lewis, Michael, Lester, Larry, Marty—lived right there. To venture by foot past Ninety-Third Street in one direction or past Ninety-Seventh Street (and the R. J. Harris funeral home) in the other, to expand beyond the broad avenues, Church and Willmohr, that lay like protective shores on either side, was, in the breast of an eleven-year-old, to court an incalculable danger. That nest of city blocks was their own on those summer days, the arena for the principal moments of their lives. They played ball in empty lots, rocky and uneven and strewn with glass and debris. Usually there was one bat among them, and a few gloves to share, and a softball that would serve until it had the mush of a month-old melon. They played a form of baseball with a pink Spalding Hi-Bounce Ball, a Spaldeen, off the apartment house stoops, and they played a form of baseball in the boxes on the sidewalk. They rode homemade scooters and glanced over at the girls playing hopscotch or chanting while they jumped rope. It could go on like that all day, no parents anywhere to be seen. Often you'd hear the sounds of the ball game, Red Barber's syrupy voice from the console radios, through the many open windows up and down the block.

No Black people lived in the neighborhood. Nor Irish. Nor Germans. Nor Italians. Nor, even, Jews who veered much outside the range of modified religious observance that prevailed. The kosher butcher might attract lines on a Friday afternoon, but so did the movie house on Saturday, Shabbos. (Ira, to put a point on it, was his own grandmother's Shabbos goy.) There were other parts of Brooklyn from which both Catholic schools and yeshivas drew, and areas where groups of Italians and Irish shared or contested ground, but on the whole, the borough was far from the demographic tapestry it would later become. You saw only white faces in the shops and schools, on the trolleys and in the parks, and, almost universally, on the theater screens. What was happening on the Dodgers in those years was not happening in many other places.

You went to the dentist, but you did not go to the doctor. The doctor came to you when bidden, and came quickly. Polio, in East Flatbush, just as anywhere, was not some distant menace. It had nearly felled Lester a few years before, and now, at eleven, he moved with a gimp. He always got picked last when the boys chose sides to play ball. *He wasn't the most athletic of the group to begin with*, the other boys told themselves. When there was an odd number of kids—four on one side, five on the other, say—the captains would shoot fingers for who got the extra guy. The loser had to take Lester. And yet Lester loved to play. He always played. He wanted to play. And if the boys were callous, even cruel, in their selection ("*You* take him") it was a callousness born of strict competitive drive. Having Lester on your team made it less likely that you'd win the game. And whether you won or lost that game of softball on an empty lot might lighten or darken your mood for hours or more.

The other boys wanted Lester to show up and play, of course, to be part of things. They would have felt incomplete without him. He belonged. They could all remember when the polio was worse for Lester: at age seven or eight, he was so debilitated that his mother pushed him from place to place in a kind of oversized stroller. They knew the stoop where Lester lived, and the shape of the book bag he carried to school, and the sound of his biggest laugh. They'd wave to his mother when they saw her on the street. And when Lester did something favorable in a ball game, knocked the game-winning hit or made an improbable catch, exceeding expectations, the cheers were louder for Lester than they would have been for any of the other boys. They would hug him and hold him up and sometimes raise him above their shoulders and carry him home.

For the boys, the calculus was simple. No special privilege. No niceties. Lester didn't want niceties. Honor the effort, honor the achievement. "There is a certain amount of fairness among athletes," Monte Irvin once said, assessing the years in which he broke into the major leagues. "A certain amount of respect for ability. The attitude is play hard."

Not much disturbed the boys from their daily romp. They might break and go home for lunch, or they'd have some errands to do. But for the most part, if you were around and free of family obligations, you were out on the streets with some kind of ball or stick, or maybe a taped-up deck of cards to play packs.

There weren't many cars on the inner streets—a few more on the avenues—so the kids ranged freely, and whenever a car did roll by, they paid attention. Larry had an older sister, entrancing at age eighteen, who sometimes got picked up in a car for a date, causing the boys to pause and watch and titter. Other times, they heard the clanging of bells. Slowly around the corner came the white rounded nose and faux shingled roof of the Bungalow Bar ice cream truck, come over to Flatbush from its rounds in Bushwick.

They'd dig in their pockets for a nickel or a dime and see other kids breaking from their own games or spilling out of doorways to get to the side of the truck, to the ice cream guy in his shirtsleeves seated behind a faux picket fence. There was not much more in the world one could want than a Creamsicle or a Dixie Cup ("Who'd you get under the lid? Weissmuller? Johnny Mack Brown?") to work on for a spell on a July afternoon while standing on the street corner, your street corner, and watching a rare, special ball game on TV.

Already, the American League led 4–0 in the bottom of the first inning. Johnny Mize had dropped a ball at first base, and Reese had fumbled a grounder at shortstop, and Spahn had walked a guy and been touched for three hard singles—DiMaggio, Eddie Robinson, Birdie Tebbetts. With that, the lead was built. The Ebbets Field crowd was up and standing when Reese led off for the National League and bounced back to the mound, and they were up and standing now with one out as Robinson followed. The cloud cover was complete, and the people in the stands were hatless and full-throated, loud and buzzing. Robinson looked out toward the pitcher, Mel Parnell, a six-foot lefty and the Red Sox ace, who always seemed to stand intentionally tall on the mound. Robinson got into the batter's box and slapped at his rear hip the way he often did.

On that afternoon, in that moment, there was no more relevant baseball player, no more impactful athlete, no greater sports celebrity alive, than Jackie Robinson. Babe Ruth had died the summer before, at fifty-three. Even on this very field, alongside the Yankees' DiMaggio and the Red Sox's Williams and the Cardinals' Musial, and even on this very day, just hours after the incomparable Sugar Ray Robinson had once again beaten back Kid Gavilan to raise his boxing record to 95–1–1 and remain the welterweight champion.

In this time, this season, this milieu, Robinson stood fully astride. No one played with more intensity and no one played better. Branch Rickey had taken to calling him "the best since Ty Cobb," and the suggestion drew no complaints. He batted fourth in the Brooklyn lineup and he knew when to take a walk and he had added a dangerous level of power to his game. After Robinson hit a thirteenth-inning home run to beat the Giants at the Polo Grounds in late May, you could have heard Leo Durocher cursing on the Sunset Strip. Wherever the Dodgers played that season, kids climbed onto the sun-heated dugout roof before the game and dangled scorecards or notebooks over the ledge, hoping that Robinson, down below, might sign his name for them. The other Dodgers were sought after for their autographs as well, of course. They all were. "One time a kid asked me to sign six different items for him," says Carl Erskine. "'Six?' I asked him. 'Why so many?' He said he was planning to trade all six of mine for one Jackie Robinson."

For five weeks now, a song had been playing on the radio, newly minted and rising in the charts just as Robinson rose among his own ranks. Bandleader Buddy Johnson's "Did You See Jackie Robinson Hit That Ball?" began with the big blowing wind instruments and featured the many-voiced choruses and tinkling piano of the times. Its lyrics, with allusions to Paige, Campanella, Newcombe, and Doby lifted Robinson to singular stature. He hits a home run, he steals home, "When Jackie comes to bat / The other team is through" went the lyrics. In the time since the song first reached American ears and up until his historic first at bat in the All-Star Game, Robinson had batted .405. Over 31 games, he had gotten 47 hits and scored 31 runs, and the Dodgers had gone 20–11. Buddy Johnson visited the Dodgers' locker room and gave Robinson an autographed copy of the record, and Robinson gave Buddy Johnson an autographed baseball in return.

The sportswriters were already forecasting Robinson for the league MVP, even with half the season to go. And it was around this time, just before the All-Star Game, that a reader from Baton Rouge, Louisiana, wrote to the *Pittsburgh Courier* with a question: "Who is the greatest Black athlete of all time?"

The *Courier* had begun publishing in 1907, and its editors went about surveying the historical landscape. That landscape included Jesse Owens, who'd won four Olympic gold medals and set four world records, as a sprinter and a jumper and a hurdler. It included the great heavyweight champions Jack Johnson and Joe Louis—the latter, in the summer of 1949, still in the full flush of his extraordinary reign. There were Bobby Marshall and Fritz Pollard, who'd gone to the NFL, and there were many Negro leaguers tall in both deed and legend: Gibson, Lloyd, Bell, Paige.

There were others too. But then, taking into account how, in college, he had starred in track and football and basketball, and, of course, bearing witness to what was happening right then in the major leagues, the *Courier* responded to the question without ambivalence: "We'll pick Jackie Robinson."

Even in that year of years for Robinson, and even for all the times he had in his life stepped onto a playing field as the focal point for an enormous crowd, Robinson was not immune to occasions of exceptional demand. He read the newspapers. He felt the surge among the neighborhood boys who gathered outside for a send-off when he set out in the morning from home. He heard specific pleas from the crowd. *First Black baseball player to start in an All-Star Game.*

"I still get a little tight in tense situations," Robinson admitted to a reporter that week. The tendency was not so problematic as it had been when he was first breaking in, Robinson added. Back then, in those tense situations, he would simply grip the bat more earnestly and narrow his gaze further still and blink back the throbbing at his temples and stay in there and hit. Often to fine result, yes, but in those pressing moments, less than his best self. Now, though, when he felt himself "all pounding inside" as he put it, Robinson would step out of the batter's box. He would breathe a long, even breath and swing the bat and look around at the things he could see, the positioning of the players on defense, the shadow or lack of it on the ground, the wind playing against a high flag out beyond the outfield wall. *To get myself acclimated* is how Robinson thought of those respites outside the batter's box.

Parnell had a good slider and a good sinker, and he could deliver strikes at various speeds—the pitch selection and approach had gotten him here. Still, as Robinson stepped in for his first All-Star at bat, he reminded himself of the principle that George Sisler had drummed into him: "Always look for a fastball, Jackie. Just look for the fast one." There would be time to adjust if the slower stuff came. The spring sessions with Sisler at the Dodgers camp at Vero Beach that preseason had been remarkable for Robinson. Transformative, in a way. Sisler was someone Branch Rickey had believed in for many years. Where Branch Rickey went in baseball, Sisler went, too—as a scout, an evaluator, a learned eye, a batting instructor. In the spring of '48, Sisler had attended daily to twenty-one-year-old Duke Snider, laying in a foundation that would help Snider to cool his inner coil, to rein himself in. Sisler was in his fifties and had been retired from his playing days for nineteen years, and he was soaked in earned baseball wisdom. He'd hit .407 in 1920 and .420 in 1922, the year before his eyesight got wrecked by sinusitis. Even so, he played another seven seasons, plagued by double vision and relying on wiles and an attention to details, and batted .320. He knew what he was doing in a batter's box.

Sisler wanted hitting to be basic and disciplined, tied to certain simple truths. He watched Jackie closely in batting practice, and they worked together, hitting off a tee. Sisler helped Robinson to keep square in his stance an instant longer, helped to eliminate Robinson's tendency to lunge. Robinson became more patient on pitches off the plate and more aggressive on pitches he could drive. Sisler would clap once sharply when he saw something he liked: "Just like that, Jackie! Just like that!"

After working with Sisler that spring, Robinson felt full of new confidence at the plate, as if suddenly in possession of a mental key. Those hitting lessons would stay with Robinson for the rest of his career. He was a quick learner, highly astute, and the huge impact of his sessions with Sisler—whose insights were crucial and well placed but not, after all, revolutionary—was a reminder of how very little coaching Robinson, now thirty, had ever received. *I'm doing just what we talked about*, he would say to himself as the season went along. *Looking for the fastball*. Now Robinson stepped back inside the batter's box, and Parnell got back up on his toes and looked in toward home plate.

The pitch came over the plate at the level of Robinson's thighs, and he sent it on a line drive over the shortstop's head, the ball landing cleanly on the grass and bounding to the right of DiMaggio in center field, to the left of Williams in left. It was a sharply struck single by almost anyone's lights, but not by Robinson's. He never broke stride as he rounded the first base bag, raising flecks of dirt as he churned toward second, raising a spray when he landed in his slide. The strong throw came in to the second baseman Cass Michaels, who wheeled and put down the tag, touching the right ankle of Robinson, who, using every inch of that size 13 shoe, already had his toe on the bag. A double for Robinson, and the crowd for the first time that day had a reason to cheer. A runner on second base with Musial to follow.

If there was a visiting player alive who had made a habit out of hitting baseballs with true authority at Ebbets Field, that player was the Cardinals' Stan Musial. "Oy, here comes that man again!" the crowd would say, in fear and admiration when he stepped out of the dugout and moved toward the plate. Musial in those years had become a part of the zeitgeist of Dodgerdom. Over 16 games at Ebbets Field in 1948 and the first half of 1949, Musial had batted .493. He'd scored 23 runs and driven in 17. Among Musial's 34 base hits in those 16 games were

7 home runs. The one that he hit now off Mel Parnell cleared the Esquire Boot Polish sign in right field and cleared the fencing behind it. Heads up on Bedford Avenue. Robinson jogged around to score, and Musial jogged in behind him. It was 4–2 now, and the fans stayed on their feet. When Musial arrived at home plate, Robinson greeted him with a handshake and a slap on the rump.

The folks in Brooklyn followed the Dodgers in the daily papers, and they listened to Red Barber call the games through the big wooden console radios in their living rooms. There was an inclination in those days to stare at the radio while you listened to it. Three and a half feet tall, two knobs, a dial, and the grille—like a little square person, practically. "Evening, baseball fans," the game might begin. "This is your redhead, Red Barber."

It was from Barber that Ira and his friends and a good number of others not only got the spirit and feel of their team and the richness and subtlety of baseball but also came to consider certain things about what was happening in America, about how people could be treated for better or for worse. The notion that there was a world that existed and operated outside the sphere of the streets of Flatbush was not immediately accounted for in a young boy's thoughts. At the Saturday movies, you went to the Westerns and then played your own version of bang-bang, acting out scenes on the street. But the details of life around the ball games were real.

The backstory on Red Barber is that he was born in Columbus, Mississippi, and moved to Florida at age ten, and as a child had once seen a Black man tarred and feathered and forced through the streets by the Ku Klux Klan. He lived in segregated communities, and he went to segregated schools, and he attended the University of Florida, which was also segregated and would remain so until 1958. Barber's first job in baseball was calling games for the Cincinnati Reds, which he did for four seasons, before coming to the Dodgers in 1939. Barber had this gorgeous southern drawl, and a curiosity and clear intelligence (he was the son of an English teacher; he graduated first in his high school class), and he really gave you a picture of what was going on out there. The folks in Brooklyn loved him. "Well, I'll be a suck-egg mule," Barber might say when a game took an unexpected turn. He called the ball field "the pea patch," and he referred to having the lead as being "in the catbird seat," and he pronounced *here* as a two-syllable word: *he-ah*.

Barber was the first person in the Dodgers organization who learned that Branch Rickey planned to bring a Black player to the team. They were sitting together one afternoon at a back table at Joe's Restaurant, near the Dodgers offices on Montague Street, after attending a meeting at Borough Hall. This was in the spring of 1945, when the war was still going on and before Branch Rickey had signed Jackie Robinson. The Dodgers' scouts and other front-office men out looking for players thought that the idea was finding talent for a potential new Negro league team, the Brooklyn Brown Dodgers.

The way Barber remembered it, in a memoir that came out in the late 1960s, Branch Rickey was working on a hard roll that afternoon at Joe's, breaking the roll into pieces and then buttering the pieces with sharp dabs of the butter knife. Bread crumbs gathered on the tablecloth and fell on the floor, and Rickey put away one hard roll and then another in this fashion while at the same time telling Barber what he really had in mind—not a Negro league team at all. He didn't know exactly when a Black player would play for the Brooklyn Dodgers, Barber recalls Rickey saying, and he didn't know exactly who that Black player would be, but he did know that this was something that would happen, that the time had come for it, and that he was going to be the baseball executive to make it so. That meant, of course, that there would then be other Black players, too, any number of others who might help the Dodgers win.

When Branch Rickey really got to talking passionately about

something, his eyebrows could seem even more enormous and thicketed than they actually were. He was a Methodist who had arrived at his decision to force the integration of Major League Baseball while silently pacing in a minister's office. He liked the idea of making the Dodgers better and more profitable, and he thought keeping Black players out of organized baseball was completely asinine. The thing he most loved in his professional life was a ballplayer who could really play the game.

Branch Rickey fully grasped what Barber meant to the Dodgers as the voice of the team, how he appealed so strongly to radio listeners and had helped increase the size and ardor of the fan base. And he knew where Barber hailed from, of course, the kind of surroundings the announcer had lived in all his life until he came north to start his career. Rickey wanted Barber to understand what was going on so that if Barber felt he couldn't broadcast a team composed of both white and Black players, now was the time to look for another job. If he waited until a Black player was actually signed and playing in the Dodgers system, and then decided to leave—well, that wouldn't be good for anyone concerned, least of all Red himself. So Rickey wanted Barber to have the early heads-up. *Don't tell anyone at all about this*, Branch Rickey said, not anyone—although he knew of course that Barber would talk things over with his wife, Lylah, with whom he lived in Westchester County, outside the city. Barber was then thirty-seven years old, and calling games for the Brooklyn Dodgers was about the best job he could ever conceive of having.

When he got home that night, as Barber recalled, he told Lylah what Branch Rickey had said, and he told her that that was it, he was going to leave the Dodgers. The prejudices instilled in him were too great to overcome, he felt, and he would look for work somewhere else. But Lylah had another idea. "Let's have a martini," she said. Then they could consider things a bit more fully, sharpen up their thinking, and go to sleep with open possibilities. Over the next few days, Barber came to a couple of what he would characterize as "self-realizations" about the randomness of his or any other person's lineage and place in the world; about the second great commandment, "Love thy neighbor"; and about his role as a reporter. Plus, it was a great job.

He would stay on with the Dodgers after all. Of course he would. What he would do, he decided, was report the game as he always had: call the ball and convey the environment in all its sumptuous detail, just describe what was happening. And so he did. Red Barber told you what Robinson was doing in the game, and what an impact he was having—a real spark plug, a fire-starter. On national broadcasts, such as the 1949 All-Star Game, he might remind listeners of Robinson's prominence. "He is certainly the most publicized player in many a year," Barber might say. He described how Robinson batted and the way he ran the bases and how his teammates embraced him after a big, game-winning hit. He called him Robby sometimes, when doing the play-by-play.

Barber was an active and curious reporter, keen on facts and nuances he thought were salient to his listeners' understanding. Before games, he would spend time in the dugouts and on the field and talk with the players on both teams about how they were feeling, about a bruise someone had on his hip, or the extra sun he had taken in the outfield the day before, or even how the bacon and eggs had gone down that morning before the game. Barber liked to assess whether a player was rested and sharp, or whether anything had occurred that might be relevant to a player's performance or frame of mind on the field. During the 1949 season, for example, he would sometimes talk with Carl Furillo about the health of Furillo's father, who was in the perilous grip of heart failure and whom Furillo visited in Reading, Pennsylvania, whenever he could.

It was this kind of thinking and approach—a style that would become commonplace for radio and television broadcasters of any worth, but which Barber was then forging as a gold standard—that led Barber to explain to listeners how, when the Dodgers played in St. Louis, the team and its traveling party stayed at the top-end Chase Hotel, but that Robinson, and, in '49, Campanella and Newcombe, were not permitted to join them. Instead they stayed at a hotel in another part of town, where accommodations were inferior. No air-conditioning, for one thing, which meant open windows all night and little relief from the midsummer swelter that could engulf St. Louis. If Robinson and the other Black players had indeed been granted an exception to stay at the air-cooled, chandelier-lit Chase and chosen to do so (as Robinson eventually did, years later), they would have been required to remain in their rooms for the most part and would not have been allowed to hang around in the lobby with their teammates or eat dinner in the hotel restaurant. By informing his audience of Brooklyn Dodgers fans of these circumstances, Barber was in a small but direct way influencing how some people thought. It was a vivid situation.

Since getting to know Robinson and witnessing his pride and grace, the determination and unfettered excellence with which he played, Barber had been even more able to shed the cold vestiges of bigotry clinging to him from his early life. There was no possible response to knowing Robinson, Barber felt, other than respect. Barber saw how Robinson inspired other players and saw how firmly he had carried himself even among quisling teammates of early years. By 1949, Barber might come upon Jackie organizing card games in the clubhouse. "Hey, Gene," Robinson would call out to Hermanski, a deck of cards in hand. "Let's get started."

Robinson said that he appreciated the way Barber broadcast the games, holding him to the very same standards and expectations as any other primary Dodger. "Just one of the guys" was to Robinson the essence of equality. "If there is any thanks involved, any appreciation," Barber would reflect many years later, "then I thank Jackie

Robinson. He did far more for me than I did for him." Barber, in his broadcasts, was neither a crusader for nor a belittler of Robinson—simply a reporter, matter-of-fact in his delivery and tone. Injustice needs no embellishment to be seen.

"When Red Barber would describe the way things were in St. Louis, I would get so angry. Like, incensed!" says Ira. The medium of sports, then, now, since Milo of Croton, has been a way into a young man's heart. "I learned about all of the race stuff from Red Barber and from the baseball pages. I don't recall Barber even saying that Robinson was a Black ballplayer. But I do recall him reporting on what was happening. I learned about Jim Crow segregation in hotels and restaurants from Barber. That was when I first heard about it, and that was when I first hated it. And the reason I hated it was not because I came from a liberal family that was steeped in civil rights. I hated it because those were my guys. If they had done that crap to Hodges or Reese for some reason, I would have hated it too."

This was 1949, and Jim Crow was not being taught by any mandate in the public schools of Brooklyn. Nor, to schoolchildren in the borough, was evidence of segregation and its insidiousness clear. The institutional racism of the North was quieter. "My father was a glazier," says Ira, "and he lost his job in the '30s, during the Depression. Then when he began to get work in the '40s—sometimes just a day or two a week—he would get jobs through the labor union hiring office. That was enormously helpful, and my father, through a lot of hard work and willingness and discipline was able to get back to full-time work and get us as a family back on our feet. He began to save some money and eventually we moved to the suburbs and bought a house. But at the time, the same union that had gotten him those jobs did not allow Black membership. Blacks were not allowed in the union. And all of those type of construction and labor jobs went to union workers. Did I know all of that as a kid? No way. Did my father know it? He must have known it, but I don't know if he thought about it. It was the way things were. And it is because of that institutional racism that I and my children are descendants of, and beneficiaries of, white privilege. Black workers, any number of whom might have been as good and hardworking a glazier as my father, were just not given the opportunity."

This was still years before Emmett Till and Rosa Parks and the Little Rock Nine. Martin Luther King Jr. was twenty years old in 1949, attending Crozer Theological Seminary in Chester, Pennsylvania. He had taken courses on the Old Testament and the New Testament, and he had read in the seminary library a biography of Gandhi, and on the Thursdays when King delivered the student sermons, his classmates crowded thick into the chapel to be sure not to miss it.

And this was eighteen years before Ira would take his first job at the New York Civil Liberties Union (NYCLU), and nearly three decades before he would move into the role of executive director of the American Civil Liberties Union (ACLU), a position he would hold for nearly a quarter century. He spent thirty-five years devoted to the advocacy and protection of civil rights, absorbing and sometimes courting controversy, and expanding the reach and standing of the organization and its principles. From the late 1970s to the start of the 2000s, few Americans embodied the idea of civil rights more visibly or prominently than Ira. And if, at any time in those years—from the moment he arrived early for his first day of work at the ramshackle, Lower Manhattan offices of the NYCLU, in 1967, until his ACLU retirement dinner in 2001—you had asked Ira why he took the path he had taken in his professional life (that is, who or what had most influenced him to embark on it), Ira would have said without hesitation, just as he would still say today: "Jackie Robinson."

Nor was he alone. "At some point after I got to the NYCLU," says Ira, "I discovered that everybody who worked there who was around my age had been Dodger fans and that the centrality of Jackie was universally shared by them." There was Art and Alan and Norman and Danny, and others. A Dodgers fan at every other desk. Not everyone was a baseball fan, and there was the occasional Giants or Cardinals fan mixed in. There was not, however, a Yankees fan among them. "I was enough of a trained mathematician to know that such universality was very unlikely to have been random," says Ira. "There was a reason. The consequences for a white kid in the late 1940s in America to be growing up with a Black man as his hero were enormous. That just didn't happen in those days. It's hard to understand today how revolutionary it was to your own subconscious psychological development. When you got older, when the seminal moments in the civil rights movement happened and the arguments were made, you always had a sense of having heard things, experienced them, before, in an intimate way."

The Dodgers played on radios almost every day of the summer in Brooklyn in those years, in Flatbush and East Flatbush, in Bath Beach and Bensonhurst and Brownsville and Borough Park and Bay Ridge, in Bed-Stuy and Bushwick and beyond. You could hear Red Barber throughout the New York area: in Yonkers, a woman shushing her daughter during a tight game; in Kew Gardens, a mailman pausing on his route to listen. Sometimes in those years and in the years to come, the great Dodgers players could be heard throughout the country as well, in the World Series, for example, or in an All-Star Game. So that if you were an athletic kid at Gibbs High in St. Petersburg, Florida; or a cross-handed-hitting teenager in Mobile, Alabama, swatting bottle caps with sticks on a dusty field; or a young boy on a family farm in Minnesota, getting a break from the afternoon chores, you, along with countless others, might have been listening too.

It was the top of the fourth inning now, and the National League, by dint of a few singles and a few walks, had taken a 5–4 lead, and big Don Newcombe was on the mound, throwing his warm-up pitches.

Truth was, the score could have been longer in the National League's favor. It was Newcombe who'd gone to bat in the bottom of the second inning, with the bases loaded and nobody out, and smacked a pitch from Virgil Trucks on a line to deep left field, toward the foul line and near the wall—right there by the MICHAELS sign—and Ted Williams, even with the taped-up ribs, had gotten on it quick, a few galloping strides and then a backpedal and then, long-armed and six-foot-three, a long reach upward to snare the ball, at once disappointing and thrilling the Brooklyn crowd. (Teddy Ballgame in our Ebbets Field!) Newcombe batted left-handed, and so the ball had been slicing away from Williams and what might have been a double and three runs for the National League was instead only one run and an out. "Williams saved my scalp," said the American League manager Lou Boudreau after the game.

Along with Newcombe, Roy Campanella had come in at catcher. Gil Hodges was now at first base in place of Johnny Mize, Robinson was still at second, and Reese was still at short. The makeup of the infield at the All-Star Game felt very much like the makeup of the infield on a given day of the Dodgers season at Ebbets Field. Jogging out from the dugout and picking up their gloves was not, even with the park gussied up and the crowd extra large and lively, so different from the usual. "All right, let's hold 'em, boys!" Pee Wee might shout out as they prepared to go onto the field. "They get nothing from us."

Sometimes during the changeover between innings, Robinson would turn toward the stands from in front of the dugout and look for Rachel. She wore her good clothes for every game, and she sat with people the Robinsons knew, sometimes Joan Hodges or Bev Snider or another of the wives. Rachel had a way of holding her hot dog in one hand. Jackie would find her in the crowd and look straight at her and allow humor and kindness into his eyes, softening the face he wore on the field. With these looks, Jackie and Rachel shared their own perpetual, lifelong inside joke, the improbability and the whirlwind, the beauty and the size of everything: Look at our lives. Jackie knew they would both be there at the end of the day. Rachel would wave gently and smile from her seat. Sometimes Jackie Jr. would be standing wedged between Rachel's knees, working through a hot dog of his own, the brim of his toddler-sized Dodgers cap turned upward from his forehead.

The top of the American League lineup was due to hit in the fourth, which meant Dom DiMaggio would start things off. This was Dom's fourth All-Star Game, and he was keen on them, not least for the chance to have some time around his brother Joe, given the distance that was so often between them. They had posed for photos together before the game, as usual—"the All-Star Brothers"—with Dom leaning nonchalantly on his bat. In such times throughout their lives and careers, Dom was sharply aware of the particular heat and attention that followed Joe, and today, he was aware of the heat and attention on Robinson as well. A similar aura, he thought.

Dom noted the anticipation that coursed through the crowd when Robinson strode toward the batter's box. He'd felt the extra claps of thunder that echoed across Ebbets Field after Robinson's double in the first inning, and the intensity of the applause that had followed even Robinson's walk leading off in the third. The crowd at a game like this—people called it a Dream Game—focused tightly on every player and every development, but even then, on some more than others. *Does it help him play better?* Dom wondered of Robinson. *When he's at the plate or standing in the field, does he think about how he is seen in other people's eyes?*

Against Newcombe now, Dom hit a ground ball to the third baseman, Sid Gordon, who threw across the field to Hodges for the first out of the inning. Then George Kell, the Tigers' high-average hitter, singled into left field, and the next batter, Williams, drew a walk. Newcombe now had some work ahead of him, with two runners on and Joe DiMaggio coming up to hit. Newcombe was six feet four inches tall and upward of 220 pounds, and the afternoon air in Brooklyn hung heavy with imminent rain. He pulled a handkerchief from his back pocket and took a moment to wipe his face and brow. He had been in the major leagues for less than two months and had appeared in just fifteen games, and he was barely twenty-three years old.

Newcombe could get distracted during games sometimes, in on himself too much, and Robinson was given to trotting over to try to help set things right. He would urge Newcombe, and not in gentle terms, to bear down and address the situation. Pull your tits up, man. In Pittsburgh, two weeks before the All-Star Game, Newcombe was pitching with a lead, but had begun falling behind in the count against modest hitters. He appeared tentative and began aiming the ball. Suddenly the Pirates had runners on base, and Robinson was standing next to Newcombe near the mound. "You should go to the clubhouse and take off your uniform and go home," Robinson said. "You don't want to pitch. You've got no business here in the big leagues." He told Newcombe to quit fooling around, and that there were three guys in the bullpen ready to come in for him. "Go on inside and shower or reach back and throw the damn ball."

For the life of him, there were times that Newcombe wanted to take a punch at Jackie. Newcombe's enormous body would stiffen in anger, and a thunderous scowl would take over his face. Not that he would ever actually take a swing at Robinson on the field! Regardless of his temper. Newcombe would never raise a hand against Jackie Robinson anywhere or anytime, no matter how fiercely Robinson goaded him. That was mainly because of his respect for Robinson. But partly for another reason: "Jackie'd kick the shit out of me," Newcombe said. Never mind that Newcombe was a head taller and had Robinson by twenty-five pounds. Newcombe knew the athlete that Robinson was, and he also sensed, in the way that someone who'd marked time in poolrooms as a teenager could sense, that Robinson knew his way around a fight. That much was true. As Newcombe saw it, "Anybody take a punch at Jackie was going to get knocked on his ass."

Newcombe and Robinson were not dissimilar, both of their emotions woven into the game as if upon a loom. For Robinson, there was no slack in the yarn. Nor did he care to see any slack in Newcombe, least of any of the teammates. Newcombe was the third Black man ever to throw a pitch in the major leagues. In that ball game in Pittsburgh against the Pirates, he got back on the mound, cowed and seething at once, and finished the inning and then the rest of the game. The Dodgers won going away. In the ninth, Newcombe struck out the final batter on three pitches. If Robinson told you to pull your tits up, he had something in mind. "He knew that I would be a better pitcher if he made me mad," Newcombe said.

Newcombe came into the All-Star Game with a 6–2 record and a 3.59 ERA, a decent number that would have been even lower, considerably so, if not for the first outing of his career, pitching in relief against the Cardinals in St. Louis in the middle of May. He had lasted a third of an inning and given up four hits and three runs, and afterward as he sat at his locker, he thought maybe that was the end of it, maybe he had botched his chance at making good in the major leagues. Newcombe was born and raised in New Jersey, one of five siblings and the son of a personal chauffeur. He got his start playing Negro league ball with the Newark Eagles during the war, and he'd caught the eye of Clyde Sukeforth, Branch Rickey's scout, because of his size and athleticism. He had a big windmill windup and a high leg kick and a rare suddenness—he finished his pitches like a massive wooden hatch door blowing shut in the wind.

Newcombe had been going to spring trainings with the Dodgers for a few years. He had been singed through to his upright core in Havana in 1947, when the team segregated him and Jackie and the other Black players to the city's dingiest restaurants. Newcombe had been with the team in Florida in '48 and '49, confronting, inevitably, the white anger and searing rejection of the South. Yet for most of Newcombe's time in organized ball, he had played in areas of relative hospitality and welcome: for two years in Nashua, New Hampshire, where you heard French as often as English on the streets, and then, for the early weeks of the 1949 season, with the Triple-A Royals in Montreal, where he would sometimes get bacon and eggs at the diner near the stadium, on the corner of Ontario and Delorimier.

So somehow when he was called up to the major leagues and flew with Branch Rickey by chartered plane from Long Island to join the Dodgers in Chicago, and then traveled in the team Pullman to St. Louis, Newcombe had different expectations. That is, with his mind focused on the opportunity to pitch in the majors, he had not been entirely prepared for what to expect. "I still remember them pulling up to the hotel for Blacks in St. Louis, and Jackie and Roy and I had to get off the bus," Newcombe would say many years later. "And none of the Dodgers got off the bus with us. None of them. They were all going to the whites' hotel, and they just watched us walk away. . . . I'll never forget how they stayed on that bus."

After the Cardinals knocked him around in St. Louis, Newcombe did get another chance to pitch, of course. Two days later, he shut out the Reds 3–0, in the first game of a doubleheader in Cincinnati. He gave up only five singles in that game and didn't walk anyone, and he also drove in two runs. (Newcombe was a seriously good hitter.) Robinson had a couple of hits; and Campanella singled and scored; and between games of the doubleheader the commissioner, Happy Chandler, came by and shook their hands. When Newcombe had his total bearings, his fastball was tough to hit, near the top of the zone, and his slider, the closest thing he had to a curveball, could be blistering.

The slider was not a pitch many pitchers threw, but it was the one that gave Joe DiMaggio the most trouble. With Kell on second base and Williams at first, Newcombe got DiMaggio to hit a ground ball to third base for the second out. Both runners moved up. Next was lanky Eddie Joost, and from the stands, it appeared Newcombe had escaped the trouble: Joost hit an ordinary grounder toward Hodges at first. But the ball struck the lip of the infield grass and veered abruptly, glancing off Hodges's bare hand and into right field. Both Kell and Williams ran in to score. The American League led 6–5 and would stay in front for the rest of the game.

It would wind up as an unusual and somewhat sodden All-Star Game. Rain finally came in the sixth inning, leading to an eleven-minute delay, and then spattered down steadily throughout the final innings. Joe DiMaggio doubled home Dom DiMaggio for the American League and Ralph Kiner homered deep into the bleachers for the Nationals, and in the end, more than three hours after the game began and with the stadium floodlights on against the darkened sky, the American League finished off an 11–7 win. Twenty-five times during the game, the *h* in the Schaefer Beer sign above the scoreboard had blinked on for a hit, and six times an *e* on the sign had blinked on for an error—both totals unprecedented in an All-Star Game. After his hard double in the first inning, Robinson had gone hitless. His most conspicuous moment came when he started a brisk double play on a ground ball in the fifth. He was one of four players to stay in the entire game. And in this, his first All-Star Game, in the midst of an extraordinary year, Robinson scored three runs, more than any other player on either team.

FEATHER

For all Robinson's open intensity—his new willingness to give glimpses of his anguish and anger, to make his feelings (and not simply his presence) known—he confined that outward simmering to the ball field. The tart tongue that might take a teammate to task or pointedly prick an opposing player did not share opinions or engage in larger ruminations off the field. Robinson had been appropriated into political and social debate from the start of his baseball journey, as a symbol of racial integration, a representation of a nation's better instincts as well as a reminder of its harshest sin. Yet he remained resolutely within the proscenium arch: a ballplayer with every diamond a stage. After a game, he'd talk about what had happened within it—a ball he'd hit, a play he had made. But that was all. He did not, at least not in any formal or dedicated way, make public judgment on issues outside the sport. Early in 1949, Robinson declined offers to have a bylined newspaper column, for fear he might stir unintended controversy or complaint.

In early July, however, Robinson was asked to go to Washington, DC, to speak before the House Committee on Un-American Activities, the then decade-old commission charged with rooting out Americans with Communist ties and sympathies. The committee's interest, in this case, was for Robinson as a Black celebrity to publicly undermine Paul Robeson, the singer, actor, and former star athlete. Robeson was a prominent activist, in America and abroad, and in April, speaking in the context of a potential conflict with the Soviet Union, he had made a charged declaration: "It is unthinkable," Robeson said, speaking at a Communist Party–sponsored congress in Paris, that Black American soldiers "would go to war on behalf of those who have oppressed us for generations against a country [the Soviet Union] which in one generation has raised our people to the full dignity of mankind." Nor had Robeson backed off in the months since. "I repeat it with a hundredfold emphasis," he said in late June. "They will not."

The committee had been wanting to bring in Robinson to denounce Communism in some fashion or another since the year he broke into the majors,[12] and now, in Robeson, a clear foil had emerged. Friends

---

12. The fact that Communist media, in particular the *Daily Worker*, had championed baseball's integration long before the white mainstream press did was not lost on

of the committee had privately established that Robinson, despite the bogus court-martial and the discrimination he'd been subjected to during his army stations, did not share Robeson's belief regarding Black soldiers. He, Robinson, would serve his country to fight any foe. It was also true that Branch Rickey, who bowed with equal piety at the altars of Methodism and capitalism—neither his right to worship nor to swing a profitable deal should be abridged by Communist ideal—was eager for Robinson to testify. And as Robinson would one day reflect: "At that point in my life, if Mr. Rickey had told me to jump off the Brooklyn Bridge, I would have said 'Headfirst or feetfirst?'"

And so, on the morning of Monday, July 18, 1949, ten days after the request had arrived by telegram from the House Un-American Activities Committee—less than a week since the All-Star Game and roughly sixteen hours after the Dodgers had beaten the Cubs on a ninth-inning home run at Ebbets Field—Jackie and Rachel Robinson set off by airplane for the broad, well-paved streets of Washington, DC.

Jackie wore a tan gabardine suit and a tie patterned with rounded squares; Rachel, a pleated dress and white summer gloves. She held Jackie through the arm as they walked, and she carried his speech in a large envelope in her other hand. The House office buildings— the sprawling, heavy beaux arts run of the Cannon and the smaller, columned face of Longworth—stood in the southern shade of the Capitol, along Independence Avenue and across the National Mall from the National Gallery of Art and the National Museum of Natural History. The natural history museum housed artifacts of ancient civilizations, a chronicling of consequential forebears, human culture, and thought. From within the exposition of old Egypt rose

---

members of the Committee for Un-American Activities, nor on many progressive leaders within and in support of the Black community.

Ma'at, the goddess of justice, portrayed with an ostrich feather atop her head. The difference between falsehood and truth, when the heart is weighed in the afterlife, is as light as a feather.

And in Robinson's words to the committee that day—he sat in open session, reading meticulously prepared sentences—the merest emphasis might have been that fine a measurement. He had been summoned to denounce Robeson, and denounce Robeson, in a manner, he did. "I think it sounds very silly," Jackie said of Robeson's claim regarding Black soldiers, although with his very next word, "But," he added a mark of hesitation, and he then went on to honor Robeson's right to promote his personal views as he wished. Paul Robeson's name appeared in one paragraph of the twenty-three paragraphs that constituted Robinson's address, a feather on top of the larger mass of what he said. But a difference-making feather it was. Those few words were enough to tip the scales of public judgment.[13]

JACKIE ROBINSON TERMS STAND OF ROBESON ON NEGROES FALSE read the headline on the front page of the *New York Times*, above the fold—a sentiment repeated in headlines and radio reports across the nation. Inside, the paper printed his statement in full. Robinson began by establishing that, for a ballplayer, "It isn't exactly pleasant to get involved in a political dispute," and he professed no expert knowledge "on Communism or any other kind of a political ism." But, Jackie added, "You can put me down as an expert on being a colored American, with thirty years of experience at it. And just like any other colored person with sense enough to look around him and understand what he sees, I know that life in these United States can be mighty tough for people who are a little different from the majority—in their

---

13. For some, Jackie's testimony verged on betrayal. In 1943, during breaks between rehearsals for his role as Othello on Broadway, Robeson had joined a delegation that met with baseball commissioner Kenesaw Mountain Landis in an appeal to allow Black players into organized ball.

skin color or the way they worship their God or the way they spell their name."

Robinson spoke of how his role in baseball had conferred on him a sense of responsibility, which was why he had agreed to go before the committee. The phrasing that Jackie delivered had been written with the help of civil rights leader Lester Granger, the head of the National Urban League. But it was Jackie who shaped the essence and intent of the message. The speech's center of gravity occupied a few paragraphs that began a little more than halfway through:

"The white public should start toward real understanding by appreciating that every single Negro who is worth his salt is going to resent any kind of slurs and discrimination because of his race, and he's going to use every bit of intelligence, such as he has, to stop it. This has got absolutely nothing to do with what Communists may or may not be trying to do."

The committee room was filled beyond seating capacity, and a microphone set up on the table in front of Robinson amplified his high-pitched voice. He wore a wedding band on his left ring finger and a watch on his left wrist. Robinson continued:

> And white people must realize that the more a Negro hates Communism because it opposes democracy, the more he is going to hate any other influence that kills off democracy in this country—and that goes for discrimination in the army and segregation on trains and buses, and job discrimination because of religious beliefs or color or place of birth.
>
> And the one other thing that the American public ought to understand if we are to make progress in this matter, is the fact that because it is a Communist who denounces injustice in the courts, police brutality, and lynching when it happens, doesn't change the truth of his charges.

Jackie in his coda rejected Communist agitators for leveraging the cruel facts of racial discrimination to suit their needs, and he emphasized the strength of Black Americans as their own best agents of change. Close to the end of his time, he added—and here the felicity of Granger's language is clear—a brief, not-so-thinly veiled reproof of the baritone, Robeson.

"I can't speak for any fifteen million people any more than any other one person can, but I know that I've got too much invested for my wife and child, and myself in the future of this country, and I and other Americans of many races and faiths have too much invested in our country's welfare for any of us to throw it away, because of a siren song sung in bass."

As he finished and lay down the sheet of paper on the table in front of him and straightened his broad back against the back of his chair, someone called out "Amen!" Rachel sat just off to the side of Jackie, near to him. There were no additional questions or official procedures, but now people were in motion all around the committee room, and they came forward to be around Jackie, staying him and offering words of congratulation until he and Rachel and a pair of committee leaders made their way out through the corridors of the Cannon, the Old House Building, and onto Independence Avenue, into the muggy midsummer air. Jackie and Rachel had a plane to get to, back to Brooklyn.

"If you focus too much on what he said about Robeson, you can miss other things," says Yohuru Williams, a dean and professor of history at the University of St. Thomas in Minnesota who was, for three years in the mid-2010s, chief historian at the Jackie Robinson Foundation. "He is staking a claim to the same principles laid out by the Founding Fathers and pointing out that the people who built the country are entitled to its fruit. There is definitely a way to look at what he said and interpret it that Jackie is part and parcel of the establishment. But if you take out the Robeson aspect, it is a really beautiful speech."

Letters praising Jackie arrived to the ballpark from precincts near and far, and a congressman with ties to the committee suggested that Jackie receive an official medal from the Veterans of Foreign Wars for his words. Editorial writers by and large clapped him on the back. And the Robeson remarks did linger. The testimony—the hard nubble of it—dropped a few more hailstones into the summer storms stirred up by the Cold War and the resentment toward Robeson. In late August, Robeson was scheduled to sing at a picnic concert for the Harlem chapter of the Civil Rights Congress in upstate New York. A mob of 350 or more military veterans arrived well ahead of time in protest, seething and violent. They marched loudly and blocked off the roads. They flipped parked cars, rolling one into a nearby stream, and then advanced on the concert area, where the organizers and early comers were, destroyed the empty stage, and splintered wooden chairs. Eleven people on the grounds were injured while a small group stood together and sang "I Shall Not Be Moved." On the hillside above the grove, protesters set fire to a cross.

News of this insurgency was given to Robinson by a *Daily Worker* reporter as he sat in unform in the dugout at Ebbets Field. Robinson's understanding that his words to the committee might now be seen by some as living in continuum with the roil and hate of that mob, invested him with a sense of gravity and the slender veins of remorse. Never in the aftermath of the HUAC testimony did Robeson criticize Jackie.[14] His respect for Robinson was immovable, and he understood that at root they were allies in a larger fight. Paul Robeson was fifty-one years old in 1949, and wise to the ways of politics. Jackie, at thirty, went to Washington new to the arena. The qualified regret

14. Neither, in later years—when documentaries and interviews gave him ample chance to respond—did Robeson's son, Paul Robeson Jr. Bigger things were and remain at stake.

that Robinson would over time express about his testimony was tied
not to the sentiments he'd shared but to the place and platform, that
committee hearing—and also to the thought of having hurt a man
who had risked so much for, and committed so deeply to, a principle.
A feather's weight can beset a conscience as well. The speech Jackie
gave in the Old House Building in the summer of 1949 would linger
with him to some degree for the rest of his days.

He was back in Brooklyn that evening for the game against the
Cubs and their starting pitcher Bob Rush, a right-hander in his second season. Rush sometimes answered to the nickname the South
Bend Skyscraper. At six feet four inches and 205 pounds, he was like
a spire rising from the mound. Back home in Indiana, he'd caught
the attention of scouts with his hard, heavy fastball. "Comes in like a
shotput," one catcher said. Rush was twenty-three years old, and before starting with the Cubs, he'd fought in Germany during the war,
under General Patton.

In the sixth inning, Robinson led off with a walk. The Dodgers
were up 1–0, and there were nearly twenty-six thousand people in
the stands, and the moment Robinson reached first base, anticipation
ran through Ebbets Field. Gil Hodges was at the plate for Brooklyn, and Rush leaned in for the sign. Robinson began striding off first
base, establishing his long and animated lead and fixing Bob Rush in
a glare. "To watch Jackie Robinson day after day, night after night, is
to gape with ever increasing amazement at the magnificent brazen-
ness with which he takes charge of a crowd—and of a game," wrote
Dick Young in his review for the *Post* that night.

Rush had whirled and thrown to first base five times to keep Robinson close, and when Rush finally did throw the ball home, catcher
Mickey Owen called for a pitchout. To no avail. Jackie sprang off
perfectly, right at the start of the South Bend Skyscraper's big kick,
and he was raising dirt at second base by the time Owen's throw came
in low and then skittered far enough into center field that Robinson

bounced up and went to third. Now the infielders all came in closer to the plate, and the crowd was up and hollering. There was still plenty of light in the Brooklyn sky, and the lights around the stadium were turned on as well. In the stands, the Dodgers Sym-Phony Band wasn't beating its drums—or playing anything at all. Everyone was watching Robinson at third base and making plenty of noise on their own.

Hodges grounded out sharply to the shortstop, and Robinson, after a feint, held at third. The hum of the crowd rose and fell and then rose again as Carl Furillo came up. On the first pitch, Robinson broke hard toward home plate. Then he stopped and hustled back to third. All through the ballpark, men and women were standing and shouting through their hands toward the field. On the second pitch, Robinson did it again, breaking full tilt down the line, then suddenly stopping and hurling himself back to third base. The count was one ball and one strike on Furillo, and Bob Rush had this awful look on his face—Owen and the shortstop, Roy Smalley, and second baseman Frankie Gustine all came to the mound to give Rush a moment to pause and gather himself. "By the time I could walk, I had a glove on my hand," Bob Rush once recalled. Rush's father pitched in organized ball, in the 1910s, and he'd told Bob early on that there were three unbreakable rules for a pitcher: "Control, keep the ball low, and don't get rattled."

Owen went back behind the plate and called for the fastball, and Furillo dug in. This time after Robinson broke from third base, he kept going, bearing down hard on home plate, legs and arms and wide-open eyes, and Rush—rattled, alas—threw the ball way over Owen's head, to the backstop, and Robinson slid in with the Dodgers' second run. Immediately the cheers and the happy yells ("Did you see that? I knew it!") began in the crowd, doses of laughter and amazement throughout Ebbets Field as the players stepped to the top of the Brooklyn dugout to greet Robinson with their arms out. Narrow ribbons of orange cloud streaked across the sky. It might have been an inning or more before the buzzing of the fans died down.

He came to bat one more time, in the eighth inning with Gene Hermanski on second base, and he hit the ball on a hard, high line drive into right-center field—over and between the outfielders and up against the exit gate—and he rounded the bases with full fury and intent, finishing with a triple that drove in the final run of the game. Less than eight hours had passed since he spoke on Capitol Hill. *I'm not going to throw it all away for a siren song sung in bass.* Rachel was pregnant with their second child, and Robinson was planning to ask Branch Rickey for a raise. The win over the Cubs meant the Dodgers were now two and a half games ahead of the Cardinals in the pennant race, in first place, with a little more than two months to play.

ST. ALBANS

For one of those Brooklyn kids whose midsummer days were a shimmer of stoopball and stickball, and softballs softened by steady use, the story and tension around Robinson's testimony at the House Un-American Activities Committee had made no impact. "Wouldn't have known one thing about that," says Ronny Glassman, who was eleven that year. "We loved Jackie, Duke Snider, all of them. I played shortstop and I was not a big kid, so you can guess who my guy was." Ronny got the Pee Wee Reese "Mr. Shortstop" glove on his tenth birthday, and for a couple of years afterward, he slept with it at night.

The second of four children, he grew up fifty blocks from Ira Glasser—each of them in separate nuclei across the great divide of Kings Highway, unwittingly part of the same asphalt bloodstream, barely a mile apart. Ronny lived in a downstairs apartment, his grandparents lived upstairs, and in the years after the war, relatives arrived from Austria and Hungary, usually one at a time. Half the old family had been killed. In those years, each time a new person came to stay—underweight, skittish, profoundly marked—Ronny would see his grandmother weeping alone in the hallway and hear the sounds of low conversations in the farther rooms. A gloominess would settle over the home.

Ronny's father, a housepainter, had worked as a newspaper reporter before the war, and for his byline he took the last name Murphy. He was from Russia, blond and blue eyed and strapping, and with the Murphy surname, people wouldn't know he was Jewish. Safer that way, he felt. To keep up the ruse, they named Ronny's older brother Dennis.

What Ronny wanted, what he most deeply wanted, was to be American—to leave behind the hard, heavy weight of history and the Holocaust, and be like the other kids at the ice cream truck, the kids he saw in newspaper ads. Fly a flag on the Fourth of July. He wanted to feel it and know it and embrace it all. That meant embracing baseball and the Dodgers. The trolley to Ebbets Field cost ten cents: a half dozen stops along Church Avenue to Nostrand, a dozen more to the stadium. If you and a friend could find the change, get hold of a ticket somehow, you could on a summer afternoon go to Ebbets Field on your own.

The experience that unfolded for Ronny—as for Ira, as for legions of fans in so many major league cities over so many years—never left. They came up through the cool, shaded tunnel toward the stands and stepped out into the open air to encounter God's green diamond: the great, clean expanse of mown and watered outfield grass, the smell of it in the air; the raked and watered earth of the infield; the stitched and snow-white bases. A brave new world if ever there was one.

The Brooklyn kids played their games in empty lots and concrete playgrounds, and they spent all summer in the urban nest. Their exposure to moving images on newsreels and on the televisions that ground-floor neighbors put by their windows and turned toward the street was entirely in black and white. Those kids had never set eyes on so bright and robust a lawn as the one at Ebbets Field. The sudden sight of that wide and welcome meadow, and of the bobbing Dodger-blue caps on their heroes' heads ("There they are! There he is!") lasted long after the day and the era were done. They would think back on those scenes for the rest of their lives.

The ballpark smelled of cut salami and hot dogs draped in sauerkraut and the smoke off big cigars. Men in jacket and tie, with fedoras, and women in dresses occupied the box seats, but in the bleachers and upper grandstand, you wore sneakers and dungarees, a T-shirt or even a tank top on the warmer summer days. Black fans and white fans sat in the same sections and in the same rows, their seats side by side.

For Ronny and Ira, and for so many others at those games, it was the only space in their lives where they might so mingle. This didn't happen at the grocery store or at school or on the playground. But at Ebbets Field, yes. And not merely mingling but cheering together in open and confluent passion, engaged. So when the Dodgers third baseman, Billy Cox, picked off a low line drive and casually looked at the seams on the ball or Hodges knocked one into the gap or Furillo, "the Arm," nailed a guy at third base from the right field corner; when Campanella got a hold of one or Newcombe struck out the side or Jackie came roaring down the line; when the game was saved or won—then you rooted for the team together, erupting, clapping beside one another, turning to spontaneously embrace, bare arms against bare arms, a young white boy and an older Black man. "At least he seemed old to me," says Ira. "I don't know, maybe he was thirty-five. I was twelve. We were two human beings." There was little else to consider apart from the joy.

It would be years before the power of this milieu would fully register, before one would look back and realize the power and significance of those moments. In the intimate upper reaches of Ebbets Field, sun

on your brow and peanut shells underfoot, everyone was a Dodgers fan. As time passed, those moments, those interactions, would be
further celebrated because nothing like it had happened anywhere
else. Was there in 1949 another public accommodation in America so
naturally desegregated as Ebbets Field?

The players lived among the fans in Brooklyn, same streets, same
grocers, same trolley lines. Erskine and Snider and Reese in Bay Ridge.
Hodges in Midwood. In East Flatbush, Jackie and Rachel rented a
place on Tilden Avenue. Any of the players might get stopped for
an autograph or local glad-handing—but the attention on Jackie was
of a wholly different order. The groups of children who gathered at
the corner of Fifty-Second and Tilden to see him off to a game or
to welcome him back afterward were larger than the gaggles that
might convene for other players. The murmurs when Jackie dropped
into a store rippled louder and wider, and lingered longer after he'd
left. When Jackie and Rachel went out to eat, they were taken to the
back of the restaurant and given a table away from the crowd. All the
Dodgers were beloved and cherished. Robinson was the most famous
athlete in the world. At Ebbets Field, mail was first sorted into two
batches: the mountain of envelopes addressed to Robinson, and then
the hill of envelopes addressed to anyone else.

On Tilden Avenue, Jackie and Rachel lived on the top floor of a
two-story brick unit that was attached to a nearly identical brick unit
beside it. Two bedrooms and a new stove, a little porch off the living
room, a redbrick stoop flanked by handsome, flower-filled planters.
Everything they needed, but tight. Jackie Jr., well into his tenacious
twos, was beginning to really bound about, and soon there would
be another child. And sometimes the attention of the neighbors was
more than Jackie and Rachel wanted. In late July, the Robinsons
moved to St. Albans, Queens—Addisleigh Park, specifically—a well-
landscaped house-and-lawns neighborhood with a golf course. Babe
Ruth had lived in Addisleigh Park for a while.

Ten and a half miles from Ebbets Field, and only a town or so over from the city line and the start of the eastward spread of Long Island suburbs, Addisleigh Park had been whites-only until the late 1930s, when Fats Waller took a house on Sayres Avenue. Over time, more Black families moved in sporadically, among them, on Waller's lead, a contingent of jazz musicians: Count Basie, Illinois Jacquet, Lena Horne, Herbert Mills. The Robinsons' house on 177th Street, a pale stucco Tudor with gabled roofs, had a row of planted hedges and a Normandy lantern by the doorway arch. Roy Campanella and his wife, Ruthe, had taken a home a few blocks away.

Norway maples shaded the backyards of Addisleigh Park—how those trees would blaze in the fall—and honey locusts ran along the side of the Robinsons' house. Rachel arranged for insulation and paneling to be installed in the sunroom, where Jackie set up his desk and hung award plaques and put trophies on the shelves. The extra bedrooms, carpeted wall-to-wall, allowed for the maternal visits by Mallie or Zellee; in the living room, Rachel positioned rounded ceramic lamps on the tabletops by the sofa. After the first snow fell that winter, covering the wide flat stones of the front walkway, Jackie went out and shoveled it off. They had never owned a house before. "Home was our place away from the world, and it was central," Rachel would say. "We made a point not to talk about every negative encounter that happened. We treated our home like a haven. Safe. You want to cherish it. You use the haven to get yourself ready for the next day."

The pennant race, taut against Musial and the Cardinals all summer, stayed that way through the very lees of the season, clinched by the Dodgers in the tenth inning of the final game, in Philadelphia. Robinson singled to drive in the first run early in the game, then drew an intentional walk (he drew a lot of them that year) in the midst of the decisive rally. When the team train arrived back in New York that evening, twenty-five thousand fans awaited them at Penn Station, a massive and whooping swarm with Borough President John Cash-more, out from Brooklyn, at the head of the platform. Even the vet-eran players were left agog.

Dodger fans had known the special pain of late defeat in the final games of 1946 and the dull ache of Brooklyn's September fade in '48, and they took no National League pennant for granted, nor lightly. Special squads of policemen tried to forge a path on the platform for the players to come through, but the police were little match for the pressing ardor. ("Pulled it out in the final inning of the final game!") Some players, Snider and relief pitcher Erv Palica for two, made their way heartily and steadily through the horde and were soon aboard the subway home. But the fans closed in around Robinson with spe-cial urgency, cheering and grabbing at him and sweeping him along, separating him from Rachel, who had stepped off the train at his side. "You clinched the batting title!" someone shouted at Robinson, and he shouted back that he was happier for having taken the pennant.

The Dodgers won 97 games in 1949 and needed every one of them to outlast the Cardinals. To get there, Burt Shotton, under the cre-ative influence of Branch Rickey, managed his players with detailed precision, tinkering ceaselessly with the lineup. Nine players batted in the second spot in the order, thirteen players batted fifth. Ten players hit seventh, ten players hit eighth. Over the course of the season, Shotton deployed no lineup more than ten times. He left no spot in the order untouched. Except, that is, for one. In every game of that 1949 Dodg-ers season, all 154 games on the schedule plus two more suspended as ties after running late or long, Jackie Robinson batted cleanup. In the heart of the Dodgers order, there was no one else.

His league-best statistics were a .342 batting average and 37 steals. On many other ledgers, Robinson finished second or third: a .432 on-base percentage, 38 doubles, 12 triples. He scored 122 runs and drove in 124—remarkable numbers made extraordinary given that he led baseball with 17 sacrifice bunts. If there was a way to beat a team,

Robinson found it. He turned 119 double plays at second base, the most in baseball. He hit 16 home runs. Robinson's 9.3 WAR—the overall player-value statistic that would gain purchase some sixty years after these facts—was the highest in either league.[15]

The welcome at Penn Station had been a tempest of spontaneous glee. Two days later came a more voluminous celebration, one marginally more controlled. Some nine hundred thousand of the faithful, equivalent to a third of the population of Brooklyn, crowded along the length of Flatbush Avenue as a motorcade of Dodgers rolled by. On a weekday afternoon, and never mind the rain. Bulb horns honked and trumpets blew and children waved homemade flags. Robinson sat beside Furillo in an open Chevy convertible, wearing a warm-up jacket and waving to either side.

For the second time in three years, the Dodgers played the Yankees in the World Series, and in the only game that Brooklyn won—Game Two at Yankee Stadium—Robinson pulled a hard double over third base in the second inning. Then he tagged up and went to third base on a pop-up caught by Yankees second baseman Jerry Coleman near foul ground. And then, with the right-hander Vic Raschi on the mound and Gil Hodges at the plate, Robinson began to jockey down the basepath toward home plate. Cowed by the memory of Robinson's past torments, Raschi came to the set as he pitched to Hodges, rather than go into the windup he typically used with two outs and a runner on third. "Robinson can misdirect a pitcher's attention," Red

---

15. Too many statistics can be hard to digest, and by whatever measurement, basic or advanced, Robinson was baseball's dominant player in 1949. No one in the nearly seventy-five years since has had a season of batting better than .340 with more than 65 extra-base hits and more than 35 steals. And there's another truly pertinent category of numbers that bears presenting: those that look at performance in high-pressure situations. In the seventh, eighth, and ninth innings of games that season, Robinson batted .406 with a 1.074 on-base-plus-slugging percentage. In 20 extra-inning plate appearances, those numbers were .412 and 1.559. And when batting with two outs and runners in scoring position in 1949? Robinson reached base more than 51 percent of the time and slugged .634. In a big moment, Jackie Robinson was the guy you wanted up.

Barber at this point observed. On Raschi's third pitch, a fastball with too much of the plate, Hodges lined a single into left field, and Robinson came in to score what would be the game's only run. "He beat me more than Hodges," Raschi would say. It was the last heady moment for the Dodgers that season. The Yankees swept the next three games at Ebbets Field.

Jackie and Rachel were home together in Addisleigh Park on the afternoon of November 18, celebrating Jackie Jr.'s third birthday, when the call came that the sportswriters had named Robinson the National League's Most Valuable Player. "The first member of his race to play in the majors makes good in a big way!" a voiceover would declare in the newsreels the following week. Jackie took the call at his desk, and from the other room, he could hear the children playing games and tugging on one another, giggling and knocking things around.

Boys and girls from the neighborhood had come for Jackie Jr.'s party, as had Rachel's dear friend Sarah Satlow and her children, and also David Campanella, Roy's eldest son. Robinson told the reporter on the phone he was very happy to win the award, and he suggested it would be ammunition for seeking a raise from Branch Rickey.[16] "I didn't have a thing before I got into this game," Robinson said. "Neither did my wife." Now, he said, they had the house and they were putting some money away. The temperature had climbed into the upper forties since morning. Robinson wore a short-sleeved polo shirt, and sunlight came in through the windows facing the yard.

And then, on the back of his greatest, breakthrough season, Robinson began to say some things on the call, the kind of things that he sometimes said in those times and would say on occasion through the

16. Robinson's salary would indeed jump significantly from $21,000 in 1949 to $36,000 in '50, still well below the highest in the game, well below what he, baseball's biggest draw, objectively deserved, but the highest salary of any Dodger and nearly three times the average in the major leagues.

rest of his career—his fine season of 1952, the championship year of 1955, all of them. He wondered aloud how long he would continue in this vortex and under these particular lights, how long he would continue to play baseball. He had flagged toward the end of the year, physically spent. "In September," he told the reporter, "my legs felt tired and the bat felt awfully heavy."[17] Robinson suggested that after another year or two, he might retire. "My wife and I have talked this over," he said.

He would soon be thirty-one, and he felt weary of the travel, and he wasn't sure that the baseball-hero lifestyle was good for his son. When reporters and photographers came to the house—in Brooklyn and now in Queens—Robinson would later explain, Jackie Jr. tended toward one of two extremes: turning his back on them completely or loudly hamming it up. "He doesn't even know me," Robinson said. "I'm not home enough."

Finally Robinson said into the phone: "The strain of the last three or four years has done something to me. Not that I have anything to worry about, but I'm jumpy and nervous all the time."

Reporters and teammates never knew quite how to measure Robinson's conviction on the matter of retirement. Did he say such things aloud as a way of trying them out, testing for a response, and for his own comfort? Were these words meant as an experiment, or as the first instrument of his will? Even Rachel was not sure, nor sure exactly what to feel. This was all a great process for the two of them—their sudden unforeseeable lives—a process of discovery.

After the phone call, Robinson joined the children at the party, bending to them in greeting and with humor. The kids put on paper party hats strapped under the chin, and they all gathered around the table, and Jackie Jr., wearing a good white shirt with buttons and a

---

17. And along with the fatigue, a level of pain—on a steal of home in early August, Robinson had strained ligaments in his left foot and thereafter took daily treatment and wore a rubber cushion in the heel of his shoe.

blousy polka-dotted bow tie, sat in his father's lap as the cake arrived and everyone sang.

Autumn progressed and Rachel's belly grew (Sharon Robinson would be born in a Manhattan hospital on January 13) and Jackie adopted a busy off-season life. With Campanella, he led baseball clinics for kids (Black groups, white groups, sometimes mixed) at schools in Westchester and Long Island. He ran lessons at the Harlem YMCA. Robinson did a radio show on the weekdays, and on a few evenings a week, he sold televisions out of an appliance store about seven miles from his home in Queens. Customers would walk in and ask for him directly, and if in the end they made a purchase, he would sign for them a bat or a ball. On one prearranged night, Joe Louis and Sugar Ray Robinson showed up personally to buy TVs. The store owner had never seen business this good. At home in their St. Albans living room, the Robinsons had an RCA Victor, with the big sixteen-inch screen, on which Jackie Jr. watched *Howdy Doody* and *Mr. I. Magination* in the evenings.

Being Jackie Robinson: that was the strategy for selling the televisions. Otherwise, there was no particular technique. "If a customer is going to buy a set, he's going to buy it," Jackie explained when visited at the store by a magazine reporter. "You can't twist his arm." Two months later, after the new year and Sharon's birth, he would leave that job and fly to Hollywood to film *The Jackie Robinson Story*, which upon its release in the spring of 1950 received critical applause. For decades afterward, the movie, though flawed and hastily made, aired regularly on television, and was treasured for telling an important story, tethered closely if not strictly to the facts. Robinson had lines to learn and scenes to rehearse, and they spent all day on the lot, yet in certain ways this was not so different from the salesman assignment he'd had at Sunset Appliance. It was not so difficult, Jackie said, playing himself.

When Fats Waller bought his home in Addisleigh Park in 1938, he, like some others, had to find a way to get around the neighborhood's racially restrictive covenant. The area was built up as a segregated community in the 1910s and '20s, and homeowners were forbidden, by a clause on the standard deed, to sell their houses to Black buyers. Some did anyway, and in response, other residents took them to court. In a 1942 case, New York State upheld the restriction. Six years later, the issue reached the US Supreme Court.

In *Shelley v. Kraemer*, which arose out of a racially restrictive covenant suit in St. Louis, the court ruled that such covenants were effectively illegal, saying the government could not enforce them, because doing so violated the Equal Protection Clause of the Fourteenth Amendment.[18] These covenants were found in communities from coast to coast, put in place as a backlash to the Great Migration. The Supreme Court decision to overturn was unanimous, a ruling of 6–0. (Three justices recused themselves on the grounds that they themselves lived in neighborhoods governed by restrictive covenants.) Across the nation, residents of those communities—including, it feels safe to note, residents of Addisleigh Park—were not uniformly welcoming of the court's decision. The Robinsons moved in about one year later.

Robinson in 1949 appeared on the covers of national magazines. He populated the movie house newsreels. He inspired boldface newspaper headlines that spanned the width of the page. He was a star in every ballpark, the most visible player on every diamond. Yet sometimes in the clubhouse, coming down from a game, Robinson's face could suddenly change. "As if he were remembering something, as if he were somewhere else," said Carl Erskine. "You were always aware that Jackie had a passion, and that it wasn't just for baseball, that he

---

18. Here's the clause: "No state shall make or enforce any law which shall abridge the privileges or immunities of citizens of the United States; nor shall any state deprive any person of life, liberty, or property, without due process of law; nor deny to any person within its jurisdiction the equal protection of the laws."

was weighing other things. He was the greatest competitor I ever played with, and some of that came from his greater awareness of things, of injustice. He'd get a look of consideration."

There were events in his experience that troubled him, something underlying. He could summon the team's trips to St. Louis and the flat cruelty that so unsettled Newcombe, how their teammates simply looked away when Robinson and Newcombe and Campanella got let off the team bus at a hotel in that part of town. Or how in spring training that year, Rachel and Jackie Jr. were refused a taxicab in Vero Beach. Or the looks that he or Rachel might get, in mufti on a subway car or in an airport waiting area. Or worse than the looks, the disregard, the feigned or real indifference from his fellow man. "When the camera lights were turned off and he left the building to board a bus, he was still treated as a Black man first and a man second," Erskine would write in a memoir, referring to that 1949 season. "And this broke Jackie's heart on a daily basis because he gave his all—body and soul—to the game of baseball."

At many times in his life, Jackie Robinson—and if Jackie Robinson, then anyone; at his peak there were not five more famous people in all of America—could by some people be seen only in one context, defined not by his achievement or ability or character but by the color of his skin. He could be overlooked as an individual, unseen, and thus, for all his extraordinary fame and the familiarity of his name and figure, never truly seen at all. An outline of himself. Almost, in a certain sense, invisible.

PART THREE

AUTUMN

—

1956

BROOKLYN

Autumn arrives fitfully to Brooklyn, feinting forward, dropping back, hinting at itself. Wool-sock mornings, shirtsleeve afternoons. A near absence of rain marks the early heart of the season—gone are the squalls of August—which is given frequently to bright days roofed by cloudless skies. Days like October 9, 1956, a Tuesday. Pumpkins crowded alongside apples at the borough markets, and the heaven trees along the avenues gripped their many-fingered leaves, so that the sidewalks were still patterned with shade. At the corner of Bedford and Sullivan, within the borders of McKeever and Montgomery, the Dodgers and the Yankees prepared to play Game Six of the World Series. The Yankees, one day after the most extraordinary pitching feat in Series history, led by three games to two. Another Yankee win, in other words, ended the season. Fall was nearly three weeks old, and a persistent pre-winter wind blew in off the bight. The Dodgers, and Jackie Robinson, were looking for one more day of summer.

Pee Wee Reese batted second in the Brooklyn lineup, with Duke Snider right behind him, and Carl Furillo and Gil Hodges and Roy Campanella were all in there too. The stalwarts, year after year. Robinson, three months shy of his thirty-eighth birthday, batted cleanup. He swung a lighter bat than he'd swung in the flush of his prime. Same length, slimmer handle, the new bat a concession to the passing years. Robinson's body had thickened, his added weight distributed through his chest and belly and hips, rendering him, on the basepaths and even in the field, a rumbling mass, his raw speed clipped but his instincts hardly dulled—sharpened, in fact, and praised—and his daring and his peculiar grace intact. Small fields of gray dusted the close-cropped hair atop Robinson's scalp, and two prominent lines ran the width of Robinson's brow. His heels and knees ached with a stubbornness befitting a player who'd traveled miles beyond his years. How much more baseball did Robinson have to give? Thoughts of a life outside the boundaries of the game, thoughts that had circulated so insistently in his mind for years, had in more recent months gained the whir of imminence. Speculation about Robinson's future, conjecture cast from all quarters of the baseball theater and beyond, shadowed him. How committed were the Dodgers—the Walter O'Malley–Buzzie Bavasi–Walt Alston Dodgers—to keeping him? How much more did Robinson want? Trade, retirement, the bench? "If I didn't think I could play regularly, I wouldn't have signed for another year. I'd have quit," he had said tersely in February of '56, just before spring training.

Eight months later, another pennant won, another October stage set, Robinson played every inning of the World Series, a changed familiar presence in the middle of the Brooklyn lineup, manning third base, and still, by voice and deed, the rousing force of the team. On the diamond, in the dugout, in the locker room. "He probably has the greatest competitive spirit in baseball," Dodgers pitcher Roger Craig said that year.

In Game Six, Brooklyn was up against a tall Yankees right-hander, Bob Turley, who, it was noted with a measure of Dodger dread, modeled his unusual no-windup delivery on the recently adopted no-windup delivery of another tall Yankees right-hander, Don Larsen. The day before at the stadium in the Bronx, with sixty-four thousand fans in his thrall, Larsen had faced 27 Dodgers and gotten all 27 of them out. No one but Reese had even pushed Larsen to a three-ball count. No one but Robinson, whose low, blistering line drive glanced off the lunging glove of third baseman Andy Carey before being secured and thrown across the diamond by shortstop Gil McDougald, had come close to getting a hit. Larsen threw 97 pitches, 71 of them strikes. The first perfect game in the fifty-three years of the World Series. Larsen, battered in Game Two, was two years removed from a 21-loss season. "Come on, guys, let's get 'em, this game isn't over yet!" Robinson had exhorted the Dodgers in the top of the ninth. Afterward, he and Sal Maglie and the Dodgers owner Walter O'Malley went over to the Yankees clubhouse to shake Larsen's hand.

Western Union telegrams arrived congratulating Larsen all that afternoon and night, and phone messages came to him from the team, and Larsen, on a call home to California, had heard the pride in his mother's voice. Gillette razors wanted Larsen for a radio spot. ("The perfect shave.") The next day at Ebbets Field, ahead of Game Six, Larsen stepped out of the visitors' dugout into the clear, cool, late morning air and found a crowd of well-wishers and autograph requests. He spoke with reporters and he acknowledged the shouts from the crowd and then he turned and went out to the outfield to run a few sprints and stretch his hips and gently windmill his arm.

There were thirty-three thousand people at Ebbets Field now, the crowd thick through the upper tier long before the first pitch. Clem Labine, normally a reliever, had the start for Brooklyn. You could see the game in color on NBC, and you could hear the radio leads, Bob Neal and Bob Wolff, unspooling the play-by-play in schoolyards and living rooms and afternoon barstools from Brooklyn to Nashville to Woodland Hills, California. One year earlier, the guys who'd take your bets by the garage on Bedford Avenue or down the street from the Rogers Theater might have given sweet odds against seeing Robinson in this World Series at all. Yes, for Robinson and for the Dodgers, too, 1956 had been a different sort of season.

The true shift had begun in 1955, when the leg injuries weakened him, and the trade talk around him surfaced and resurfaced (the

Dodgers would listen to offers, their front office said), and when, in moments private and public, he continued to spar with Brooklyn manager Walt Alston. Robinson played in only 105 games in '55 and batted a soft .256. Eight home runs. Six doubles. Two triples. This was a 100-watt bulb suddenly throwing off 25 watts' worth of light. Over his first eight seasons, Robinson had batted .319, averaged 15 home runs and 53 extra-base hits, and made six straight All-Star teams—brilliant.

When, on October 4 of 1955, the Dodgers beat the Yankees 2–0 in Game Seven of the World Series, at long last delivering a title—the most significant game in Brooklyn baseball history—barkeeps across the borough and beyond called out through unchecked tears, "Free drinks for every beautiful bum in the house!" A collective, pent-up roar went up and, if you listen to the voices of those who were there, can still be heard. For that game, Robinson sat on the bench. He had a sore Achilles tendon, and after producing the Series' most stirring moment, a steal of home in Game One, he had at times seemed over-matched. Alston was a man given more to caution than to faith, and benching Robinson caused him no angst. He played Don Hoak, a .240 hitter with a copper glove, at third base instead.

"Jackie and I sat next to each other for a lot of that Game Seven," says Carl Erskine. "It was tense. Over the years in those kind of games, something always seemed to go the Yankees' way, so we were wary right to the end. Jackie was shouting out encouragement to Johnny Podres, and clapping for our guys all game long. That's how he was. It hurt him not to be playing, though. No question. I don't know that he looked at Alston once that whole game." There were times all through the late stages of Robinson's career, and during that Game Seven in 1955, when he gave off a kind of heat, as if sheeted in anger, which would then subside.

Robinson danced in a conga line with Rachel and his teammates at the Hotel Bossert that night, and he rejoiced in the days that followed. The championship, the vanquishing of the Yankees was deeply rewarding. And yet beneath that satisfaction lived the sting of not having been out there, on the field, on the front lines of a competition that he had helped to establish, with the team he had pushed and prodded and driven to sustained and now absolute success. After the final out—ground ball, Reese to Hodges—Don Hoak was the first infielder to reach the mound and get his arms around Podres.

There'd been friction between Robinson and Alston from the start. The relationship lacked the partnership that Robinson had felt with other managers, and it seemed clear to him that Alston did not truly have his back. He remembered moments like the game in Chicago during Alston's first season, 1954, when Duke Snider hit a ball just over the ivy-covered wall for a home run. But the ball bounced back onto the field, and the second base umpire Bill Engeln, confused, ruled the hit a double. This was in early September, in a game the Dodgers needed for the pennant race, and Jackie burst from the Brooklyn dugout and ran straight to confront Engeln. Other Brooklyn players were also shouting about the blown call, but only Robinson had gone onto the diamond. Alston, coaching third base, didn't move. "After I got out there, I looked around, and there was my skipper still in the coaching box," Robinson said. "Boy, I felt foolish. All of a sudden, I realized I was standing out in the middle of Wrigley Field all alone."

"I didn't go out there, because in my opinion the ball was clearly a double," said Alston. As if that were a reason! As if that were a reason to not hustle over to support and protect and stand beside the best and most important player the Brooklyn Dodgers had ever had. Loyalty was not a currency Robinson and Alston were going to traffic in. The fans in the Wrigley bleachers and the photographs that followed confirmed that Robinson had been right: Snider's hit was a homer and Engeln had missed the call. Of Alston, Rachel once said, "He and Jack found it difficult to relate as men."

As time went on, every reporter around the Dodgers learned how

Robinson felt. "If he's got any complaint, he should come and see me instead of going to the press," Alston griped once in an unusual show of pique. The press had taken to calling Alston "the Quiet Man."

In January of '56, with that Game Seven win and the Dodgers' first-ever title still echoing through the chambers of the sport, Robinson, speaking at a dinner banquet, was asked to rank the four managers he'd had in the major leagues. He did not pause: "Dressen is first," he said. "Leo Durocher second, Barney Shotton third, and Alston fourth." Another time that off-season, he went on record to say that in his mind, the 1955 Dodgers, despite the world championship, despite winning the pennant more handily than ever, were not as good as the Dodgers teams of 1947 or '49 or '53. This was, in some ways, a period of reckoning for Robinson.

There were many other banquets and events that off-season. In Calgary and Toronto, in San Francisco. In Brooklyn, Queens, and Manhattan. An arthritis telethon. An awards luncheon. A party at a radio station on Long Island. A charity for disabled children. A black-tie ball at the Savoy. At Temple Hesed Abraham in Jamestown, New York, Robinson shared a dais with Lucille Ball and Desi Arnaz. In New Haven, he spoke at Blessed Martin Church. Late in the off-season, he presented a plaque on behalf of the National Conference of Christians and Jews. Along with the busy event schedule and the time spent working out or volunteering at the YMCA, Robinson hosted two sports-themed shows a week on NBC in New York. Never had his celebrity been so entrenched. And yet, as the 1956 spring season neared, Jackie and Rachel—now living in Stamford, Connecticut, with three young children—understood that this stage of their lives was coming to a close. Robinson's baseball evensong had begun.

The Dodgers traded for a third baseman—thirty-year-old Ransom Jackson, who'd hit 21 home runs for the Cubs in '55—and soon afterward, Robinson, his 1956 contract still unsigned, wrote to his friends Caroline and David Wallerstein. David was the president of a chain of movie theaters. "I'm not sure whether I'll be playing next year or not, so I am looking for other things," Robinson said in the letter. He told them about the weekly TV spot he did with Marty Glickman, and how they took on provocative issues, and that his outspokenness had helped him make new allies and win good reviews, along with inevitable resistance. "Some don't like it," he wrote, "nevertheless I'll always say what I believe."

When he did sign his Brooklyn contract, Robinson took a pay cut—from $35,000 to $31,500—acknowledging his poor preceding season, even though he remained, a decade on, the club's outsized star and singular draw. A profit driver beyond his statistics. He was why, even in 1956, the Dodgers continued to leave Florida's East Coast and travel through the South to play exhibition games, knowing that Robinson (and his Black teammates, to a lesser extent) would bring people out, droves of them, who had never or only rarely seen him play. The Dodgers crossed the state by bus to Clearwater and Sarasota. They broke camp and traveled to Louisiana, Alabama, Tennessee, and Kentucky, hundreds of miles from their spring home, and the big crowds came in support, or sometimes in derision. In the ten years since Jackie and Rachel took their first bus ride through the South, down to Daytona Beach, few of the larger parameters had changed. At Holman Stadium in Vero Beach, the Dodgers' gussied-up baseball compound, the restrooms were segregated. And when the white players and their wives left that Dodgertown haven to shop or see a movie in downtown Vero Beach, the Black families went instead to nearby Gifford, a poorer town with humbler amenities. When the team traveled, Robinson and the other Black players stayed in private homes or at Black-run hotels. Not even the Dodgers' primary hotel in Miami, the McAllister, the team's home away from Vero Beach, allowed Black guests.

Robinson was jeered that spring in Mobile and Birmingham— caustic cries from a stirred-up crowd on the same state soil then being churned and tilled by the Montgomery bus boycott. In New Orleans, during a game against the Southern Association's Double-A Pelicans, Black fans, infuriated that the Pelicans had failed to integrate after years of promising, booed their home team so loudly that, said Robinson, "you couldn't hear anything else." From the other side of those segregated stands came the old, hard taunts, launched at Robinson in particular, and with enough animosity to curl a rookie's hair. "The fans called him the worst possible names," said Don Drysdale, who was nineteen years old that spring: "'Gator bait.' It was brutal." When the Dodgers played the Braves in Louisville a few days later, the air was unseasonably cold—morning frost on the bat racks at Parkway Field—and Robinson felt every bit of it.

He played well in the spring games. And he allowed himself, or a part of himself, to imagine that perhaps the failures of the previous season were more a product of short-term injury and poor luck than age, that he might in 1956 return to his form of earlier years. "Ransom Jackson will have to be a whale of a player to beat me out," Robinson said in the clubhouse. "My legs are strong, and that's the main thing. And I weighed out at 208. . . . I haven't been down to that since 1950."

He competed with his customary verve, and engaged with his customary cheek. "When we played over there, we had to go through their clubhouse to get to ours," says Ralph Terry, who was a Yankees rookie in '56. "We walked right past their trainer's table, and Robinson was lying on it, getting worked on. He looked overweight. It always made an impression to see him. It was Jackie Robinson! He had that high-pitched voice, and when he saw us Yankees come through, he started yelling, 'Yeah, we're going to get you guys again this year! Two in a row!'"

A measure of bravado mixed with Robinson's belief. "Only" 208 pounds, perhaps, but Robinson didn't carry that weight so comfortably as he used to. His first steps were not so quick. On another day that preseason, he said of his battle for third base with Ransom Jackson, "I'm in the fight of my life."

Robinson missed Branch Rickey that spring, as he had during each of the five springs before, ever since the Dodgers president had been forced out in the fall of 1950. No one in Robinson's athletic life had meant more to him as an advocate, partner, guidepost. "Jack loved him," Rachel said.

It was Walter O'Malley, rising from part owner to principal, who'd shunted Branch Rickey aside. O'Malley couldn't stand him. He viewed the credit and respect that Rickey received from the baseball world as a smudge on his own pride. Branch Rickey had built the foundation for these enormously successful Dodgers and, in the process and at some personal risk, orchestrated a stroke against racial injustice that had reshaped the sport, and goaded the nation. Yes, O'Malley and the rest of the board had agreed to move forward on Robinson, and certainly O'Malley had vision of his own, but these Dodgers were formed at Branch Rickey's impetus and by Branch Rickey's design. O'Malley could not change that, nor could he fully disentangle his feelings toward Robinson from his hostility for Rickey. In O'Malley's view, Robinson was a "Rickeyman." As soon as Robinson's play began to slip, O'Malley tasked his baseball brain trust—Buzzie Bavasi, Fresco Thompson, Walt Alston, head scout Andy High—to conceive a post-Robinson Brooklyn team. It was a prospect Bavasi, the leader of that trust, was reluctant to pursue. "With Robinson you win, without him you lose," he explained to O'Malley.

Robinson got along fine with Bavasi. As de facto general manager, he was disciplined and creative, the sharpest of the front-office lot, and in disagreements with O'Malley, Bavasi had earned the slack to stand his ground. Robinson and Bavasi might even share a look if the owner began to bluster or referred to himself as "the O'Malley." Yet when Jackie was in need of counsel or of conversation around the workings of the game, when he wondered which way the baseball winds might blow and how he might be blown by them, those were the times he felt most alone. Branch Rickey had gone straight from Brooklyn to become president and general manager of the Pirates. Afterward, every time the Dodgers were in Pittsburgh, Robinson would make his way to the Pirates offices, to sit awhile and talk. Now Rickey had left the job in Pittsburgh and retired.

Even in their early years together, in the thick of it, they hadn't spent all that much time together. There was great warmth—Rickey described his relationship with Robinson as "filial"—but always set in a professional framework, around their common purpose. Robinson carried with him the force of Rickey's convictions, the way he had spelled things out in the first stages of his career. Rickey would tell Robinson what he needed to do on the ball field and in his public life, and how he needed to do it, and Robinson trusted him. He did not regard Rickey as imperial or exploitive but recognized in him a certain wisdom, and saw seeds of compassion within the rough husk of Rickey's demands: *You can't fight back on the field or in the press. You must accept the living conditions. Swallow your pride and anger. Push yourself aggressively on the bases, even when you're criticized.* "You got a girl? You're going to need her," he had said upon first meeting Robinson. Rachel herself came to think of Branch Rickey as Jackie's father figure.

Over the years, as they sat together, as the blunt instructions gave way to an exchange of ideas, Rickey unfailingly conveyed a sense of calm and surety. He kept his hat on even in the office. He didn't seem to blink much. He would pause for the briefest moment before barreling ahead with his thoughts. When he made a point, he extended his arm in front of him with the sure sweep of a conductor's baton, as if he were indeed determining how things would play out: "Look at it this way, Jackie," he might begin. Or: "Jackie, think about what's happening in America and in baseball."

Branch Rickey had a swagger about him (the O'Malley might have said an arrogance), and he didn't yield much on the principles he had set. In no one else could the twin nicknames "the Mahatma" and "el Cheapo" have been so apt or so seamlessly paired. Robinson was reasonably compensated under both Rickey and O'Malley, but never did he, baseball's biggest draw, even remotely approach the salaries of the other top stars in the game. The Dodgers, as a rule, were underpaid.

"You would come to see Rickey in the off-season about your salary," says Erskine, "and he'd start off saying how you had done all these nice things and helped win such and such games, like he really had it down. You'd start to feel pretty good about yourself like maybe you were in line for a nice raise. Then he'd say, 'So, good news, Carl . . . we've decided to keep you.'"

If Branch Rickey could assume a superior air as he ran and organized a baseball team, he seemed less self-impressed by his agency in the matter of Robinson. In the spring of 1956, the two men were together at an event in Atlanta, where Rickey received a commendation. "It seems to me unique," he said in his acceptance speech, "that I should be given an award for hiring Jackie Robinson at a time when he was the best-qualified man in the world for the job."[19]

When the Dodgers opened the 1956 season at Ebbets Field— unfurling their WORLD CHAMPIONS banner in front of fans full of verve

---

19. Rickey's overall achievement, in a front-office career that began in St. Louis in the 1910s, defies simple measurement. It was he who designed the baseball complex at Vero Beach—with its pitching machines and batting cages, many instructors, and hordes of players, a blueprint so many teams would later follow. From his first days as an executive, he emphasized scouting in counterintuitive, underscouted areas. As far back as 1913, Rickey dispatched a colleague to watch games and track how many bases each batter got, and also how far he advanced the base runners in front of him.

Famously, he created the farm system, transforming the sport. He put in defensive shifts against certain batters. He encouraged platooning. He valued on-base percentage over batting average. He articulated, in the 1930s, the notion of some players being "above replacement level" and others not—a bedrock principle of twenty-first-century analytics. Alfred North Whitehead suggested that the last 2,500 years of Western philosophy can be viewed as a series of footnotes to Plato. It's as easy to see the last century of baseball player development as a series of footnotes to Branch Rickey.

after parading down Flatbush Avenue—Robinson was indeed in the starting lineup, playing third base, batting sixth, in back of Hodges and ahead of Furillo. The pride of a just-won championship can carry the better part of a fan's heart, and the faithful were hardly bothered when Brooklyn lost to Philadelphia that afternoon. Two days later, before a crowd far less entwined with the Dodgers' long-craved status as defending champions—indeed, not at all entwined but demonstrably indifferent or worse—the Dodgers hosted their "second Opening Day," a designated home game in New Jersey, at Jersey City's Roosevelt Stadium. From Brooklyn, this was a comparatively distant outpost: twelve and a half miles, two rivers, a maze of unfamiliar asphalt, and a state line away.

The Dodgers raised the championship flag in ceremony before this game as well, in a strange and cynical appeal. The Jersey City game was a gambit, one end of a many-faced wedge, that O'Malley hoped to use as leverage in his negotiations for a new ballpark. The Dodgers had outgrown Ebbets Field. At forty-three years old, the stadium felt cramped for its time. Too many cracks ran along too many seatbacks, and the clubhouse odor stood stiff and corporal as a mammal's lair. Most damning to convenient access and the bottom line, the surrounding neighborhood offered no proper parking for a fan base suddenly dependent, like much of the nation, on the automobile. Roosevelt Stadium, once home to the International League's Jersey City Giants, had space enough for seven thousand cars.

This might have been a warm encampment for Robinson, and game day itself a spiritual homecoming. It was here, tight against the winds of Newark Bay, where ten years and one day earlier he had made his gorgeous, earth-moving International League debut, integrating baseball, thrilling openmouthed fans with his daring on the basepaths, receiving the sturdy, post–home run handshake from George Shuba, and feeling the roar and the love of a massive crowd. Now, in 1956, there were just 12,214 in the stands, a fraction of stadium capacity, and they booed from the start; Jersey City was still Giants country. The Dodgers were booed over the whole, but Robinson bore the brunt of the rancor—just as he had heard the greatest swell of cheers and affection on Opening Day at Ebbets Field. This was Jackie Robinson's team, so long as he was on it. The *Pittsburgh Courier* had taken to calling him "the greying interracial pioneer" as well as "the game's most controversial figure." Dodger fans had never loved a player more.

"Give them back to the Giants," Robinson said of the Jersey City fans after the game. "There was no justification for their booing me. I don't know why they did it. That kind of reception from hometown baseball fans I resent." Even the field itself was a letdown. The infield dirt was soft: Reese stumbled while turning a double play, the Phillies' Richie Ashburn lost his footing and fell on the basepaths. And Snider described the outfield as "bumpy as hell." Combined, the two teams made eight errors. When Robinson declared in the clubhouse that he wouldn't want to play twenty-four games at Roosevelt Stadium, an allusion to the three-year, eight-games-a-year deal the team and the venue had struck, the words did not land well with the Dodgers' brass. Bavasi bristled. "The way he's playing"—Robinson had gone 1 for 7 and made two errors over the first two games—"he won't have to worry about three years. He'll be out of here in three months," the general manager said. Bavasi checked in with the O'Malley and then came back and bristled some more: "Robinson will play in Squeedunk if the Dodgers want to play there."

Robinson responded that if that's how Bavasi felt, he might as well bench him or trade him. (As a result of O'Malley's dangling, several teams had already expressed interest in Robinson: Pittsburgh, Baltimore, the White Sox, the Giants, even St. Louis.) But then Bavasi and Robinson spoke directly. And Bavasi acknowledged that even slumping Robinson was playing hard and helping the team—his sacrifice bunt, for example, had led to the winning run in the tenth inning at

Roosevelt Stadium. ROBBY MAKES UP WITH BUZZIE read one headline. By now, the Dodgers' transformation was well under way. The team was changing, Brooklyn was changing—the borough, the country, the world. Before the game in Jersey City, Robinson had looked back on his first game there in 1946, as a rookie attempting to lie as low as his extraordinary circumstances would allow. One thing had not changed: Robinson, just as the *Courier* observed, was the most controversial figure in the game.

Even with the wind blowing out toward right field—the flag beyond the scoreboard stiffened at times toward that way—the Yankees played Robinson to pull the ball. He came to bat in the bottom of the first inning. No score, two outs, Duke Snider on first base. Game Six of the 1956 World Series was six batters old. The Yankees had gone down easily in the top of the inning, and now Snider's single had produced the Dodgers' first base runner in two days. Robinson stood deep in the batter's box, and a rustle ran through the crowd. In center field, Mickey Mantle took a couple of strides leftward. At third base, Andy Carey, even with the bag, moved closer to the line.

O'Malley watched from his customary box along the first base line. It was his birthday, and the Dodgers Sym-Phony had struck up a tune in acknowledgment. He had been born not twenty miles to the north, in the Bronx, on a Friday—October 9, 1903—marked by record rainfall that not only swamped the city but also caused the rainout, in Boston, of Game Seven of the first World Series ever played. There were any number of things that O'Malley—aware now, at every game he attended, of being a broad man in a narrow old ballpark seat—might have wanted for his fifty-third birthday, although nothing more earnestly than a new stadium, a new place to perch.

He'd been agitating for years, appealing to New York City's parks commissioner (and gatekeeper, kingmaker, puppeteer), Robert Moses, for approval on a new place in Brooklyn. A no go so far. O'Malley was also in more promising ongoing discussions with the Los Angeles County Board of Supervisors, especially the principal contact, Kenneth Hahn. It was no secret that Los Angeles wanted a major league team. (Any team—they'd even courted the lowly Senators.) Three days after Game Six, with the Dodgers on a stopover en route to a series of exhibition games in Japan, O'Malley and Hahn would meet over breakfast in Los Angeles. For now, O'Malley said, all he wanted for his birthday was a Dodgers win in Game Six.

Bob Turley had a serious fastball. Mid-90s, at least, and when he got it to the right spot, up in the zone, forget it. Plus he threw a curveball that could put rope in your knees. In 1954, as an Oriole, Turley had led the American League in strikeouts—and also in walks. Bullet Bob was one of Turley's nicknames. Wild Bob was another. His new half-windup sliced a mile or two off the speed in exchange, he hoped, for greater command. Robinson took the first pitch, a curveball on the outside corner, for strike one.

Robinson had batted cleanup throughout the World Series, and before running into Larsen in Game 5, he'd been hitting .357. An old-time peak Robinson number. Turley's second pitch, a fastball, ran too far inside. Then Robinson fouled the third pitch straight back into the high seats. One and two. Turley came with the fastball once more, and now Robinson lined it hard—pulled, indeed, and on the button—into the glove of shortstop Gil McDougald. Inning over. Later, in assessing the game, Robinson would downplay Turley's sheer speed, saying the Dodgers had faced pitchers throwing harder earlier in the season. Then the reporter took the same idea to Campanella, who felt differently. "I'm telling you," Campy said. "I ain't seen anything faster this year." When it came to Robinson and Campanella, the sports editors knew, any split of opinion was notable. And braising in a little "he said, he said" between them, even over a trivial matter, could only help a story along.

They were different: different backgrounds, different paths, different temperaments. Physically different. And different in attitude. Yet they were inevitably and closely linked by time and circumstance: the two Black stars in the Dodgers' lineup for nearly a decade. "When I talk to Campy, I almost never think of him as a Negro," Dick Young, the newspaper writer, told Robinson. "Anytime I talk to you, I'm acutely aware of the fact that I am talking to a Negro." If Young's observation was crude and reductive, full of assumption and caricature—and if it reeked as well of the judgment and unease and bigotry that marked the institutions around the game—Robinson nonetheless recognized within the observation a facet of truth. And sparked to it. (You *should* know who I am! You *should* know you are talking to a Negro!) The differences between Robinson and Campanella were not of a kind to leave alone.

Robinson might from his locker-room stall reflect on civil rights, segregation, the implications of, say, *Brown v. Board of Education*, just as soon as he might remark on the Dodgers' hotel arrangements in the South. In these last years, issues narrow and wide, within the team and without, drew comments and responses from Robinson. In 1955, the Dodgers had held Pee Wee Reese Night at Ebbets Field to honor Reese for his long and beloved tenure with the club. It was the eve of Reese's thirty-seventh birthday, and Dottie and their daughter, Barbara, attended a ceremony on the field. Pee Wee received a 250-pound candlelit cake and telegrams from President Eisenhower and General MacArthur, as well as a brand-new Chevrolet. Before the top of the sixth inning, the stadium lights went down and fans lit matches and flashlights and serenaded Reese with "Happy Birthday to You."

The Dodgers beat the Braves that night, Reese hit two doubles, and afterward the feeling in the clubhouse was upbeat and light. Brooklyn led by 14 games in the National League standings. Then word came that someone on the grounds crew had raised a Confederate flag to the top of the stadium flagpole, ostensibly in homage to the Kentucky-born, Kentucky-raised Reese.

The players looked toward Robinson, and could immediately sense his anger stirring, like water in a kettle. "Who let Jim Crow back in the building?" he demanded, his voice taut and high-pitched. "Who let him in?" Robinson's eyes sharpened, and he began to move toward where the grounds crew was housed. The Dodgers were still in their uniforms, and a few writers milled around. Suddenly this special birthday event, one that Robinson had rejoiced in with his dear and valuable friend, was on the edge of becoming something else.

"We tried to calm him down, and remind him it was Pee Wee's night," says Erskine. He and Labine, two of Robinson's trusted friends on the team, had come to stand beside him. "We were not in the business of asking Jackie not to speak up—he showed us the way usually. But we wanted him to let this one go, let us get the flag quietly taken down. It was Pee Wee's night, and he hadn't had anything to do with that flag business. Jackie finally settled down, but it was another one of those times you could feel what was always inside him."

During the summer of 1956, the Louisiana legislature passed a law prohibiting interracial sports competition. In response, a columnist at the *Times-Picayune*, Bill Keefe, applauded the law and suggested in print that Jackie Robinson and his oft-heated manner provided justification for it. At that point, Keefe had been writing from a place of fear and ignorance on the matter of racial integration for nearly three decades. He described Robinson as the "persistently insolent and antagonistic trouble-making Negro of the Brooklyn Dodgers" and said that he "has been the most harmful influence the Negro race has suffered in the attempt to give the Negro nationwide recognition in the sports field, and the surprising part of it is that he wasn't muzzled long ago."

Robinson replied to Keefe in a letter that he made sure was circulated among the press. "You call me 'insolent,'" he wrote. "I admit I have not been subservient, but would you use the same adjective to describe a white ballplayer . . . ? Am I insolent or am I merely insolent for a Negro (who has courage enough to speak against injustices such as yours and people like you)?" Wrote Robinson in closing: "I am happy for you that you were born white. It would have been extremely difficult for you otherwise."

Campanella, along his way, generated no such clubhouse stirrings. He was not eager to challenge or provoke. He rarely argued with umpires. He did not raise a public fuss. He was an exceptional athlete who had no designs on pushing the bounds of the game or testing authority. "I'm no crusader," Campanella told Robinson once.

He had played in his first game for Brooklyn in April of 1948, eleven years after he began catching in the Negro leagues at age fifteen, and two years after breaking into the Dodgers system, playing in Nashua for Walt Alston. In his seven full seasons as a Dodger, Campanella was named the National League MVP three times. He hit with power, he drove in runs, he threw out base runners better than any catcher in the league. Ahead of the 1956 season, Campanella received a salary raise to $42,000, the highest in Dodgers history and the first contract of $40,000 or more ever agreed to by the organization. Upon signing, he talked about how good the Dodgers could be in '56, especially now that they'd brought over Ransom Jackson from the Cubs to play third base. "A good fielding third baseman, and a fellow who can hit," Campanella said, aware that the other player vying for the third base job was Robinson.

Campanella's continued fealty to Alston was not of particular annoyance, or surprise, to Robinson. Campy was loyal in general—to all the Dodgers brass, to organized baseball, and to the good way of life he had earned. He was, as an employee, excellent and reliable, like King Lear's Kent behind his mask. If Campanella was not always the type to deliver a plain message bluntly, he could certainly keep honest counsel. He could, as it were, ride, run, and mar a curious tale in telling it. And the best of both men—Campanella and Robinson—may have been their diligence.

In St. Louis that season, Robinson stayed with the rest of the

Dodgers at the Chase Hotel, having worn down the proprietors there and forced aside the segregation policy that had barred Black guests. Robinson checked in alongside everyone else, and he pointedly took some meals in the hotel restaurant. Often, though, he chose not to eat dinner downstairs, ordering up to his room instead. That the hotel preferred it that way was, for Robinson, immaterial. Freedom meant having dinner wherever you wanted.

Robinson would invite his friend Tom Villante, an advertising man who sometimes traveled with the team, to eat with him. After chocolate ice cream, they'd place a water glass on its side on the carpeted floor and take out a golf club and practice putting, wagering a little something on every putt. Double or nothing when you lost. "We'd play and play until we wound up even," Villante says. Jackie read the newspapers, and he phoned Rachel just about every night. Campanella and the other Black players didn't go to the Chase but instead kept to the Black-only hotel where they'd been staying for years. Campanella said he didn't want to go to the Chase now, after the hotel had barred them in the past—nor was he keen to the suggestion that Black guests stay away from the restaurant and the lobby.[20]

Campy and Robinson weren't wholly dissimilar. Campanella had his own engines of principle. In truth, the friction that attended them—a friction often leveraged by Young or other writers as a current of mutual opposition—was touched all the while by mutual respect and by their years of shared endeavor. Robinson liked Campanella. He was enormously agreeable, kind and generous and sweet, shining from a face round and vibrant as his voice. They had roomed with each other in the South and in Panama. They were booed together

---

20. For Robinson, the vision was always longer than the day at hand. What might his staying at the Chase Hotel now mean for a path to equality there in the future? In his letter to Bill Keefe, at the *Times-Picayune*, Robinson had dismissed the notion that integration meant economic risk for a whites-only establishment: "The hotels I am staying at in St. Louis and Cincinnati have not gone out of business," he wrote. "They are prosperous."

in Beaumont. Roy's wife, Ruthe, attended Robinson's historic first game, in 1947 at Ebbets Field, and sat cheering in her longcoat along-side Rachel and Jackie Jr. For years in Addisleigh Park, their children had known one another. In the off-seasons, Campanella and Rob-inson gave clinics together at the Y. The truth was that the Dodg-ers would not have been winning pennants in those years without Robinson, and they would not have been winning pennants without Campanella. By the summer of '56, both men and their families had left Addisleigh Park. The Robinsons lived to the north, in Stamford; the Campanellas to the east, in Glen Cove, Long Island. Both men drove in to work at Ebbets Field.

BOUNDLESS

The National Association for the Advancement of Colored People began awarding the Spingarn Medal in 1915, six years into the or-ganization's existence. Per instruction of J. E. Spingarn, the award's creator and then chairman of the NAACP's board, the medal was to honor "the highest or noblest achievement by a living American Negro during the preceding year or years." (Today the language reads: "for the highest achievement of an American of African de-scent.") The medal, made of solid gold, is awarded annually, with the recipient determined by committee. The first Spingarn Medal went to Ernest Everett Just, a cellular biologist and a professor at How-ard University. W. E. B. Du Bois received the award in 1920, George Washington Carver in '23. Mary Bethune Cookman in '35, Thurgood Marshall in '46. Over its first four decades, the Spingarn Medal went to educators, writers, civil rights advocates, scientists, musicians, po-litical leaders, lawyers, historians, actors, activists, and businesspeo-ple, among others. Never did it go to an athlete: not Jesse Owens or Joe Louis or Sugar Ray Robinson—or others who had broken bound-aries or achieved the pinnacle of their sport.

When, in the late spring of 1956, the NAACP committee prepared to select that year's Spingarn Medal recipient, powerful candidates emerged. Conspicuously, there was Autherine Lucy, a twenty-six-year-old English teacher who, after a three-year court battle, had won the right to attend the University of Alabama as the school's first Black student. Her presence, in February, led to campus rioting—a car she rode in was pelted with rocks, her classroom came under siege by a mob—and soon thereafter, the university expelled her, defying a court order. "They stoned me, they cursed me, they burnt me in effigy, but they did not discourage me," Lucy wrote describing the riots. In articles and in public speeches, Lucy vowed to press on until she "and others of [her] race" had their rightful access to education.

"For the life of me, I can't understand how the NAACP could pass over a great and courageous person like Autherine Lucy in making the Spingarn Award," wrote Ralph Ewing, a reader from Detroit, to Baltimore's *Afro-American* after the medal winner was announced.

Another candidate for the Spingarn Medal that year was Martin Luther King Jr. Since December of 1955, he had been at the forefront of what was developing into a watershed of the civil rights movement, the Montgomery bus boycott. Already, the boycott's implications beyond the bounds of the city, and the state of Alabama, were becoming apparent. "We are in the midst of a great struggle, the consequences of which will be world-shaking," Dr. King said from his pulpit at the Dexter Avenue Baptist Church in Montgomery. He and other leaders of the boycott had been arrested, threatened, and buffeted by violence—someone had exploded a bomb on the porch of the Kings' home—and had not bent. When Dr. King came to Brooklyn in March, to speak at the Concord Baptist Church, ten thousand people turned out and gave him a reception, as one newspaper described it, "usually reserved for its favorite heroes, the Dodgers." By late April, more than a dozen bus companies in the South had abandoned their policies of segregation.

At twenty-seven, Dr. King was determining the tone of the larger movement and defining the principles that would sustain his leadership in the decade to come. "If we are arrested every day, if we are exploited every day, if we are trampled over every day, let nobody pull you so low as to hate them," he preached to a massive crowd in Montgomery. "We must use the weapon of love. We must have compassion and understanding for those who hate us. So many people have been taught to hate us, taught from the cradle."

In the words that he preached and in the words that he told himself during that time, King echoed the spirit that had guided Robinson through his groundbreaking years in baseball, the same bottom line: "You must be willing to suffer the anger of the opponent and yet not return anger," King said in self-admonishment after succumbing to rage and indignance during the bus boycott. "You must not become bitter. No matter how emotional your opponents are, you must be calm." He had completed a doctorate in systematic theology, and had found along the way a lodestar in Gandhi, who, as King described it, had "lifted the love ethic of Jesus above mere interactions between individuals to a powerful and effective social force."

Dr. King also did not receive the Spingarn Medal in 1956 (he received it the following year), although both he and Autherine Lucy attended, and addressed, the NAACP's annual convention, where the medal was traditionally presented. In San Francisco, over several days of speeches and events in late June (Thurgood Marshall, the NAACP's lead lawyer, delivered the keynote; Marshall and King debated policies around school segregation), the Spingarn Medal, while cited, was not, in fact bestowed. Its recipient hadn't made it to the convention, on account of his having work obligations in Brooklyn.

"It is beyond question the thrill of my lifetime," Robinson said when told he had been named the Spingarn winner. He'd taken the phone call at his home in Stamford. Plaques commemorating his many years of athletic achievement hung densely on a paneled wall, and the garden outside the windows was entering its summer bloom. "You can't emphasize too much how very pleased I am."

According to the NAACP's executive secretary, Roy Wilkins, Robinson was chosen for "his superb sportsmanship, his pioneer role in breaking the color bar in organized baseball and his civic consciousness." News of Robinson's honor received considerable attention, within and without the Black press. A baseball player! There had come to be a greater understanding of how far outside the boundaries of sports Robinson resounded. "His entrance into organized baseball has done as much as anything else to bring about understanding in this country," suggested Muriel Richardson of Charlottesville, to the *Afro-American*. A columnist for the *Alabama Tribune* in Montgomery wrote, "Those who have known second-class citizenship, the humiliating scars of denial, segregation, discrimination and those fringe monsters of Jim Crow will understand the torment that Jackie suffered in breaking the colorline. Few Americans have been more deserving of the Spingarn than Jackie."

That December, at a Saturday luncheon in the Palm Room at the Hotel Roosevelt on Madison Avenue in the center of Manhattan, Robinson accepted the medal. The newspaper columnist and television host Ed Sullivan presented, and when he did, and Robinson went to the lectern, the room stood in prolonged ovation. "To be honored in this way means more than anything that has happened to me before," Robinson said. "The NAACP represents everything that a man should stand for—for human dignity, for brotherhood, for fair play."

Thurgood Marshall and W. E. B. Du Bois and Floyd Patterson sat among the audience, and all the tables were full, and Robinson's speech kept getting interrupted by applause. "And now, with your indulgence, I would like to ask my wife to come and share this honor with me," said Robinson, and as Rachel rose from her seat on the dais, so, too, did the guests rise from their seats at the tables, and the room rocked again with fervent clapping and the chandeliers shook as Rachel came forward and stood at Jackie's left side. "It is hers fully as much as it is mine," he said of the Spingarn honor. "My career and whatever success I have attained were made possible by my beloved wife. . . . She is the principal reason I am standing here today." Jackie Jr., ten years old, sat on the dais alongside members of the NAACP board of directors.

Robinson lauded the organization as a "tireless champion of the rights and the well-being of the colored people of America. . . . It is even more than that because its cause is the cause of democracy, which makes it the champion of all Americans who cherish the principles on which this country was founded." He pointed out that the NAACP had of late come under attack, which was "designed to bring its great work to an end, at least in the South where it is needed most," and said he hoped "to help in its defense" in any way he could.

He thanked Rudolph Thomas, director of the Harlem YMCA, and called out Lester Granger, head of the National Urban League, for the work Granger had done on Robinson's speech before the House Committee on Un-American Activities. And when Robinson saluted Branch Rickey for his insight and courage and his long, steady plank of support, the room broke into applause again.

On that afternoon—buoyed by the weight and the implication of the Spingarn Medal—Robinson was in part looking toward his time after baseball, for ways he might extend and enhance the mission of his life. He knew that his public strength would always emanate from his immutable accomplishment as a ballplayer. "He was a freedom rider before freedom rides," Martin Luther King Jr. would later say. For all Robinson's activism and stoicism in the years to come, for all the stands he would take and the language he would use, Robinson's most searing eloquence would remain rooted in the way he shook the foundation as a young man. From the first moment he stepped onto a baseball field as a Montreal Royal to the last time he left the diamond with the Dodgers logo stitched across his breast, Robinson gave to the world a profound and enduring expression, articulated in the way that he played the game.

AFFINITY

The story goes that when they first met, on a ball field in a schoolyard on the first day of seventh grade, at PS 156 in Laurelton, Queens, Ira and Ronny spotted each other and sensed something that drew them near. "Jackie Robinson," said Ira to Ronny. "Pee Wee Reese," said Ronny in return. And they both laughed and pounded their fists into their small gloves. They have been together in friendship for seven decades since.

Each of their boyhoods had been upended by a move out of Flatbush, and the exit of each of their families would become part of the descriptive historical statistics of the 1950s—the changing demographics, the changing faces of Brooklyn. Now, in Laurelton, they rode bicycles to each other's houses and played softball on dirt fields on the weekends and played on those yellow-painted macadam diamonds behind the school during the week. Ira still mimicked Robinson's batting stance, as expertly as he could, slapping at his right hip as he settled into the box for no reason save that Jackie did it. Any number of the kids emulated Robinson, keeping pigeon-toed at the plate and as they ran to first base, and some adding the pigeon-toes as a kind of swagger to their everyday gait, into the hallways and the classrooms. "You'll ruin your feet walking like that!" a teacher might say, but they would walk like that anyway.

A particular affinity bonded those Dodger fans, something other than the shared joy and heartbreak of the results on the field. Young fans in Brooklyn or Queens may not have dwelled on Robinson's opinions and societal views—certainly not in the way they beheld his burst out of the batter's box, or his dangling hands on the basepaths—but they had an understanding of Robinson, and the Dodgers, as a larger force. In Mobile, Alabama, teenagers such as Hank Aaron had drawn inner purpose from Jackie. ("He gave all of us, not only Black athletes, but every Black person in this country—a sense of our own strength," Aaron would write.) And in small Louisiana villages where Lou Brock passed by whites-only schools on the way to his own, and listened to baseball on KMOX radio from St. Louis, Robinson and the Dodgers suggested greater possibilities than might otherwise have been imagined. In and around New York, Dodger fans realized that what was happening in the mid-1950s in America, and what had been happening on the ball field they adored, was part of the same stand, the same insistence.

By fielding Robinson, Campanella and Newcombe, Jim Gilliam and Sandy Amorós, through the late 1940s and early 1950s—as well as the briefly brilliant right-hander Joe Black and the talented but wild and ineffectual right-hander Dan Bankhead—the Dodgers defined an organizational approach. It was one that the Giants, under Horace Stoneham, followed too: Monte Irvin; Hank Thompson; the beautiful, incomparable, extraordinary Willie Mays; the pitcher Rubén Gómez; the backup catcher Ray Noble. The makeup of those New York teams' rosters created in some young fans a certain indifference, exquisite, in its way, and unforced. A ballplayer was a ballplayer. "I hated Jackie Robinson," says Larry Raphael, a Giants fan and dear cohort in Ira and Ronny's boyhood clan in Laurelton. "I hated him because the guy killed us! I don't recall ever thinking about whether he was Black. I didn't particularly think about whether Mays was Black. I just loved Willie Mays. I loved Monte Irvin. And I couldn't stand Robinson—or Snider or Hodges, for that matter—because I'd get this awful feeling in my stomach when he came up against the Giants." For Ira and Ronny, a Giants fan of otherwise redeemable character was someone you could befriend. "But a Yankee fan, you could not," Ira says. "To be a Yankee fan was beyond the pale—unforgivable."[21]

"Contemporaneous with loving the Dodgers, you hated the Yankees, of course," says Danny Greenberg, a retired antipoverty lawyer who was eleven in 1956, and scrounged for Borden's ice cream wrappers on the ground outside Ebbets Field. Four wrappers and a quarter got you a general admission seat. "Whether we thought about it or not, part of it was because we knew that we had Jackie Robinson and they didn't, and that meant something. Even though the Dodgers usually lost in the World Series, we were righteous. You could still feel good. You wouldn't trade losing for winning and being a Yankee fan."

Robinson shared in that distaste—a learned resistance to Yankeedom that derived an edge from the Yankees' autumn dominance, and a depth from the Yankees' imperial manner and damning, hidebound ways. Three baseball teams played in New York, and the Yankees had been, without apology, the last to field a Black player—by nearly six years. "We don't want that sort of crowd," a Yankee executive had said privately during those intervening seasons. "It would offend box-holders from Westchester to have to sit with n——s."

"We'll get those Yankee bastards," Robinson said before the start of a World Series.

In late 1952, responding to a question on a television interview

---

21. Never, however, no matter how close that friendship—through first girlfriends and sandlot triumphs and high school escapades, and later through wives and children and careers and homes with distance between them—has the matter of the opposing fandoms ever faded from relevance. At some point, thirty years or so removed from the singular event, Larry began a tradition: every October 3, he sends Ira (now to his home, previously to his office at the ACLU) a photograph of Bobby Thomson. October 3, 1951, is the day that Thomson's ninth inning home run, struck off Ralph Branca, cleared the left field wall at the Polo Grounds, dooming the Dodgers and giving the Giants the National League pennant. Decades passed before Ira retaliated. But now, each August 16 since 2010, the date on which Bobby Thomson died, Ira sends Larry a copy of Thomson's obituary.

show, Robinson had evenly pointed out the Yankees' lack of Black ballplayers, and he later expanded on his thoughts to a newspaper reporter: "It seems to me the Yankee front office has used racial prejudice in its dealing with Negro ballplayers. I may be wrong, but the Yankees will have to prove it to me." The TV comment caused a stir (Robinson popping off again, groused the Yankee brass), but Bavasi and O'Malley stood firmly by him, and when baseball commissioner Ford Frick called Robinson in to discuss the matter, he told Robinson that next time he needn't mince words.

Those feelings hadn't softened by the 1956 World Series, as Game Six moved, scoreless, to the middle innings, the sun high above Ebbets Field, the wind blustering through the second deck, the crowd— batter to batter and pitch to pitch—on tenterhooks. The Dodgers lineup included Gilliam and Amorós and Campanella. Newcombe, the best pitcher in baseball, who'd pitched in Game Two, was ready to start Game Seven if Brooklyn could get there. The only Black player on the Yankees roster, the second-year outfielder Elston Howard, hadn't gotten into the Series at all. It would be 1963 before a Black pitcher joined the Yankees rotation.

Robinson's antipathy toward the organization did not extend to disdain for individual players. Just as he had gone over to congratulate Larsen on his perfect game a day before, he had in an earlier October appeared in the Yankees clubhouse to praise Mickey Mantle. "He shook my hand and said, 'You're a hell of a ballplayer and you've got a great future,'" Mantle would recall. "I became a Jackie Robinson fan on the spot." Robinson complimented Yankees shortstop Phil Rizzuto for his skill and his savvy on the field, and he hailed second baseman Billy Martin for his hustle. As for Yogi Berra, who was now coming to bat to start the top of the fourth inning of Game Six, Robinson described him as "the greatest competitor in the clutch."

Berra's and Robinson's careers had run in parallel lines, a series of interconnections, of games against each other and shared headlines and banter at the plate—a long and coincidental association that by 1956 had turned almost numinous. They'd been together in the International League in 1946, both rookies: Robinson, with the Montreal Royals, reshaping the sport. Berra, a catcher with the Newark Bears, and as often called Larry, declaring himself on the field as a force of exceptional promise. At age twenty-one, Berra hit .314 and slugged .534 and had, as the *Scranton Tribune* put it, "a flair for hitting scorching line drives."

They played against each other at Delorimier Stadium in June and at Ruppert Stadium in July, and if Robinson was always the starring attraction, Berra had won a place on the marquee. In one midsummer game, Robinson dived to catch Berra's liner with the bases loaded, preserving a Royals win. In an August doubleheader, Robinson had three hits to lift Montreal in the first game; Berra knocked in two runs to lift the Bears in the second. In September, the teams squared off in the postseason.

Robinson and Berra met in the postseason the following year as well, as major leaguers, in the 1947 World Series. In the first inning of Game One, Robinson stole second base—Berra never had a chance—and over the course of the seven games, Robinson's basepath cheekiness, his bluffs, his feints, his dodges, unnerved Berra to the point that the Yankees wondered if he belonged at a position other than catcher. In 1948, Berra played 50 games in left field. "We knew that with Jackie Robinson in Brooklyn, we'd be facing the Dodgers lots of times in the future," Berra said after the '47 Series.

Both of them really knew how to talk on a baseball field. They needled and chattered with one another in the Dodgers–Yankees spring exhibition games each year, and they saw each other again in the World Series in 1949 and in 1952—when Robinson stole twice more off Berra, still without being caught—and in 1953, when Berra hit .429. And then, in the opening game of the 1955 World Series, they met again in the play that would link them from that day forward, the play that endures as the most memorable of both players' careers.

The Yankees led by 6–4 in the eighth inning at the Stadium, and Robinson was on third base with two men out. It was not a time or place for high risk-taking by a base runner. Not down by two runs, not with the Dodgers rallying and the Yankees starting pitcher beginning to wilt, and not, ostensibly, by a then thirty-six-year-old player who would later say in moderate jest that he had "a pretty good day for an old, gray fat man." But this was Robinson. And the Dodgers had at that point lost four World Series in eight years to the Yankees. The plucky call of the Brooklyn faithful—"Wait till next year!"— was beginning to lose its charm. *I may not be here next year*, Robinson thought as he moved off the third base bag and looked down the line toward home plate. *I'm tired of waiting.*

The pinch hitter Frank Kellert was at bat for the Dodgers, and Whitey Ford, a left-hander, was on the mound. Yankees manager Casey Stengel called out to Ford from the first base dugout: "Hold him on—don't let him get too big a lead." The Yankees third baseman, Gil McDougald, played in and close by the bag. Berra crouched behind the plate. There were sixty-four thousand fans in the crowd on a Wednesday afternoon, and every person in every part of the ballpark knew exactly who was leading off third base.

Robinson broke briefly down the line, then stopped and broke back, as the pitch to Kellert came in a little high and a little outside and the umpire, Bill Summers, called it a ball.

Ford would later say that he "knew Robinson was going to try to steal," but in the moment, it did not appear that Ford knew it at all. Robinson saw that Ford was deploying his full windup, raising his hands high above his head, then swinging them back behind him. *He is not giving me much of a look*, Robinson thought.

So Ford went into that windup and Robinson broke from third again and this time he came barreling down the line. The pitch arrived low and over the plate, where Ford had wanted it, and Berra caught the ball and put down a tag as Robinson's right foot touched home plate. Summers put out his hands flat. *Safe!*

Robinson stood right up at the end of his slide and turned to jog back toward the delighted Dodgers dugout. Berra reacted otherwise. He whirled around immediately and hotly toward Bill Summers. He tore off his catcher's mask and rose up into the umpire's face, complaining that Robinson was out, that he'd gotten the tag on him in time. Berra followed after Summers as Summers tried to move away. He thwacked his catcher's mask on the ground and gestured in various, sudden ways, and he appeared just as angry at an umpire's call as a player could be. Summers was the most experienced umpire in Major League Baseball—twenty-three years, seven World Series, six All-Star Games—and he seemed completely unimpressed by the ranting. After the game, Berra would say, "It was a close play but I had him easy."

Robinson didn't agree: "I was safe—no doubt in my mind at all. I could see the plate when I slid in. Yogi was back of the plate."[22]

Later, Berra, embarrassed as well as incensed by the result, illogically called the play "bush." Other observers more reasonably pointed

---

22. Berra's vehement reaction may have conjured memories for Robinson. He had seen such an outburst from Berra before, during the 1946 International League playoff series between the Bears and the Royals. In the bottom of the ninth inning of Game Six, in Montreal, with the Royals leading three games to two, and hoping to clinch the series, the score was tied 4–4 with two outs and a runner, Tommy Tatum, on first base after singling. The crowd's cries of "Ta-ta-ta-tum!" echoed through the park. Berra knelt behind the plate for the Bears, and Robinson stood in the Royals dugout. Montreal's Herman Franks came up to bat and lined the ball off the scoreboard, and as Tatum rounded third base, Clay Hopper, coaching there, waved him home. The throw beat Tatum to the plate, but the umpire ruled that Berra missed the tag. Tatum was safe, giving the Royals a 5–4 win and the series. Berra went bonkers, dropping his glove and mask to the ground and charging furiously at the umpire. Livid Bears joined him, and quickly players from both teams milled on the field, along with fans down from the stands. Police needed to break things up and get the umpires safely away. Nine years later, in 1955, watching Berra's excited response to his steal of home at Yankee Stadium, Robinson knew that the eruption had precedent.

out Robinson's poor judgment in risking the steal of home with the tying run standing at the plate. Alston, as one might have guessed, was quick to distance himself: "Robby was strictly on his own stealing home," Alston said.

Robinson understood that the timing of the steal did not make baseball sense, no debate there, but he had felt that the moment was one to seize, as a way to assert both himself and the Dodgers against Yankee hegemony. The Yankees won that Game One, 6–5, meaning that the stolen run proved immaterial to the outcome. Whether it had a lingering impact on the Dodgers in that 1955 World Series, helping to spirit them toward their eventual yoke-snapping win is plausible but debatable. What's certain is that Robinson's steal of home became symbolic of the Dodgers' long-awaited championship, and symbolic as well of the heightened, air-tight tenor of the Yankees–Dodgers rivalry. The steal—a daring, improbable, immediately vintage steal— bequeathed a lasting image of a great player in a moment of greatness.

Robinson's steal of home was discussed widely and intently in the days afterward. The Dodgers batter, Frank Kellert, disclosed that he thought Robinson was out, and the next day incurred a blistering dose of Robinson's locker-room wrath. (In mid-October, Brooklyn cut Kellert from the team.) After the Series, reporters contacted Robinson, seeking further comment about the steal while he vacationed with Rachel and the kids at Grossinger's resort, in the Catskills. Film of the play showed at various off-season events. Nor did it end there. Robinson's confronting moment against Berra and the Yankees in 1955 has entered the baseball registry, alongside Joe DiMaggio's kick of the basepath dirt in the 1947 World Series; Willie Mays's over-the-shoulder catch in 1954; Sandy Amorós's snare of Berra's tailing line drive in 1955; Bill Mazeroski's being engulfed after his Series-winning home run in 1961. They form the enduring visions of a long, precious, resonant era in the game. Robinson's play, alone among them, has taken added dimension, the particular symbolism of him sliding in safely, his right fist clenched, his body fiercely extended against Berra guarding the plate, has become imbued as well with a sense of defiance, determination, and triumph. A painted version of the image—three stories tall, with Robinson's fist held high, his ball-cap flying off—adorns a building in North Philadelphia.

Long after Jackie's death, for years and decades beyond, Berra and Rachel would encounter each other from time to time, at this event or that. Always it was a version of the same greeting. Yogi would grin at Rachel with his wonderful, broad, reliable grin. "Out," he would say. And Rachel would return with her own, gentle smile and say, "Safe." So that the greeting became a link between them, to the times of their lives, to the beauty of baseball, to the extraordinary, continuing power of Jackie himself.[23]

BROOKLYN

Now, it was one year and eleven days after that steal of home. It was October 9, 1956, and Robinson, playing third base, looked in at Berra leading off the fourth inning of Game Six of the World Series. In his first at bat, Berra had knocked the ball over Furillo's head, off the screen in right field, and because of Furillo's unearthly arm, held at first base with a single. This time Berra swung at Labine's first pitch. He hit a routine ground ball to Gilliam at second base, the first out of a quick half inning. The score remained 0–0, and then in the bottom

---

23. The most endearing example of the "out, safe" exchange comes by way of Lindsay Berra, Yogi's granddaughter, who described in a television interview a ninetieth birthday party held for Yogi at his museum in Montclair, New Jersey, in 2015. "Grandpa was in the theater surrounded by a whole bunch of people, and he was in a wheelchair at that point," Lindsay said. "Rachel came walking in, down the hallway there, and they could just sort of see each other through the arms and legs. And it was actually really sweet. You saw Rachel go like this [Lindsay swept her hands out, palms down, *safe*], and Grandpa just went like this [*out* sign with the right hand], and she gave him a big smile and went over and gave him a big hug."

of the fourth, Robinson came to the plate with one out and nobody on base.

The Dodgers had not scored in twelve innings, and Turley had struck out five batters already in the game, and you could hear some yawping out of the Brooklyn crowd, a restless feeling. Robinson took the first pitch low. The Yankees were again playing him to pull and at third base Andy Carey was well back of the bag, not guarding against a bunt. Enos Slaughter stood deep in left field beneath the high beating sun. Robinson stepped out and reassembled his grip on the bat, and then stepped back in and took the pitch low for ball two. When the next two pitches both rode high, and trailed inside, Robinson jogged to first base with a walk.

Billy Martin scurried over to talk with Turley and then went back to second base. Turley adjusted his socks and stepped onto the mound. Gil Hodges was up, and Robinson took a big lead, drawing a look from Turley. On the first pitch, Hodges flew out to right field. Two out.

Now Sandy Amorós stepped in, and he swung and missed at Turley's first pitch. Robinson continued to press his good-sized lead, edging off. "Always worrisome for a pitcher when a fellow like Robinson gets on those bases," the radio announcer Bob Neal said.

But on Turley's next pitch, Amorós popped up harmlessly to third base. Another scoreless inning was over. The energy ebbed in the crowd. And Robinson would have to wait for another chance to assert himself, to continue his stirring revival of 1956—his final, proud stand on the field.

When Alston had benched him in June of '56, Robinson said little in complaint, certainly nothing in the way he had fumed about a benching by Alston the previous year. Robinson was never shy to argue against what he believed to be wrong or unjust—not in small matters, not in large. But he did not argue idly or without cause. He was batting .236 at the time Alston sat him down and the team was in a pennant race. Robinson knew that over the first six weeks of the 1956 season, he had not proved himself to be among Alston's best nine. "I don't blame him," Robinson said of the move.

That did not mean he was resigned to it. Complacency never hampered Robinson's athletic life, and it would not hamper it now. During his time on the bench, at Alston's bidding, Robinson took out his other fielding gloves and practiced at all the positions he'd played during recent years—first base, second base, left field as well as third—to give himself and the manager more options. He applied himself with a specific intensity, and he stayed at the center of the spirit of the team. Before the start of innings, if Campanella was still getting on his gear, Robinson came out and crouched down to warm up the pitcher. In the dugout, he exhorted and encouraged teammates—his replacement, Ransom Jackson, among them—and chided umpires, and kept his edge. Robinson might go four days without getting into a game, start once, then sit out for three more. And so on. He pinch-hit sometimes or played a couple of late innings in the field. He got ejected from a game for throwing his helmet after arguing a call. Teams inquired about Robinson in talks with Buzzie Bavasi, and Bavasi said no, not now. They did not want to trade him. "I think he can help us win the pennant," Bavasi said, sensing something.

Then, on the night of June 25, at Ebbets Field, with the Dodgers scuffling and slipping in the standings, Alston gave Robinson a start for just the fifth time in 25 games, at first base against the Cubs left-hander Jim Davis. Robinson homered in the first inning. He homered again in the fifth, and the Dodgers won 10–5. The next day, Alston again started Robinson at first base, and he singled and scored. The day after that, same thing. What began then, and what continued despite another period on the bench nursing a pulled groin in July, was a show of considerable will and determination on the part of Jackie Robinson.

He was Brooklyn's oldest player, save pitcher Sal Maglie and, by a few months, Reese. Robinson weighed thirty-five pounds more than Pee Wee did. The years of football had visited upon Robinson's hips, heels, and back an accumulation of minor traumas. Fatigue ran through the trunk of his body, heavy as sap against the heartwood. Every day was a new demand. He knew, though, that his voice, the respect he commanded, was still tied to how he performed on the ball field. There remained an expectation—his own and surely that of others—defined by the standard he had set. That summer, Althea Gibson was continuing her rise through the amateur ranks of tennis, becoming the best female player in the country. She was referred to, practically pro forma, as the Jackie Robinson of her sport. The phrase had entered the American lexicon, here to stay.

Gibson won the French Championships in May, took the doubles title at Wimbledon in early July, and in between ran off a string of tournament victories as a kind of all-star American ambassador on European soil. As for the comparisons to Robinson, she acknowledged the inspiration and spoke of the statement he made through his play. "In the field of sports, you are more or less accepted for what you can do rather than what you are," Gibson said that summer. "That's been true since Jackie Robinson's time."

After games, Robinson sat heavily on the stool by his locker and worked his ankles and his knees with his strong hands. He soaked his feet, and on the table each day, a trainer kneaded his shoulders, neck, and spine. Robinson's eyesight was not so sharp as it once had been. He conserved energy where he could. In terms of his day in, day out influence on a game, his performance had fallen sharply from just two seasons before. And yet, just as he had in that June start against the Cubs, he summoned moments—stirring moments, full games, and then games on end—of the old Robinson greatness. In that last summer of 1956, in the games that mattered most, Robinson was there. Reese was the Brooklyn captain and Hodges the steady hand on the rudder, and the Dodgers' overall talent was fathoms deep. But no one held sway as Robinson did. This was still Jackie's team. "Never," says Erskine, "was there any doubt about that."

"The aura around him, the way that he played, it made an impression on me that never, ever left," says Bob Aspromonte. He was eighteen when he joined the Dodgers in late July of 1956, a few weeks out of Lafayette High School—same school as Sandy Koufax, just six miles from Ebbets Field. Dodgers scout Al Campanis had been going to his games. Aspromonte had power and an understanding at the plate, Campanis reported to Bavasi. "An old head on young shoulders."

When Aspromonte arrived at the ballpark that first day—after getting dressed in his boyhood bedroom and walking out the family kitchen and onto the streets of Bensonhurst on his way to play with the Brooklyn Dodgers—Alston told him to take some ground balls with Robinson and Reese and Hodges. "I couldn't move for a minute. I just stood there," Aspromonte recalls. Sixty-five years later, the day could not be brighter in his mind. "Then I finally go out there, and Jackie comes over and he sees my glove, this big outfielder's glove I had. And he pulls off his second baseman's glove and says, 'Here, use mine.' He's watching me take grounders and he's happy. He had a high-pitched voice. He says, 'Isn't that so much better with the smaller glove?' and it was. I was still kind of in a dream. I'm fielding ground balls and throwing them to Gil Hodges. After a while, I go to give the glove back to Jackie, and he shakes his head and says, 'No, that's yours now. Keep it.'

"I got sent to the minor leagues for a few weeks after that, to Macon, Georgia, and I took Jackie Robinson's glove with me. And I had it when I came back up to Brooklyn in September. What I remember about Jackie was how proud he was and how caring. You could tell that some things were an effort, physically. But he played *hard*. And I remember that he was always very aware—on the field, in the dugout, in the locker room. Very aware."

Over a span of that summer—a good, solid span, 104 times at bat in 36 games—Robinson hit .386 and got on base 48 percent of the time and slugged close to .560. Milwaukee led in the standings for much of the season, and against the Braves on July 31, with the Dodgers five games back, Robinson drove in all of Brooklyn's runs in a 3–2 win: a two-run home run in the second inning, then a single to send home Reese in the bottom of the ninth. The next night, Robinson scored the game-winner in the eighth, and the Dodgers were just three games back. In late August against the Braves, in Milwaukee now, Robinson, weakened by a stomach bug but in there nonetheless, doubled in the seventh inning and scored to tie the game. An inning later, he came around from first on a hit by Campanella, taking off for home plate when the throw came in behind him. Heads up. No hesitation. As one newspaper photo caption described it the next day: "Robinson turns back the calendar and scores from first base on Campanella's single." With that win, Brooklyn trailed Milwaukee by one game in the loss column.

The Braves were a new rival, lifted into contention partly through the effectiveness of their starting pitchers and the contributions of their Black players. Major league teams employed about three dozen Black ballplayers in 1956. On some days, three of those players were in the Braves outfield. Bill Bruton, the line-drive-hitting center fielder, chased down balls in the deepest part of Milwaukee County Stadium. Rookie Wes Covington showed power and promise in left. And playing right field and batting in the middle of the lineup: Hank Aaron, twenty-two years old and the best everyday player in the National League.

Aaron, on his way to leading the league in hits, a season away from winning the MVP, viewed Robinson with open admiration As a teenager in Mobile, Alabama, he had seen Robinson up close, heard his voice, and felt his presence. And as a rookie in 1954, when the Braves traveled north from spring training with the Dodgers, Aaron stayed in hotels with the Dodgers' Black players. He would go to Robinson's room, and, as he described it, sit off to the side, "thumbing through magazines, as Jackie Robinson and his Black teammates—Roy Campanella, Don Newcombe, Junior Gilliam and Joe Black—played cards and went over strategy: what to do if a fight broke out on the field; if a pitcher threw at them; if somebody called one of them a [n———]." Aaron understood from Robinson's example that the time had come for pride to conquer meekness. "Jackie made sure that younger Blacks like myself were soldiers in the struggle."

Aaron also learned that part of the reason that clutch of Dodgers stayed in and played hand after hand of cards like that, all through the evening, was because Robinson could not go out without drawing so much attention. Robinson "handled an awful lot inside of him," Aaron later wrote in a preface to Robinson's autobiography. Aaron recognized, in a visceral way, that the pressure Robinson lived with— from his first day in the major leagues to his last—was of a kind that most people didn't know about or could not understand.[24]

Not every Milwaukee player regarded Robinson with that level of respect or deference. The pitcher Lew Burdette was a committed bench jockey, a prankster, and a wag. He once posed for his baseball card portrait as a lefty. He sneaked snakes into the pockets of umpires. He frittered around nervously on the mound and was widely suspected of throwing the spitball. In that August 1956 series at County Stadium, Burdette took to razzing Robinson for his increased weight and his swagger. All season, Robinson had heard the barbs from opponents. ("Hey, Jackie, gettin' big for your britches, aren't ya! More ways than one!") But in Burdette's words, Robinson heard something else. The pitcher had been chirping at the Dodgers' Black players for years, and a few summers earlier, he had gone after Campanella

---

24. Aaron's admiration for Robinson never waned. Up until the time of Aaron's death, in January of 2021, he had a half dozen photographs of Robinson displayed in the living room of his home in Atlanta.

during an at bat by hurling, Campy said, a racial slur—as well as two knockdown pitches. That led Campanella to charge the mound with his bat.

Now, as the Dodgers warmed up on the field between innings, Burdette was getting on Robinson aggressively from the first base dugout, calling out with a reference to watermelons, a racist trope. Robinson made sure through Hodges that he had heard right, that Burdette was talking to him. Then Hodges rolled Robinson another warm-up ground ball, and Robinson picked up the baseball and threw it across the diamond, full force into the Milwaukee dugout.

"I aimed it right at Burdette's head," Robinson later said, still simmering. "Lucky for him, it missed." Burdette denied any racist intent. "I saw a picture of Robinson in a magazine, and he really looked fat. So I kidded him about it. . . . I never said anything off-color." Robinson let it be known that he was ready to meet Burdette in the lot outside the stadium anytime, although this was not an invitation Burdette was of any mind to accept.

All summer, Robinson kept his fire, kept his awareness. He groused about Alston's erratic use of the twenty-year-old Sandy Koufax—talented but wild—and privately called Alston "dumb." He sent a telegram to Herbert Lehman, senator of New York, on-site at the 1956 Democratic National Convention in Chicago, backing Lehman in his push that the party adopt a plank insisting on the enforcement of integration laws.

"It was very thoughtful of you to wire me. I greatly appreciate it," Lehman wrote back to Robinson a few days afterward. "I was of course disappointed that our minority report on civil rights was not adopted at the Convention." Robinson supported Lehman, but not, in general, the Democratic Party. On the whole, the party was not close to where it needed to be on matters of civil rights. Added Lehman, signing off: "I have long been one of your fans. I watch the Dodger games on T.V. as often as possible."

During the crucial end stretch of the 1956 season, the last two weeks as the Dodgers climbed into first place, Robinson batted .311, scored 9 runs, hit safely in all but one of his last 13 games. In the third inning of the season finale, against the Pirates at Ebbets Field, he drove a home run over the left field wall. Brooklyn won the game and, with it, the pennant. The players gathered and rejoiced in a mob on the field.

"I went over and hugged Jackie so much," Aspromonte says. "I'm not sure what came over me. I grabbed on to him and didn't let go. He was laughing, and some of the guys were laughing at me. I felt like I had just gotten there, and I didn't want him to leave!"

Robinson's regular-season numbers in 1956—a .275 batting average, a .793 OPS, 10 home runs, 61 runs scored, 43 RBIs, 37 extra-base hits—appear ordinary, even meager, beside the gleaming statistics of his first eight seasons as a Dodger. He was no longer elite, or even near to it. Yet by every measure, his results were significantly stronger than those of the previous season. And Robinson's WAR of 4.3, as we see that player-value number from here, trailed only Snider and Gilliam among Brooklyn's position players. Robinson simply would not, it is worth acknowledging once more, go gentle.

For the first time since 1953, Robinson received votes for the National League MVP Award, and here is one reason why: In the games that Robinson started, the Dodgers won 61.5 percent of the time, 64–40. In the games he did not start, they won at a rate of 58 percent, 29–21. Milwaukee finished a single game back in the standings; Cincinnati, two. There is no imagined scenario in which the Dodgers would have reached the 1956 World Series without him.

Game Six moved into the fifth inning, then quickly into the sixth. The sky remained bright, wind still gusted out toward Bedford Avenue, and the tension at Ebbets Field was such that the crowd became even more riveted, and sales of hot dogs and peanuts declined. Robinson's third at bat came in the bottom of the sixth. Still scoreless. Gilliam on second base. Snider on first. Turley had walked them both, creating sudden movement in the ballpark: the Yankees' Johnny Kucks began warming up in the bullpen, and the crowd began to stand and stir. The Dodgers had not had a lead in three days. The outfield played Robinson straightaway this time, and on Turley's first pitch, he popped the ball softly into shallow left field, where the shortstop McDougald, just in front of Slaughter, caught it for the second out.

One pitch later, Hodges popped out as well, to Billy Martin at second base. Another fruitless inning was over. The Yankees were coming up again against Labine, and the familiar dread and unease returned to the breasts of Dodger fans—conditioned as they were to brace for disappointment, a persistent feeling that not even the World Series win of 1955 had had the power to banish.

Even then—and surely now among those who recall—there was the sense of an ending around this World Series in Brooklyn, a sense of imminent change. The borough's trolley lines had all but shut down, the *Daily Eagle* had published its final issue, and O'Malley's restlessness, his persistent talk of needing a new place for the team to play, had beaten an ominous tattoo into the heads of fans. And Robinson, by whose lights and presence this great Dodgers era would be firstly and finally defined? The latest speculation was that he would retire and take a job managing the Royals in Montreal. "I'd be interested if they offered it to me," Robinson told a reporter during the World Series.

Rachel hadn't gone to Ebbets Field for Game Six, but rather stayed in Stamford to spend a few extra hours with the children, look over some last things at the house, get her hair done, pack. Hours after whenever the World Series ended—whether after Game Six or after Game Seven—the Dodgers were scheduled to leave by chartered flight to Japan, by way of Los Angeles and Hawaii, for a series of exhibition games. Not all the players were going (no Furillo, no Amorós, no Maglie, no Koufax), but many of the front-liners were. From the first planning discussions, Japanese officials had asked the Dodgers to guarantee that Robinson would be on the roster.

A few games in Hawaii, then nineteen more over twenty-five days in twelve cities in Japan. Robinson would be draped in leis in Honolulu and don kimonos in Osaka and dance with traditional geisha in Tokyo. Japanese children gathered around him after the games with baseballs and ball caps for him to sign. He hit home runs and he stole bases and he slid hard into home. In one game, against a local all-star team in Hiroshima—and what hard sense of history and sadness and outrage was felt there then, eleven years after the bomb?—Robinson argued so vehemently against an umpire's call at first base that he was ejected. From an exhibition game. On a goodwill tour. In front of twenty-five thousand bemused spectators familiar less with such outbursts than with a baseball culture steeped in decorum. Robinson had irked the umpire, Jocko Conlan, by yelling across the diamond that Conlan had blown the call by being out of position. "Everybody knew that Jocko missed the play," Robinson said. "But when I told him, he got angry."

Many of the players (as well as O'Malley, with his wide suit and big cigar) drew crowds of fans on the street, and in each new city, the team would be welcomed grandly, sometimes with a motorcade and signs hung all over town, on streetlamps, trees, and storefront windows: WELCOME BROOKLYN DODGERS! On game days, taxis trailed the team bus from the hotel to the ballpark, the taxi passengers hoping to glimpse a Dodger, any Dodger. Robinson, though, carried a greater and more particular power—to the Japanese, he represented something right in America and served as a reminder of what was terribly wrong. On the eve of the games, the *Japan Times* wrote in an editorial, "One of the notable achievements of the team from Flatbush Avenue was its success in breaking the color line in organized baseball. It indicated that progress is being made in the United States toward solving the problem of racial prejudice."

There is at once a beauty and an irony to the fact that Robinson—
the most famous Dodger by an order of magnitude, and the man who
lodged Brooklyn into the global imagination as a place of progress in
civil rights—would play his final games in a major league uniform on
distant ball fields, a missionary in Dodger blue. Shizuoka, Sapporo,
Sendai, Shimonoseki, Kofu. When the tour ended, the US ambassador to Japan, John Allison, wrote to personally thank Robinson for
being there and for playing baseball with his signature verve. A few
weeks later, at home in Stamford, Robinson received a letter from the
US State Department asking if he, independent of the Brooklyn club,
would consider a trip across South America. His presence there, the
government letter said, "could do a lot of good in winning respect and
understanding for our country."

In Japan, Rachel and the other players' wives—Bev Snider, Carolyn
Craig, and Betty Erskine among them—traveled on the same trains
as the team but were sequestered in separate cars, apart from the men,
conforming to the Dodgers' decree that they follow the local Japanese
custom regarding gender roles. And yet on the same train, up front
in the car with the plush seats, Kay O'Malley and Lela Alston rode
beside their husbands, a brazen management-player double standard
that Robinson could not abide. As the countryside rolled past the
windows of the train, he stood up and complained loudly to the team
about the slight. Reese, watching Robinson in his pique, leaned over
to Roy Campanella and said, "How much do you want to bet that
Jackie won't be back next year?"

That Robinson chafed against the Dodgers brass, refusing to let
the exclusion of the players' wives go unremarked, did not, however, limit how eagerly Robinson embraced the experiences of Japan
and the time he spent there with his teammates. They visited Shinto
shrines and ancient temples, and they stood somberly at the ruins in
Nagasaki. They ate sea urchin and yuzu. At the bar at the Imperial
Hotel in Tokyo, Jackie, a teetotaler, even had the smallest sip of sake.

He and Rachel wore good clothes and bought souvenirs for the kids and Willette and their mothers and friends. Jackie was into it, game for spontaneous outings and new flavors in a way that Rachel did not often see at home. He chatted and laughed as they wandered through a site or shop, behaving with what seemed an intentional openness and vigor. As Jackie and his teammates pulled on happi coats and headbands for a social meeting with Japanese baseball officials, it occurred to Rachel that he was leaning in to these days as a Dodger because there were not many of them left. "He knew the end was in sight," she would tell a biographer.

One day in the arcade of shops at the Imperial, Jackie and Rachel were browsing around with some of the others. Bob Aspromonte, still eighteen, was among them. "We were looking at things, kind of picking them up and putting them back. I was in awe of everything—where I was and who I was with. Then I saw this beautiful set of china on a shelf, really nice stuff, and I said to myself, really under my breath, 'Wow, would my mother love that.' Well, Rachel heard me, and that was all it took. She went up to the clerk and she got it for me. Paid for it, had it packed up and sent. I was a young kid with not a lot of money, and a few weeks later, this set of china arrived for my mother in Brooklyn. Rachel was like that. Jackie was like that."

Jackie and Rachel would reminisce about this trip time and again over the years and recount it to their children and their friends. ("When we were in Japan, we saw this man riding past on a bicycle, holding a large fish on a string. . . .") Moments preserved in time, jewels in the beautiful, rich sweep of their lives together.

All of that, though, had not yet come to pass on the afternoon of October 9, 1956, as Rachel reassured Jackie Jr. and Sharon that they would be okay while she and Jackie were gone (Zellee had come to stay in Stamford), and Jackie and the Dodgers tried to break ahead of the Yankees in Game Six, to keep the World Series alive. When Labine led off the bottom of the eighth by doubling deep into the left field corner, it was Brooklyn's third hit in seventeen innings. The left-hander Whitey Ford and the right-hander Bob Grim got up in the Yankees bullpen.

Gilliam struck out after failing to bunt Labine over to third, and Reese flied out to Mickey Mantle in center field, bringing Duke Snider to the plate. Snider batted left-handed, and the wind blowing out toward right field made Casey Stengel nervous. *If Snider gets hold of one . . .* Stengel came out of the Yankees dugout to talk things over on the mound with Turley and Berra.

As they conferred, Labine sat down on second base and looked around at the teeming corrals of Ebbets Field, the vendors in their white shirts standing in the aisles, the men in suits behind the dugouts, the people in ball caps in the highest bleacher rows, the pennants and the bunting that flapped in the wind. Labine was thirty years old and had spent most of the season as a reliever, coming in for one or two innings at a time. He had never started in a World Series before. This was the greatest game that Labine had ever pitched.

The Yankees chose to walk Snider intentionally and try their hand against the right-handed Robinson. "Jackie, an ever-dangerous man with the wood," Bob Neal told his listeners as Robinson prepared to hit. Eighth inning. Two out and two on. No score. Already in the sixth inning, Robinson had missed a chance like this. Now a big hit could all but win the game. He took his firm stance and slapped at his hip, and then for the second straight at bat, he swung at Turley's first pitch, overeager, and popped up the ball to Andy Carey at third base. Inning over.

Robinson was angry, unhappy with himself, and sorry that he had let the team down. He knew he could hit Turley. He'd been all over him when he lined out in the first inning. And in the '55 Series, Robinson faced Turley twice and singled both times. Maybe he was too anxious, could have waited another pitch, let the at bat unfold. But when he liked a pitch, he liked a pitch. Manning third base in the top of the ninth, Robinson kicked at the dirt and circled around his position. "Robinson's a little perturbed," Neal said.

The Yankees didn't score in the ninth, and neither did the Dodgers. Brooklyn had now gone eighteen innings without even getting a runner as far as third base. In the top of the tenth, the Yankees again went down easily against Labine, 1-2-3, and now it was the bottom of the inning, two outs, and the Dodgers had Gilliam on second base and Snider on first. Robinson was coming up to face Bob Turley for the fifth time in the game.

He stepped across home plate in front of Berra, rolled his shoulders, and gently wagged his bat before finding his place in the batter's box. Sweat stuck to Robinson's brow. *I can't fail again*, he thought. *I can't let that happen*. Robinson stood in shadow, looking out at Turley in sunlight on the mound. Turley had a circular face and evenly set eyes and brown hair closely cropped at the sides. Thin, curling lips. His control problems were evident: eight walks so far in the game. He looked in at Berra for the sign, then looked back at Gilliam leading off second base, and then he stepped forward and threw to the plate. Robinson rocked and swung—going after the first pitch once again—and fouled the ball back into the stands. Strike one.

A pleading chorus came out of the crowd, and out of the Brooklyn dugout too. ("C'mon, Jackie! Send us home! Here we go, Robbyyyyy!") One hit was all the Dodgers needed. Moments before, as Robinson strode from the dugout toward the plate, Pee Wee Reese had called out: "Thrill me, Jack."

The edge of the shadow line touched the front slope of the mound, and the wind had lessened and shifted away from right field. The Yankee outfielders played Robinson deep and swung over toward the left side. Mantle in center, Hank Bauer in right, Enos Slaughter in left. Earlier, foxed by the bright sky, Slaughter had misplayed a ball, allowing a looping hit by Gilliam to land in front of him. Robinson had no love at all for Slaughter, the old nemesis who in 1947 had spiked Robinson on a play at first base, gouging his calf so that the blood ran down. "One of the lousiest things I've seen in baseball," said the Dodgers' Eddie Stanky about the spiking. Slaughter said he hadn't meant any particular harm.

Slaughter played the game as hard as anyone, Robinson gave him that. He'd been a ten-time All-Star for the Cardinals, busted his ass all over the field, and scored the winning run of the 1946 World Series on a hell-bent dash from first base. He still played that way at forty years old. "I ain't no pantywaist," Slaughter liked to say. He had been raised on a ninety-acre family farm in North Carolina, strengthening his wrists by milking the cow and his shoulders by scything the wheat. Slaughter's father carved him his first baseball bat from the durable wood of a mulberry tree, and from time to time, the two of them traveled by horse and buggy to watch the local minor league team play ball. Slaughter went by the nickname Country, which to some people connoted a ruggedness and folksy charm, but to other people implied something else.

Bob Grim was up and throwing again in the Yankees bullpen as Robinson got back into the batter's box. He took his solid stance and fixed his eyes on Turley. Robinson's left shoulder looked to be the size of a linebacker's. McDougald at shortstop was playing well over into the hole, allowing Gilliam to take a substantial lead at second base, and the second baseman Billy Martin kept dodging over to try to bluff Gilliam back to the bag. Turley went into his stretch, looked back toward Gilliam, and threw to the plate again. Robinson laid off. Outside. One and one.

So very much would happen in Robinson's life over the weeks and months to come. Japan. The Spingarn banquet. The job at Chock Full. The trade, authorized by Walter O'Malley, of Jackie Robinson to the New York Giants. Retirement from the game. Meetings with the NAACP. Letters to Martin Luther King Jr. But right now for Robinson there was none of that or anything else. There was only this.

Turley caught the ball back from Berra and got up on the mound and then stepped off and drew a long breath and then got back onto the mound again. Gilliam kept his hands on his hips as he edged off second base, and then, as he moved farther away from the bag, he dropped his arms so that his hands hung below his knees. Then he got up on the balls of his feet, ready to run. Turley looked in toward the plate, stepped forward and threw the ball, and Robinson swung.

You could tell it had a chance by the sound of it—CLOCK!—a high line drive out toward the gap in left-center field. Slaughter moved sharply toward the ball and leaped with his glove hand outstretched. But the ball got over him and landed on the cinder path, one hop against the ad for Schaefer Beer. Gilliam gathered speed as he rounded third, and when he touched home plate, his fellow Dodgers streamed out of the dugout and some fans spilled out of the seats. The big Brooklyn crowd thundered and roared, and the old stadium shook and shook and shook in the autumn air. The Dodgers had won! There would be a Game Seven. When Clem Labine reached Robinson in the thicket of teammates surrounding him on the field, he kissed Robinson's cheek for all he was worth.

This was in the late afternoon on October 9, 1956: 10 years and 175 days since Robinson had played his first game as a Montreal Royal, 9 years and 172 days since he officially broke in at Ebbets Field. It was the 314th day of the bus boycott in Montgomery, Alabama—and another 74 days would pass before the boycott ended in success. This was the day on which the Brooklyn Dodgers beat the Yankees in a World Series game for the final time, and it was the day that Jackie

Robinson stroked that game-winning hit, the 1,550th hit, the final hit, of his Dodgers career.

There was still Game Seven to be played, the next afternoon at Ebbets Field, with Don Newcombe pitching for the Dodgers. Newcombe won 27 games in 1956, threw 5 shutouts, and allowed fewer base runners per inning than any other pitcher in baseball. He was voted the National League's Most Valuable Player.[25]

But in Game Seven, Newcombe did not pitch at that level. He gave up a two-run homer to Berra in the first inning and a two-run homer to Berra in the third inning, and he left the game in the fourth with Brooklyn trailing by five runs. The Yankees would go on to a 9–0 win, champions once again.

Robinson was the last World Series batter, swinging and missing at strike three and then, when the ball bounced away from Berra, racing to first base, in full flight, squeezing the last life out of the game, and the Series, never mind the score. But Berra got to the ball and threw to first base for the out. The Yankees gathered near the mound in celebration, and Robinson turned off to his right and into foul ground.

He would be back at Ebbets Field after that afternoon, to collect his things and say goodbye to the staff—Robinson always tipped the clubhouse guys well, home and away—but he would not be back on the diamond. And even then, he knew that this might be true.

You could see Jackie Robinson pausing there after the final out on that October afternoon, and looking out over the ballpark, at the fan of the infield and the white bases and the green outfield grass and the bleachers beyond. His office. The ground where he had plied his

---

25. In the eleven seasons beginning with Robinson's Most Valuable Player Award in 1949, a Black player won National League MVP nine times. As Willie Mays accurately observed of those years, "Did you notice that the teams that signed more Black players tended to win more games?" Dodgers, Giants, Indians, Braves. The Yankees were the era's most glaring exception.

craft and defined his mission, established himself and asserted himself again and again. Robinson had the quality of being witness to his own life. You can see him there, still and thoughtful at a standing rest, solemn as a lion in a tender moment, and then turning his great, thick body—the big shoulders and powerful arms, the sturdy trunk, legs thick as the thickest mattress springs, the body that had done its part to change the world—away from the field and beginning to move in his aching gait down off the field and into the dugout and on through the tunnel to the locker room, where he would talk to the newspapermen and feel the fresh disappointment of the World Series loss and then peel off his flannels, his Dodger blues, his uniform, for the last time in his life.

PART FOUR

WINTER

—

1972

GIFTS

There's this wonderful story that Sharon Robinson, the middle child of Jackie and Rachel, likes to tell about her father. It comes from the years when she was growing up and he was retired from baseball and the whole family—the three of them as well as Jackie Jr. and David, the youngest—were living in the big, many-roomed house on Cascade Road in Stamford. Sharon often points out that because she was just six years old when Jackie retired, her memories of him don't revolve around baseball. As a child, she learned much of what she knows about his playing career not from Jackie but from listening to other people, from within her close circle and without, the many who remembered it well.

What Sharon most associates with Jackie, along with the personal, fatherly things, the outings they shared and the quiet talks they sometimes had, is his attention to and involvement with the civil rights movement—the extraordinary events that they witnessed or influenced, her father's presence and concern in the arena, and the strong, sometimes controversial public opinions he held. Topics related to civil rights, and justice more broadly, circulated around the dinner table in Stamford on the nights when Jackie was neither out nor traveling and they were all at home, together.

Each year, a few weeks before Christmas—and this now is the story that Sharon likes to tell—Jackie would return home from New York City one evening carrying bags of men's clothes. Golf shirts, slacks, dress shoes, socks, perhaps a sport coat. He would take the clothes into his room and lay them out on the bed that he and Rachel shared, and then he would call out, "Jackie! Sharon! David! Come on in here." The kids would scramble over themselves upon hearing his voice, and when they got to his room, Jackie would say, "Now, why don't each of you pick out something you would like to give me for Christmas."

They would make their selections and then carry off the clothes to their own rooms and conscientiously hide them away until at some point, with help from Rachel or on their own, they would box and wrap the gifts and place them under the tree for Christmas morning. They all loved Christmas. The smell of the pine sap, the early morning, the cooking, the way they all gathered round, and also how, as the day unfolded, memories of past Christmases would resurface and the family stories were retold.

Rachel and Jackie recalled their snowless childhood Christmases in California, or the sweet, rounded trees they had put up by the Steinway during their years in St. Albans, or the time in 1948 specifically, when the young couple and Jackie Jr. lived on Tilden Avenue in Flatbush and Jackie had gone out and bought a Christmas tree as a gift for their new (and destined to be dear, lifelong) friends, the Satlows. Sarah, Steve, and the kids.

This particular reminiscence came up every year and always entertained. Jackie had believed the Satlows were without a Christmas tree because they couldn't afford one, not because, as was the case, they were Jewish. He took the tree right up to their front door. ("Surprise!") And Sarah after just a moment's pause had seen to the heart of the gesture and smiled so broadly and decided to herself that never mind what her parents or the other neighbors might say, they would put up that Christmas tree that year. Jackie and Rachel and Jackie Jr. helped the Satlows string the lights.

By the hearth in Stamford, on the apron beneath the tree, the gifts waited to be opened. Jackie would pick up one of the boxes addressed to him and inspect it on all sides, as if mystified. He'd hold the box by his ear and shake it gently, raising his eyebrows. "Now, I wonder what this could be?" he would say. They all giggled ("Aw, Dad!") and shook their heads—all the more so when Jackie unwrapped the gift and pulled out the cream-colored collared shirt or dark trousers or whatever it might have been, and fell back with an exclamation of wonder, as if he'd had no idea what the box contained and now was flush with unexpected joy. "What good taste you have, Sharon!" he might say with a smile.

Sharon has written a memoir that traces through happy as well as difficult times in her family. She also has written autobiographical books for young readers that illustrate Jackie's courage and hark to his achievements and to the Robinsons' connection to the front lines of history. (*Child of the Dream*, for example, tells of the Robinsons' trip to Washington, DC, on August 28, 1963, when Sharon was thirteen.)

She has so many powerful memories of her father—he died when Sharon was twenty-two—but the memory of the self-bought Christmas gifts retains a particular warmth. That's partly because of her father's humor and good nature, but also, perhaps, because it reflects something deep and essential about Jackie Robinson. That he viewed his agency as something he could share. That he understood that the giver and the receiver of a gift are more closely aligned than one might imagine, and that he was always, even in smaller family moments, aware of how his actions have an impact on the lives of others in a memorable way. For any number of reasons, when Sharon is asked to tell one story about her father, the story of the Christmas gifts is the one she chooses to tell.

PASSAGES

Robinson couldn't see well. But he was driving himself there anyway, sticking, as best he could, to the right lane of the Hutchinson River

Parkway. His peripheral vision was shot, and there was not much at all coming into his right eye. For months now, people he met for a meal noticed how he'd come into the restaurant and stand for a moment to get his bearings. Then he'd start making his way to the table, trailing the hostess but along the way bumping into chairs, or knocking unintentionally against a diner's back. If Rachel were there, she might try to take his hand and guide him, but Jackie wouldn't have that. ("I'll get there fine, Rae.") He just wished the lights weren't so damn dim in these places. He wished there were a little sunlight coming in. If you were standing near Robinson as he navigated through a restaurant like this, you might hear him quietly cuss.

It was just like that on the day a few weeks earlier, when he had gone into Midtown to meet Tommy Villante and a couple of baseball executives for lunch at Mike Manuche's. Villante was floating an idea for a charity dinner in behalf of Jackie Jr., in partnership with a rehab facility or drug awareness group maybe, something baseball-backed to honor Jackie Jr. and remember him by. They had ordered steak all around, and iced tea.

"If Rachel hears about this idea, she is going to cry," said Robinson, dabbing quickly at his own eyes. His face was wider now than it had been, his forehead rucked and touched by sorrow. But his smile, when he showed it, took years off his age. Robinson was still a handsome man.

At least it was daylight now as he drove, a crisp morning in early April. Robinson, keeping to fifty miles an hour, gripped the steering wheel and stared intently at the road, drawing a breath each time he neared an on-ramp where traffic might merge in front of him. His knuckles hurt. He drove past the exits for Rye and Harrison and New Rochelle, bound for the Whitestone Bridge. He had the route mapped in his mind. He would pass Shea Stadium and then go down to the Interboro Parkway and get off at the Bushwick Avenue exit and into

Brooklyn, Midwood, to the Church of Our Lady Help of Christians. Gil's funeral. Some of their old Dodgers teammates would be there.

Robinson had spoken with Villante that same morning and turned down the offer of a ride to the funeral. Ralph Branca and Villante were driving there together, and it would be no trouble for them to pop up from Westchester and pick him up, they'd said. But Robinson decided he would handle this one on his own. It had to do with how he was feeling. Fifty-three and with the extra weight. His knees balked, and in the mornings, sometimes his ankles felt on fire. His sorry eyesight. But this—a ninety-minute drive, at a time like this—was something, he felt, he could do.

Gil. Robinson could hardly believe it. Forty-seven years old. And he'd looked not only fine but fit too. A newspaper account put it like this: "Gil Hodges, the popular first baseman of the old Brooklyn Dodgers, who later managed the Mets to their surprising baseball championship, died of a heart attack today after playing 27 holes of golf." Hodges had had a heart attack once before, and so had Robinson. Along with the other health issues that affected Robinson, his blood pressure had been too high for years.

He had driven this route, southward along the Hutch, for close to seventeen years, ever since they'd settled in Stamford. He'd commuted in to Ebbets Field and then to Chock Full o' Nuts, to the bank and the Y in Harlem, to Nelson Rockefeller's office, to his many appearances and engagements in and around New York and Brooklyn over the years. He and Rachel loved their home in Connecticut, inside and out and right down to the name of the road it was on: Cascade, for the waterfall just beyond it. They had pushed through the human muck to buy a place like this, through the real estate agents who kept steering them to other communities, through the houses they'd seen and bid on that then suddenly vanished off the market when it became known who the buyers were. St. Albans was one thing; an enclave in Stamford was another. The Robinsons were the only Black family in the neighborhood. When they moved in, some folks on the street sold their homes.

Cascade Road took a slight curve just before it reached the Robinsons' house, number 103. It was an uphill curve that didn't allow for any perspective of approach—you got to the top of the curve, and suddenly it was there: the mouth of the shaded driveway. Home. Six acres, maybe a little more, and woods surrounding the sloping back-yard, and a pond that the kids could swim and row a wooden boat in. They had built the house—Rachel had, with a meticulous builder—virtually from the ground up. The broad-stone facing was a nod to the glacial till so common to the landscape of the coasts of southern New England. A wooden deck wrapped around the second floor, and below the deck, wide doors opened onto the patio at the head of the backyard lawn.

Some of the boulders on the property were intentionally kept in place. One, dubbed "the Big Rock," served as a site for family confer-ences. Another remained exposed inside the playroom, jutting prom-inently out of a wall beside the pool table and the soda fountain. The finished house yielded other pleasing quirks: two-way dresser draw-ers that opened into both the master bath and the bedroom, brass bathtub faucets in the shape of fish, tall fireplaces set into smooth gray stone, a fireman's pole. There was ample room for Willette and Zel-lee to stay, and ample outdoor space for the unforgettable summer-time concerts the Robinsons hosted. Overall, the home itself and the grounds around it offered an openness that called California to mind.

Things had not always been easy in Stamford for the Robinsons, even after they got settled in. They were rejected from joining the country club at High Ridge in a membership vote, and they knew exactly the reason why. Jackie made sure news about the rejection got out, then said he'd play golf somewhere else. At every new school, Jackie Jr. and Sharon and David felt the gawking and the whispering of their white classmates, and they heard much harder things at times in their teens.

But the Robinsons joined a good Congregational church a quarter of a mile from home and they developed full, deep friendships and they found that the neighbors who did welcome them were prepared to pull them close. Friends were always coming over to the house, children and adults. When the pond froze over, the boys sometimes played hockey out back. On the nearby local ball fields, Jackie occasionally held clinics with the Babe Ruth and youth baseball leagues. Of the things that Robinson had come to regret, and in this last year some of those regrets had become profound, the home he and Rachel had made on Cascade Road in North Stamford was not among them. The place was a blessing, a sanctuary, a nest that they cherished.

Halfway to Our Lady, Robinson almost wished he'd accepted the ride with Branca and Villante after all. He had a history as a terrific driver—precise, aggressive, and, as his passengers joked, unencumbered by speed limits. Now his skill and muscle memory, the reflexes he retained, carried him at his slower speed. The highway remained manageable. But he knew that once he got into Midwood, and onto the narrower streets with smaller signage and tighter turns, the challenge would be greater. He wasn't familiar with the roads; it would be hard to get around.

Robinson did not at first notice them driving right behind him, Villante flashing his headlights in greeting. Nor did he turn to look when they swung out alongside and slowed and tooted the horn. Branca, in the passenger's seat, rolled down the window and began shouting and waving to get Robinson's attention. Villante pushed on the horn again. Finally, Robinson did notice, and he nodded and grinned at Branca without taking his hands off the wheel. "Follow us!" Branca got across. "We'll go together!" Robinson, as he later allowed, felt relieved.

The drive continued without incident, with little traffic to speak of. Soon after pulling off the parkway, Robinson, trailing behind, found a parking spot at the end of a line of cars on Avenue L near Twenty-Ninth Street, just a couple of blocks from the church—a stroke of luck given the crowds. Villante and Branca drove on, turning at the next corner to find a spot of their own. Robinson parked cleanly. But when he shut off the engine and tried to step out of the car, he found that he could hardly move. He couldn't raise his legs more than an inch off the seat. "It was like I was glued down, weighted down," he would say. "Like in a dream." He was stuck.

This happened to him sometimes after he had been sitting for a while: his whole body going stiff, his lower half seemingly thickened and weighted, legs like heavy, water-soaked logs. Rachel noted it on occasion after a long dinner. Or when he rose from his chair on a weekend afternoon. For a few steps, he would lumber and creak— almost dragging his feet with each labored step—until he began to loosen up and the suggestion of his old grace and power returned, glimpses of the strides that had once set the world on end.

This sensation was different, though, weightier still. He sat alone in the car, his ring of keys still in his right hand. The day was overcast. Gray squirrels bantered on the coarse, rectangular front lawns. The leafless branches of the gingko trees along the sidewalk showed their earliest buds. It was Thursday, middle of the morning. An older couple walked by, all bundled up, and then a kid passed on his bicycle. You could see little clutches of people, many of them women, moving in the direction of the church to show respect for Gil, and to see who on this day had come to their neighborhood.

Tom Seaver and other Mets players had arrived, Commissioner Bowie Kuhn, and Howard Cosell from ABC Sports. Robinson knew that Pee Wee Reese would be at the funeral, as well as Sandy Koufax, Carl Furillo, and others. Newcombe. There would be guys Robinson had known twenty-five years but had not seen since Jackie Jr.'s death, ten months before. Ten months. A cruel irony hung on the agony of the loss. Robinson had felt as though they only recently got Jackie Jr. back.

"It started a long, long time ago," Robinson said, recalling Jackie Jr. soon after his death. "He resented people talking to him about his father. He was very young, you know, and it built up something in him, I think, and all of a sudden, he rebelled against it, and it came about after he developed some potential as a Little Leaguer.

"There was always that comparison," Robinson added. He had agreed to sit down with the Associated Press, to lay bare the burden. "And even though at that time there was a great deal of warmth and a great deal of love between us, the pressure started to get real hard on him, and all of a sudden he, you know, just kind of started to pull away."

They had seen him drifting at Stamford High, out of place and out of sorts. Sports were not the thing for Jackie Jr., nor did he seem sure what was. He didn't quite fix on anything. "I was haunted by the image of being the son of a father who was a great man," Jackie Jr. would later say. They tried boarding school, but it worked out for only a year. Jackie Jr., the school administrators said, did not fit in. As Jackie Jr. grew deeper into his teens, he and his father, in Rachel's words, "became increasingly unable to talk with each other or embrace."

At seventeen, in 1964, Jackie Jr. joined the US Army. At eighteen, he began serving in the infantry in Vietnam, writing letters home about the death he saw—soldiers alongside him, children and innocents in the villages. They smoked weed in the infantry and took pills and dipped their joints in opium oil. At nineteen, Jackie Jr. took shrapnel in his hip in an explosion that killed two men. He left the army in '67, honorably discharged with a Purple Heart, and tried to begin again. He spent a stretch of time in Stamford, doing odd jobs, then a stint out in Colorado, where he'd been stationed in the army early on. "He'd go out for two months and be perfectly clear of heroin,"

Robinson said. "Then he'd come back to Stamford and get back on it again." In truth, he was using out in Colorado as well.

When Jackie Jr. was arrested in March of 1968, charged with possessing packets of heroin, a bag of marijuana, and a .22—as well as luring the police into a car chase in an attempt to flee—Jackie and Rachel and Sharon went to pick him up at the jail, to post bail. "We have obviously failed somewhere," Robinson told the reporters gathered by the jailhouse entrance. "My wife and I were probably away too much instead of being home where we were needed. . . . I went running around everywhere else." Robinson would later say that he had "had a feeling that something was wrong" with Jackie Jr., but that the distance between them was too great. He couldn't reach him. "If I could do things over," Robinson said, looking back through the years, "perhaps I would reduce my work schedule and try to be closer to my children."

The trauma of the arrest created drastic change. Jackie Jr. went into rehabilitation—a condition for avoiding jail time—got himself clean for months, then for years. He took a job counseling at the rehab facility, Daytop Village, in Connecticut. He gave public talks about the dangers of addiction, at times with Jackie standing by his side in support. The Robinsons held a picnic for the staff at Daytop, fifty-some people mingling out on the lawn, and when the afternoon was over and everything had gone so well, Jackie Jr. put his arms around his father in thanks. This was in the years when the Robinsons hosted jazz concerts to raise money for civil rights, and they decided to earmark the revenue from the next one, set for late June of 1971, for Daytop. Jackie Jr. would organize the event.

He was driving his brother David's 1969 MG Midget, a two-seater with a soft convertible top, northbound on the Merritt Parkway in the first hours of June 17, 1971, when the car—as best as the police could determine—spun out of control. It demolished guardrails and struck an abutment at the New Canaan overpass, and when they found Jackie Jr., he was pinned in the wreckage with a broken neck. He could not be saved. A single-car crash. He was eight miles from home, from the boyhood bedroom on Cascade Road where he had been staying in those weeks, from the note of greeting that Sharon, just up from DC, had left on his pillow. Eight miles from the site of the upcoming jazz concert, from the continuance, at age twenty-four, of his reclaimed life.

In the darkest hour of that dark, fell night, a police officer came to the door at Cascade Road and roused Sharon and Jackie from their sleep and delivered the unspeakable news. And then David agreed to go to Norwalk Hospital to identify his brother. Jackie and Sharon drove up to Massachusetts, where Rachel was attending a conference, and broke the news to her in a hotel room there. The resilience that had long bonded Jackie and Rachel, that had been part of their connubial marrow from the start, would never be needed more.

So now here was Robinson, April 6, 1972, sitting in his car in Midwood, Brooklyn, stuck in the front seat, a few blocks from Gil Hodges's funeral service. The crowd swelled within the church and without. Photographers and television cameramen found their places. Robinson knew that any words to him from old friends and baseball people would be kind ones, and kind the looks he would receive. Still, he could not find a way to move. At home, he and Rachel sometimes went long stretches in silence. When you've been scalded, even the softest touch hurts.

On the one hand, Robinson was in no hurry to get of the car. On the other, he couldn't bear to sit there any longer. Joan and the Hodges family would soon be at the church. This was a day to honor Gil. And there were not many men in his baseball life more worthy of honor. *What am I going to do?* Robinson thought. He kneaded his thighs, massaged his battered and repaired right knee, and waited for the feeling, the immobility, to go away. *Think of something else. This will pass. It always does.*

And then, suddenly, the car door was open and Ralphie was leaning in and taking hold of him, and Villante had him under his other
arm and they got him out and onto his feet on the street. He wore a
long, dark overcoat over his suit. Robinson leaned on both of them
as he straightened himself, took a few shuffling steps, and then stood
still for a moment. Some of that deadweight feeling began to ebb, and
he felt a little freer, and soon he was okay to walk toward the church
between his two friends, slowly but no longer leaning on them, moving forward on his own legs.

Even with so many mourners in attendance, Gil's was a quiet funeral,
the service dignified and sweet. Father Curley talked about how
Hodges had never been thrown out of a ball game by an umpire, how
he had been a leader marked by self-discipline and even temper, and
that these were the traits that helped him to lead the "beloved bums"
in 1955 (and then, as manager, the beloved, chronically inept Mets) to
their World Championships. The church was filled to capacity. A few
dozen kids from the Gil Hodges Little League had come, wearing
the league jackets with the orange patch. Mayor John Lindsay was
there, with an entourage of city officials around him. Pin-setters from
Hodges's Brooklyn bowling alley stood among former and current
major leaguers alongside the overstuffed pews. In all the spheres of
his life, Hodges had reached up, down, and across.

The organ music and liturgical voices carried outside to where by
now thousands stood on the sidewalks, rows deep behind the wooden
police horses. At some neighboring houses, people climbed onto their
roofs to watch as the funeral came to an end. The casket and the honorary pallbearers—Erskine was among them—emerged first from
the church. "It scares you," Robinson said to the reporters when he
stepped out shortly afterward. "I've been somewhat shocked by it all.
I have tremendous feelings for Gil's family and kids. Next to my son's
death, this is the worst day of my life."

Erskine had seen firsthand what Hodges had done for Robinson during those crucial early years of his career, how with his manner and his presence, Hodges had been a defuser when Robinson, by his presence and nature, lit many fuses. "Gil prevented fights and pulled guys off the piles at second base," Erskine would later tell Hodges's biographers. "Nobody running between first and second challenged him because he was big and strong and was respected." The influence, Erskine would say, ran deeper than dispassionate accounts might suggest. "If you didn't play with him every day, you might not even have realized it was going on. But he helped Jackie by keeping the peace around second base."

Hodges was younger than Robinson by more than five years, but he was preternaturally mature: calm and steadying. He made the most difficult plays at first base with an ease of movement that belied his provenance as a catcher. Hodges was everywhere that he needed to be on the field. He would lead all first basemen in putouts and assists. He hit, and he hit for power. He played every day—averaging 152 games a year through the long heart of his career—and he made every All-Star team and he established himself, along with Robinson and Reese, as a yearslong pillar of the best infield Brooklyn ever had. Some reporters noted that with his power, consistency, and excellence, Hodges reminded them of Lou Gehrig. "I appreciate the compliment," Hodges said, "but Gehrig had one advantage over me."

"What was that?" asked Arthur Daley of the *New York Times*.

Hodges grinned. "He was a better ballplayer."

Living in Flatbush in '49, when Jackie Jr. was a toddler and before Gil Jr. was born, the Robinsons and the Hodges ate dinner together sometimes, sat down over coffee, went out for scoops of ice cream. In the Dodgers clubhouse, Jackie and Gil played cards, and for a time the two men lockered side by side. Hodges and Ralph Branca were the only white Dodgers who played on the Jackie Robinson All-Stars in the fall of '53, when Robinson took that barnstorming team down south.

On so many days and nights during those fierce, beautiful summers at Ebbets Field, Robinson and Hodges sat next to each other in the dugout. Robinson was always chirruping, calling out to the players on the field, sassing an umpire. Hodges not so much. He breathed deeply and evenly, and he took everything in. The other Dodgers recognized that, even when you included big Don Newcombe, Robinson and Hodges were the strongest men on the team—both of them even more imposing in their bearing than by their physique alone. "He was as big as a statue," said Bob Aspromonte of Hodges. "All he would need to do was look at me."

No one in baseball was surprised when Hodges went on to become a manager, or when he, abetted by Seaver, transformed the way the Mets carried themselves. What he left behind in the Mets dugout on the day he died was an attitude that would prevail for years to come. The shortstop Buddy Harrelson described Hodges's gift as "the belief that it was something special to be a Met." He had instilled similar feelings in teammates throughout his playing career. There was a standard that you held to, a sense of professional honor, and you did things just so.

Aspromonte played (and briefly roomed) with Hodges for a few months in 1956, and again in Los Angeles during the latter years of Hodges's career, and that was more than enough to impress the young player. When he was drafted by the expansion team in Houston, and then again when he was traded to Atlanta, Aspromonte wore uniform number *14*, just like Hodges, as a tribute. "Finding out he died was devastating," said Aspromonte. He had been traded back home to New York and played for Hodges and the Mets in '71. "It was just unbearable to realize that the relationship was gone." Aspromonte attended the funeral with his brother Ken, and he remembers the plain numbness that surrounded him, and coming up to Gil's widow, Joan, whom he knew . . . but not finding any words to say. Disbelief attended the sorrow in the church that day.

"He was the best manager I ever had," says Jerry Koosman, the Mets left-hander, "and it was a privilege to be part of his process." Koosman drove to Hodges's funeral in his Oldsmobile station wagon with the old Brooklyn Dodgers pitcher Joe Black and the Mets pitching coach Rube Walker. They came over from the Travelers' Hotel by LaGuardia Airport, and when Black stepped out of the car and up onto a curb near the Our Lady Help of Christians Church his pants tore right down the seam of his backside. "What are you going to do now, with your pants ripped like that?" Koosman recalls asking. "So we said, 'Joe, you go in front and we'll walk behind you and protect you so it's not seen.' We did the same thing on our way out. In a way, it was kind of a good thing that happened. I remember thinking that Gil would have laughed about it."

Koosman had been on the mound for the Mets in Atlanta a few years before, late September of 1968, when in the middle of the game Hodges left the dugout with chest pains. After Koosman got knocked out in the sixth inning, he went back into the clubhouse and saw Hodges lying on the trainer's table, his face reddened, but saying that he felt more or less well. The doctors termed it a mild heart attack, and Hodges spent more than two weeks in a hospital. But he recovered nicely from that and soon returned to lead the Mets with all his dedicated force.

So Koosman did not think the worst, or even close to it, on that early April day in 1972, when he came out of the shower in his hotel room near spring training camp in St. Petersburg, Florida, and heard sirens and then learned that Hodges had been taken to Good Samaritan Hospital. This was during the major league players' strike, and many of the Mets had left Florida. Koosman, though, had stayed to get in some more throwing, and that afternoon he had seen Hodges on the golf course playing with Walker and two other Mets coaches, Joe Pignatano and Eddie Yost. The coaches played 27 holes that day, and then when they walked back to the hotel room, just as they were making plans for dinner, Hodges suddenly collapsed and could not be revived. "I went to the hospital expecting to talk with him but he was already dead," Koosman says. "And then a few days later we were in the funeral, with all those different people, all those players, and I had this feeling that everything was in limbo: the Mets, baseball, everything. You saw Jackie Robinson there and Pee Wee Reese and it felt like something so significant had ended."

Branca kept a hand on Robinson's elbow as they came down the steps of the church and moved onto the sidewalk among the dispersing mourners. The neighborhood crowd gawked and snapped photographs and Robinson stopped here and again to shake hands and exchange words of commiseration. He might have liked to just go home, or to go sit with Ralphie and Villante and talk somewhere. But among the people on hand was Howard Cosell, the great television broadcaster, and Cosell asked if Robinson would take a ride with him, back to the old neighborhood, maybe film a few things he could use on ABC. So Robinson got into the back seat of the car and a driver took him and Cosell over to where Ebbets Field had been, driving along Flatbush Avenue, and then over to Tilden, and past the old trolley stops and what was left of the shops. Robinson talked with Cosell about how things had been in those glorious, hard, wonderful times, and the way that he had felt coming up to bat in that ballpark, with the crowd all stirring and shouting as he stepped in, and how it felt to be out on the Ebbets Field grass with his glove on, and how the sun tended to play in the afternoons, and the things that he missed and remembered most about Gil. He talked to Cosell about how very much more baseball, and all the more so the country at large, still had to do when it came to the rights and the dignity of its Black citizens.

Robinson had a sense of something after attending Gil Hodges's funeral, a sense that he carried with him as the rest of that year went on, and that he talked about sometimes as he pressed forward with his views on civil rights, and as he suddenly began to reengage with baseball: that so much of what he had in his life was precious and rare, and that there were things he very much wanted to do and things he hoped would happen in the world around him, and that the urgency was as real as it had ever been. Robinson had suffered from diabetes for fifteen years, and his blood circulation was very bad. At one point on the day of Hodges's funeral, while talking with Roger Kahn and Don Newcombe, Robinson said in a simple assessment of the old crew of Brooklyn Dodgers teammates, "I thought I'd be the first to go."

LOS ANGELES TO CINCINNATI

Robinson had not been inside a baseball stadium for years. Since his retirement, he'd had no official or professional connection at all to Major League Baseball—which he openly criticized as negligent in its treatment and integration of Black players in their post-playing careers. How could he not? Twenty-five years after Robinson broke in, more than fifteen years after his final game, no team had hired a Black manager or general manager, and very few Black players held jobs of significance in the game. It was a conspicuous element of Robinson's protest that he did not attend Old-Timers' Games or other stadium celebrations. He'd stopped being invited, because his answer was always the same.

But then, at Hodges's funeral, Robinson had seen so many of the old guys together, and he had spoken with Newcombe, for whom he retained a warm affection. Newcombe did have a connection to baseball, as a community relations liaison for the Dodgers and team president Peter O'Malley. Sensing in their conversations and reminiscences the earliest edges of a thaw, Newcombe invited Robinson to come to Dodger Stadium later in the spring, on the first Sunday in June. In an on-field ceremony before that season's Old-Timers' Game, the Dodgers planned to retire the uniform numbers of three

former players who'd reached the Hall of Fame: Roy Campanella's
39, Sandy Koufax's *32*, and Jackie Robinson's *42*. Newcombe, Reese,
and Jim Gilliam would be there and others as well. A bunch of the
old Yankees. Musial. Newcombe worked on Robinson a bit, and so
did Tommy Villante, who recalls, "We had to kind of convince Jackie
that Peter O'Malley wasn't just the same guy as Walter, who Jackie
still felt wary about." Robinson said yes.

JACKIE ROBINSON-DODGER FEUD ENDS read a headline in the Long
Beach *Press-Telegram* on the day of the event in Los Angeles. Separate
and apart from his dissatisfaction with baseball as a whole, Robinson
had a more particular friction with the Dodgers themselves, stem-
ming not from issues around race but from his divide with Walter
O'Malley and the galling trade of 1956. Trade discussions had circulated around Robinson for some time, and to many, a trade made
sense: Robinson was an older, expensive player with his best years behind him but still capable on the field and, as ever, a draw at the gate.
And yet it seemed that Robinson, with his long and numinous reach,
should have been beyond such mundane calculus. Trading him was
akin to excising the lion's heart. O'Malley, then, exhibited a particularly pointed flex of might when on December 13, 1956—a little more
than two months after the final out of the World Series, and 299 days
before O'Malley officially pulled the Dodgers out of Brooklyn, bound
for Los Angeles—he traded Robinson to the rival Giants.

Bavasi delivered the news by telephone to Robinson, who smiled
(or did he grimace?) on his end of the line. Privately, Robinson had
already moved on. Shortly before learning of the trade, but already
with an inkling of it, he had decided to retire from baseball, accepting
a position as a vice president overseeing personnel at the Chock Full
o' Nuts restaurant chain in New York. Robinson, keeping those plans
private (to be revealed weeks later in a paid-for *Look* magazine story),
made no mention of the Chock Full job to Bavasi. So the trade to the
Giants was announced, and it rent a gash through the Dodger zeit-

geist. Robinson publicly thanked the Giants owner Horace Stoneham for wanting him, and in the following days, he and Jackie Jr. held up Giants' pennants and posed for the photographers who came to visit the home in Stamford. During the time between the trade and Robinson's writing to Stoneham, in early 1957, on Chock Full o' Nuts letterhead, to say that he would not in fact report to spring training, that he was leaving baseball for "business opportunities," Robinson received a welcome-to-the-team telegram from the Giants' twenty-five-year-old center fielder, Willie Mays.

Robinson knew that Walter O'Malley remained an ally in baseball's path to progress, and he knew that Rachel had a fine and gentle relationship with Kay, and yet in the aftermath of the trade and in the decade and a half since, Robinson and the Dodgers had not gone anywhere or done anything hand in hand. In 1972, the conflicting emotions of a breakup—*I don't need you. I love you*—still weighed on Robinson. "I couldn't have cared less about the trade, because I had already made my decision to retire," he said as the Old-Timers' Day in Los Angeles approached. "But I was hurt by it, yes. After you give everything you have to one team, it's hard to be traded."[26]

---

26. The larger rub of the O'Malley–Robinson conflict traced beyond the trade to their respective feelings toward Branch Rickey—the same wall of contention that had shadowed the two men during Robinson's career. By 1972, O'Malley's map-shifting move of the Dodgers to Los Angeles had proved bold and prescient, a success that reshaped baseball with enormous benefit to the sport. Over their first 15 seasons in Los Angeles, the Dodgers drew upward of thirty-one million people to their home games. No other National League team drew even twenty million during that span.

And yet O'Malley knew that whatever he did in baseball (the move, presiding over Brooklyn's World Series win in 1955 and then over three more titles in Los Angeles, his own progressiveness on integration) would never be what Branch Rickey and Jackie Robinson had done together in 1947. The O'Malley, a man with the intellect and the ego to take on Robert Moses, understood that there are few gods among us and fewer still among high-salaried sports executives, and he knew that Branch Rickey's square face and heavy brow, not O'Malley's own, was destined to be carved into any metaphorical mountainside of baseball builders. Along with that envy was a matter of money, a sting. Back when O'Malley had forced him out of the Dodgers ownership group in 1950, Rickey bit back, craftily exploiting a contract clause to draw an extra $50,000 out of O'Malley's hands.

In 1970, Walter O'Malley had moved himself into the Dodgers' chairmanship and given daily control of the team to his son, Peter. During the repatriation of Robinson in '72, Peter O'Malley said he could not imagine allowing a trade such as the one of Robinson. The franchise's greatest player? The critical baseball figure of his time? That would never have happened on his watch, Peter O'Malley said. He framed the trade of Robinson as an organizational regret.

Robinson's job at Chock Full o' Nuts drew naturally on his celebrity. Sharon recalls going with him to work and staying downstairs by the counter in the restaurant and listening to the women who worked there and the customers who came in talking of her father (and the extraordinary baseball he had played) with unqualified reverence. When Chock Full o' Nuts opened a new restaurant or store or negotiated with a coffee distributor, Robinson might be deployed for publicity and goodwill. And yet the consequence of his job often lay in brass tacks: paperwork, which he despised, and the general day-to-day facets of employee relations, "ironing out their problems and keeping personnel changes at a minimum," as Robinson described it.

Early on it fell to Robinson, for the first time, to fire someone. "He hated to do it," said Dan Blumenthal, an executive at Chock Full. "But he dealt with the man with such charm, compassion, and understanding. Eventually the man was gone." For a few minutes afterward, Robinson sat silent at his desk. He looked out the window. Then he looked over at Blumenthal. "I never had so many butterflies in my stomach in all my life," he said. A few months into Robinson's tenure, a newspaper profile described him as having made the clean

---

Robinson's allegiance to Branch Rickey, however, remained as deep and immovable in 1972 as it had been for more than a quarter century, his devotion as enduring as O'Malley's distaste. There had been no more important man in Robinson's life. "He was like a father to me," Robinson said upon Rickey's death in 1965. "He was one of the most knowledgeable men I ever knew. Not just about baseball, but about everything. He was warm and human and kind. He was thorough and exacting. We will never see another like him."

transition from the ball field to being "the man in the gray flannel suit."

He was a hit, naturally, at the company picnics, held fifty miles north of the city, in Warwick, New York, where Chock Full owned land and a summer camp. Mitchell Ostrove's father, Samuel, worked for Chock Full o' Nuts for twenty-five years, the last three as president. "One year, there was a softball game between management and the employees," says Mitchell. "The employees had a pitcher and a catcher who had played semi-pro baseball, so you can imagine how they pitched. There was no way anyone in management was going to hit it, because it was so fast. After a batter or two, Jackie walks over to the employee and says, 'We're here having fun. Just lob it in there.' The guy says, 'That is not how I pitch.'

"So Jackie says, 'Tell you what. You strike me out, and you can pitch however you want.' Well, they're still looking for the ball that Jackie hit. That pitcher didn't give up, though. He says to Jackie, 'That was lucky. Try it again.' And now they're still looking for the second ball that Jackie hit. That's how he took care of it. Jackie said to the guy, 'Now you see the difference between being a professional and semi-professional.' Everyone understood what he meant. The pitcher lobbed in the ball from then on, and we went ahead and had a great afternoon. Now, that is not something you see at every company picnic."

Robinson could have kept things right there in those early years of his retirement, made good money, rested on his name and achievement, quietly gathered the long threads of praise that continued to come to him. Cloaked that way, he might indeed have found a glad-handing role with baseball, settled in. Not Robinson, though. Not even close. "I like his type," said William Black, the Chock Full o' Nuts president who pursued the Robinson hire. "He's feisty, not afraid to speak his mind."

Along with the desk job, Robinson in 1957 took over as the leader of the NAACP's Freedom Fund, a program that targeted January 1, 1963—the centennial of the Emancipation Proclamation—as the day to end segregation. Later he joined the NAACP's board. He toured widely on the organization's behalf, giving speeches from podiums and pulpits, raising funds, recruiting members.

During a visit to Greenville, South Carolina, Robinson and others traveling with him were ordered by an airport manager and a police officer to leave the whites-only waiting area at Municipal Airport. They did not leave. Robinson believed that as interstate travelers, they were protected by law. He knew also that the airport was federally funded, creating, in those chaotic evolving years, some legal gray area.

He asked the officer what the law was in Greenville. "He just stood there dumbstruck," Robinson later told reporters. "He did not say a word." The officer made no arrests, but the event caused active dismay. Weeks later in Greenville, several hundred protesters descended peacefully on Municipal Airport singing "America the Beautiful." Black ministers read prayers aloud in the whites-only waiting room.

Robinson's determination to be heard never wavered. He wrote letters—often, with William Black's blessing, on that Chock Full o' Nuts letterhead—to the prominent ears he knew he could bend. In 1958, he heard President Eisenhower suggest to a gathering of Black leaders that they have patience in the push for civil rights. "I felt like standing up and saying 'Oh no! Not again,'" Robinson wrote to President Eisenhower the next day, "17 million Negroes cannot do as you suggest and wait for the hearts of men to change. We want to enjoy now the rights that we feel we are entitled to as Americans." Added Robinson: "I respectfully suggest that you unwittingly crush the spirit of freedom in Negroes by constantly urging forbearance."

There was a warm history between Eisenhower and Robinson, who had earlier written to the president, praising him for sending federal troops to ensure school integration in Little Rock, Arkansas.

Robinson could still summon the honor he had felt when, at an anti-defamation banquet in 1953, President Eisenhower stepped off the podium and walked through the crowded room, all eyes on him, to shake Robinson's hand. That history did not, however, put Eisenhower above Robinson's reproach. With friend, foe, or formidable figure, frankness may have been Robinson's most constant virtue. When he thought you were wrong, he told you so.

There were many, many such letters, to and from civil rights allies, business leaders, politicians, and the like. (So much correspondence that thirty-five years after Robinson's death, many of the letters were curated and published in a book.) His writing tended toward the cordial, colored at once by assertiveness and a core humility, and built firmly around his concerns. Usually, he had a bone to pick.

In 1960, exchanges unfolded with key presidential candidates—Hubert Humphrey, John F. Kennedy, Richard Nixon. Robinson supported Humphrey over Kennedy in the Democratic primary, then campaigned for Nixon over Kennedy in the general. Independent by affiliation, Robinson had joined the slender ranks of Black Republicans. A line of conservatism had long buttressed his views on the economy as well as on certain social values, even as the one progressive value stood above the others.

The Democratic Party, Robinson felt, took the Black vote too quickly for granted. He thought that perhaps in his dissent he might help spur more urgency on both sides when it came to civil rights. Wary as he was of the creeping right-wing element in the Republican base, neither could he look past the Democrats' tether to the Dixiecrats of the South. The idea that Alabama governor John Patterson, a Democrat and a staunch segregationist endorsed by the Ku Klux Klan, had emerged as an active supporter of Kennedy's presidential bid, was too troubling for Robinson to ignore.

Around that time, during a radio interview with the CBC in Canada, Robinson was asked why in his post-athletic life he had chosen the more arduous path of engagement—chosen, as the interviewer phrased it, "to be a fighter for your people"? Robinson responded: "I remember in my childhood going to the YMCA when I was young and being told I could come back one night a week. Going to the swimming pool in Pasadena, California, and being told that Negroes could use the pool once a week."

During his baseball career, Robinson explained to the CBC,

> I received a great number of letters from Negroes all over the country. And I feel that because of what they did for me during my tough years in baseball, just because now that I have had a certain amount of success, and that I could live certainly on my reputation and perhaps do a lot better than I'm doing now, that I would not only be letting my kids down, I would be letting a great number of people down who helped me tremendously. I sincerely believe that a person who has had the kind of luck that I have had to move ahead, needs to get into this particular fight because we do have a battle on our hands. And if we lose out now, I'm afraid my kids may have to go through the same thing. And I don't want my kids or any other kids having to go through the same kind of things.

No former athlete had taken up the cause so vigorously as Robinson did in the late 1950s and early '60s. His *New York Post* columns, begun in the spring of 1959, appeared three times a week beneath his name and smiling visage. "I've always tried to give as honest and sincere an opinion as I could," Robinson wrote in his *Post* debut. "Unfortunately, some people don't always appreciate this." He grappled with sports, feuding in print with the *Herald Tribune* columnist Red Smith over an analysis of the Yankees, or breaking down the National League pennant race. When Pumpsie Green broke in with the Red Sox, the last major league team to field a Black player, Robinson's column ran as an open letter to him: "All that will be required is that you conduct yourself on the field in a manner that befits your worthiness as a member of the Red Sox," Robinson wrote. He closed with "Congratulations again on being a 'first.' You may not always find it the easiest or most pleasant category in the world. But it's an opportunity at which I know you'll do your very best."

The *Post* column proved a platform for more. Robinson's sentences were sometimes crafted with the help of a ghostwriter. Opinions were his own. He wrote with plain and pointed outrage after the lynching of Mack Parker in Mississippi. He wrote about his own testimony at a Senate hearing on juvenile delinquency. He wrote about matters of integration and housing and education, and he routinely tackled, as he said, "the ticklish subject of politics." Robinson's endorsement of Nixon for president in 1960 would lead to the end of his regular work in the *Post* (as well as to a temporary enforced leave from Chock Full o' Nuts), but he soon found new space, writing other columns, syndicated, that appeared in the *New York Amsterdam News*, and the *Chicago Defender*.

When Robinson chastised Malcolm X, objecting to his brand of militancy and to his separatist views, Malcolm X responded with unveiled ire in the *Amsterdam News*. He rebuked Robinson for his allegiance to his "White Boss" and his "white benefactors," and for supporting Nixon, and for his general approach. "You never take an interest in anything in the Negro Community until the white man himself takes an interest in it," Malcolm X wrote. Robinson did not blink. "Coming from you an attack is a tribute," he wrote back, adding that he was proud of his associations with Branch Rickey and William Black and Governor Nelson Rockefeller of New York (whom Robinson backed and would work for), and proud to associate with "decent Americans of either race who believe in justice for all." He characterized Malcolm X's leadership as "a sick leadership."

The sparring between the men was not limited to this exchange.

And yet Robinson maintained his appreciation for the critical importance of Malcolm X and the voice he represented. In the aftermath of
Malcolm X's assassination in 1965, Robinson wrote his column, then
called Jackie Robinson Says, from Miami, where he was on vacation.
"A little blue went out of the sky and a little warmth left the sun
here . . . when the news came that a hail of bullets had silenced Malcolm X.

"I have been on record," Robinson wrote, "as being opposed to
Malcolm's philosophy. But I have always respected the man as one
who said what he believed." Robinson went on to mourn that the
murder of Malcolm X had "stilled his articulate voice" and added:
"Many of the statements he made about the problems faced by the
Negro people were nothing but the naked truth. However, we are often far apart in our opinions of how these problems should be faced."

Robinson's greater kinship, as he traveled his post-baseball journey of insistence, was with Martin Luther King Jr. They had known
each other since the time of Montgomery—each man sought out the
other in the months after the bus boycott—and they came together
in common cause as King's national influence broadened and took
firmer hold. In 1957, each received an honorary degree from Howard University. Rachel and Coretta sat with each other at commencement. The next year, Robinson and King spoke at a rally in Harlem,
joining to help spur the Youth March for Integrated Schools, at which
cadres of Black students and white students moved arm in arm down
Constitution Avenue. Together, King and Robinson worked through
some of the ongoing friction (and competition for fundraising dollars) between the NAACP and King's Southern Christian Leadership Conference (SCLC). Whenever the two men met, they gathered
each other in and held their grip and looked directly into one another's face. Robinson began letters "My Dear Martin." King began his
"My dear Friend Jackie."

When in 1962 Robinson was elected to the Baseball Hall of Fame, he donated the proceeds from a dinner in his honor to the SCLC. Later that year, after still more Black churches were burned in the American South, this time in Georgia—Shady Grove Baptist, Mount Olive Baptist, Mount Mary Baptist—Robinson arrived with an aide of Dr. King's to tour the ghastly rubble, the ashes that covered the remains, the fallen church bell on its side. He was asked by King to lead the effort to rebuild. Robinson immediately secured a $10,000 check from Nelson Rockefeller and a $5,000 check from William Black. Over the course of the Robinson-led campaign, more than $100,000 came in, as well as gifts of paint, wood, tempered glass, and quarried stone. Others donated a few days of free labor, a few weeks, months. Robinson and King appeared together when the new buildings were done, taller and finer than before. "Two years ago, I stood among the smoldering ruins of these churches," Dr. King said. "Those days told us of man's potential for evil. Now we see the goodness of man reflected."

Twice in 1963—in June and then in September, two Sundays within the hot swirl of a year scarred by hate and marked by moral courage—the Robinsons hosted jazz concerts on the wide and sloping backyard of their home on Cascade Road to raise money for the SCLC and the NAACP. The concerts were Rachel's idea, and she was both the principal organizer and engine behind the events. They called old neighbors from St. Albans, and other musicians they knew from along the way, and assembled a run of headliners: Dizzy Gillespie on his trumpet. Dave Brubeck on his piano. Billy Taylor on his saxophone. Jackie and Jackie Jr. directed cars where to park and shook every guest's hand. Sharon and David sold hot dogs and cold cans of soda down by the stage. Rachel and Zellee made sandwiches, and plates of chicken and layer cakes, and Rachel helped bring the food around to the crowd. Neighbors rowed over on the pond and left their boats by the shore. Someone sold T-shirts. The set ran ten acts long—from the Duke Ellington alumni to the Randy Weston

Quartet—through the afternoon into the evening. In June, some six hundred people turned out. Twice that number attended the reprise in September. The Robinsons raised more money than they'd ever imagined they might: bail money to spring hundreds of peaceful protesters from southern jails. Rachel barely stopped moving on those long days. She wore her orange sundress with the big pockets, her smile as bright as the light on the hill.

The Afternoon of Jazz concerts would continue as a near-annual event for more than two decades. Thelonious Monk would come and Sarah Vaughan and then Jesse Jackson, on that heartbroken afternoon in 1971, days after Jackie Jr. had left. The money always went to a different facet of the cause. One year during the 1960s, in the late-morning hours before the day had truly gotten under way, a neighbor heard from his bedroom some unmistakable vocal strains and said to himself: *That sounds like Ella Fitzgerald!* And then leaned out his window to see that it was indeed she. Ella stood right there, warming up her pipes on the lawn. You might see anyone on those afternoons at Cascade Road. Judy Garland, sitting quietly up top on the patio with a drink, listening to Gillespie blowing his horn.

The attendees on that September Sunday in 1963 included Martin Luther King Jr. He arrived in midafternoon and spoke kindly with the Robinson kids. (Sharon later wrote that standing beside him, she felt "close to God.") He moved through the crowd, shaking hands and exchanging words, and descended toward the gathered musicians. "I'm Martin King. What's your name?" he said to Quincy Jones. This was eleven days after the "I Have A Dream" speech in Washington, DC. "It was still echoing in our ears," Robinson said.

Roy Wilkins, the head of the NAACP, addressed the crowd from the stage, and then King took the microphone. He described Robinson as "one of those great unselfish souls," and then he spoke with more earnestness and invoked the tale of Rip Van Winkle: "When Rip went to sleep, there was a picture of King George on the wall of the inn," said the Reverend King. "When he awoke, he found a picture of George Washington. During the interim, a revolution took place which old Rip missed. This is what the Negro community is doing now. We are in the midst of revolution. Don't go to sleep."[27]

That evening, as dusk began to encroach and some of the tables had already been folded up and the crowd was just beginning to thin, the great jazz singer Joe Williams, who had gotten his start singing gospel in churches on the South Side of Chicago, delivered the Lord's Prayer in song. Guests who had been walking toward their cars stopped and turned to listen. This was the same year as Bull Connor in the streets of Birmingham and the same year as George Wallace's inaugural address, and it was one week before the bombing by Klansmen of the 16th Street Baptist Church.

A decade and a half removed from breaking into the major leagues—from those steely early years of self-restraint—Robinson allowed that he could not imagine adhering to nonviolence in the way that King and his many followers did. "If anyone punches me or otherwise physically assaults me, you can bet your bottom dollar that I will try to give him back as good as he sent," he wrote. His admiration for King's Gandhian style, however, was unqualified. He saw it as a sign of absolute strength. "It takes real guts to go through what they endure and suffer."[28]

---

27. The day's event raised more than $30,000. Six weeks later, Rachel received a letter from King, thanking her directly. "Without your dollars for freedom the Conference would be unable to work effectively toward its goal of the full integration of the Negro into all aspects of American life," King wrote. "Without your moral support we would be in a dungeon of despair."

28. The Robinson–King relationship was not without some disturbance. Later in the 1960s, King spoke out vehemently against the Vietnam War, condemning it on multiple grounds: a larger religious objection to war; the specific motivations and politics at work; and the conflict's appalling violence and the innocent lives it claimed. King's objections were not driven by civil rights concerns per se, but such concerns were relevant. Sermonizing at Manhattan's Riverside Church in April of 1967, the Reverend King emphasized the hypocrisy in a war that was "taking the Black young men who had been crippled by our society and sending them eight thousand miles away to guarantee

King on numerous occasions and in numerous contexts expressed a debt to Robinson—for what he had done and the manner in which he had done it—and never more succinctly than when he said to his chief of staff, the pastor Wyatt Tee Walker: "Jackie Robinson made it possible for me in the first place. Without him I would never have been able to do what I did." Hank Aaron sometimes referred to Robinson as "the Dr. King of Baseball."

The Robinsons were there for "I Have a Dream," all five of them in Washington, DC. Jackie had been designated as the face of the Connecticut delegation (some three thousand people traveled down from the state), and the family had seats on the platform at the foot of the Lincoln Memorial. Before the march began, Jackie stood beside

---

liberties in Southeast Asia which they had not found in southwest Georgia and East Harlem." He characterized the US government as "the greatest purveyor of violence in the world today."

A few weeks later, Robinson devoted his syndicated column to an open letter to King: "I feel you are utterly on the wrong track in your stand on Viet Nam," he wrote. Robinson praised King as "the greatest civil rights mastermind and leader which the movement has ever had" and honored King's overriding stance against violence. But, Robinson added, "I have a deep respect for our country. I know that our country is not always right and that, in fact, on the domestic front, our country has been and is so terribly wrong with respect to its treatment of the Negro. . . . But, Martin, aren't you being unfair when you place all the burden of blame upon America and none upon the Communist forces we are fighting?"

Robinson said he felt "confused" that King supported Cassius Clay in Clay's refusal to serve in the war and, overall, Robinson allowed to being perplexed by King's stance: "I am confused because I respect you deeply," he wrote. "But I also love this imperfect country."

King phoned Robinson after reading the column, and the two men quickly restored goodwill. Yet the incident proves instructive in the measuring of Robinson. His views on Vietnam—the theater, remember, where Jackie Jr. served and found struggle—were no aberration. Robinson's speech at the House Un-American Committee in 1949 had over the years been denounced (by Malcolm X, for one) as a betrayal of Paul Robeson. But Robinson owned his larger sentiment. His worldview incorporated an underlying faith in American governance and social philosophy, as well as an allegiance to the nation's military. He was firmly anti-Communist. Robinson's challenging of King further underscored his unyielding commitment to his own principles, as well as his readiness to antagonize. At one time or another Robinson raised his voice against so many personal allies: Roy Wilkins and Adam Clayton Powell. William Black and Nelson Rockefeller. The Dodgers. Baseball. And so on. Everyone, more or less, except Branch Rickey.

King at Lincoln's feet and addressed the crowd. "I know all of us are going to go away feeling we cannot turn back," he said. The sun shone and the masses clustered and shouted as they marched, and Robinson wore a coat and tie and kept an arm around David. There was great energy and excitement along the way—Sharon, thirteen, fainted in the crowd and had to be revived in an aid tent—and then for the speeches afterward, the Robinsons sat together, right up front and as close as could be as Reverend King spoke to the world.

Robinson in his post-playing life understood the sound of his own voice, and the image of his own figure, and the place that he occupied in the conscience and the tension of the time. "An attendant lord," as it were, able "to swell a progress, start a scene or two." When he spoke, people came to listen, and when he walked a city street with his pigeon-toed gait, people stopped to look. At restaurants, autograph-seekers came to his table between courses. He wrote his pointed letters and he got letters back. He strode onto the set of *What's My Line?*, the star mystery guest, and the platform shook with the roar and applause of the studio audience. He gave addresses in the teeth of civil rights, as he did at the St. Paul's AME outside St. Augustine, Florida, after another stand, another round of arrests. He spoke at synagogues and Jewish centers and articulated the shared pain and goals of the persecuted. He could be bluff, direct, and unhesitant. Free of pretense. Full of judgment. No gnostic proclamations, no grander illusions of power. "I don't claim to be a leader," Robinson wrote in a column in the mid-1960s, "but I have a right, a duty and a responsibility as a citizen and a Negro and I intend to go right on speaking out for what I honestly believe."[29]

---

29. Robinson's voice attracted an audience through celebrity but developed heft through experience. Wrote Rev. Martin Luther King: "He incessantly raises questions to sear America's conscience. Some have challenged his right to ask these questions. He has the right—more rightly—because back in the days when integration wasn't fashionable, he underwent the trauma and the humiliation and the loneliness which comes with being a pilgrim walking the lonesome byways toward the high road of freedom."

He was constrained in part by his health. Circulation issues, eyesight, surgeries, a staph infection, his heart—a body too soon ridden with indignities. Robinson accepted the challenge of diabetes with quiet courage. Right at the outset, he learned to inject his own insulin and test his own levels. Rachel called it a "declaration of independence." Robinson rarely spoke publicly of the disease. Even physically limited, adjusting to a body changed and changing, Robinson had the bearing of an athlete and projected physical strength.

He played tennis on the courts at Grossinger's or over at the Ostroves' in Harrison. Once he brought along Hank Greenberg for doubles. "My dad and his friends were really pretty decent, pretty avid tennis players," Art Ostrove recalls. "But one rally, and you could see the athlete that Jackie was—even if he did labor a little between points and look a little older and heavier. His reflexes and his precision—he was just in another class." Robinson tamed the ripple in his golf swing, got his score down. (Once, out with Rachel, he broke 70.) At home on a winter's day, he went out onto the frozen pond—a nonswimmer vanquishing his fears—and under the broad, gray sky cleared away snow with a shovel and pounded on the ice to test its thickness so that the kids could come out and skate. Sharon, in one of her picture books, recalls seeing him moving around alone on the uncertain ice and thinking, *My dad is the bravest man alive.*

At the banquet dinners and the meals out, Robinson rolled his shoulders and stretched his neck and did his best to stay away from sweets. "Don't tell Rachel," he would admonish with a wink, ordering his slice of strawberry cream pie from the counter at Chock Full o' Nuts.

He left Chock Full in 1964 to campaign and later work for Rockefeller, as a special assistant on community affairs. He took a figurehead position as a co-chairman at the Hamilton Life Insurance Company, which wanted to show some interracial bona fides. The hiring, Robinson said bluntly, may have been a "grandstand play . . .

but as long as Negroes are brought into the mainstream of American business, and young Negroes are encouraged by my career that's all that counts." He helped found the Freedom National Bank in Harlem and he drove in for the morning hours in his green-gray Lincoln, a heavy foot on the gas when traffic was light. At the bank he opened the doors, greeted people, gave advice to first-time borrowers. He fell out from the NAACP in '67 and broke (temporarily, though) from the Republican Party in '68. In 1970, through the carriage of a committed group of investors, he started the Jackie Robinson Construction Company to build low- and lesser-income housing. Robinson took an office at headquarters in New Jersey, and the company would break ground on a two-hundred-unit apartment complex. In pursuit of a meaningful life, idleness was not part of the Robinson makeup.

Nor was it part of Rachel's. She finished a degree in psychiatric nursing and began teaching as an assistant professor at Yale. She took a second job as director of nursing at the Connecticut Mental Health Center. Sharon married young, and then divorced. She enrolled in the nursing program at Howard University and two years later received her cap. David graduated high school, from Mount Hermon School for Boys in Massachusetts. "In a land where we declare that we have 'liberty and justice for all,'" said Jackie, speaking at the Mount Hermon commencement, "it seems that slogan really means 'liberty and justice for all as long as you do and say what some people want you to do and say.' It may not be the most popular position, but to build for leadership, one must base his standing on what is right, not what is expedient." In the fall of 1970, David went off to Stanford University.

The days and nights on Cascade Road were much quieter than they had been when the kids were young and at home—when Rachel was more about the kitchen and more often had her music on—and the silence in the house was at times weighted with sadness. Branch Rickey had died in 1965 and Mallie in 1968, collapsing suddenly in

Los Angeles at the age of seventy-eight. She died in May barely one month after the telephone rang in Stamford on the night of April 4.

"I'm shocked, oh my God, I'm frightened," Robinson said when he learned of the murder of Martin Luther King. The world at times seemed full of loss, and compassion in short supply and Robinson's body ached in its decline. "As he grew older he kept painful thoughts to himself," Rachel later wrote. "And so did I." She would sit on the couch and he would come beside her and quietly rest his head on her lap. Being with Rachel, his troubles didn't seem so near.

Sometimes during his later life journey, Jackie would remark that baseball seemed far away from him and somehow part of a different, other life. He observed that if he had remained in the game, as he had once wanted to do as a manager or front-office sharp, he would have been confined to "a narrow strata" that he was now pleased to have outgrown. The environment and details of baseball—being embedded with his teammates, sharing the priorities and urgency of the effort, having the competitor's inevitable in-game notion that the outcome of an at bat or an umpire's call bore some existential truth—all of that had changed. He didn't go to the ballpark or watch games much on TV. He didn't parse the standings. His closest friends had no connection to the sport.

Upon his induction into the Hall of Fame in 1962, Robinson asked that his plaque make no mention of his role in integrating baseball. The plaque cited his career batting average and his MVP Award, his stolen bases and his defensive excellence at second base. Nothing else. Nothing about being the first Black ballplayer of the twentieth century. No discussion of his brilliant, attacking approach on the field. No nod to the circumstances under which he played. The plaque read as Robinson wanted it to. His aspiration hadn't changed: *Hell of a ballplayer, Robinson, and just one of the guys.*[30]

---

30. In 2008, with Rachel's oversight, the Hall of Fame updated Robinson's plaque, recasting the language. Along with citing the personal statistics and the Dodgers team success, the plaque now refers to Robinson's "electrifying style of play" and concludes:

Aeschylus in framing his legacy decreed that the inscription on his gravestone bear no allusion to the plays that had made him famous, but only to his service as a solider in the defense of Athens and Greece—even though his written words, the tragedies, were what publicly distinguished his irreplicable life and would make him immortal. All of it, of course, intertwined. No *Agamemnon* or *The Persians* had Aeschylus not gone to war. Nor, in the case of Robinson, could there ever be any extrication of baseball from his message, or his message from the arena of baseball—no matter what the plaque in Cooperstown read. For all the years that he and the sport kept each other at arm's length, and for all the emphasis Robinson placed on a life outside the game, there was something more than simply fitting, but rather inevitable, that in the final year of his life, 1972, Robinson came back to baseball, and baseball came back to him.

Robinson stood talking with a couple of the Dodgers executives—team president Peter O'Malley, the PR director Fred Claire—and some former players on the field at Dodger Stadium, just in front of the dugout on the third base side. Newcombe and Koufax and Gilliam were gathered with them, and it was about an hour before pregame ceremonies. The low clouds of morning had moved away, and the late spring air and warming sunshine, Robinson said, reminded him of his youth. Robinson always liked going home to California. Sometimes he saw his brother Mack. Recently, at a studio on Sunset Boulevard, Robinson had filmed an episode of the *Sports Challenge* quiz show, competing on a team with Snider and Erskine against three members of the 1972 Dodgers: Wes Parker, Frank Robinson, Maury Wills.

Batting practice was under way, and from the stands fans shouted

---

"displayed tremendous courage and poise in 1947 when he integrated the modern major leagues in the face of intense adversity."

players' names, as they always did before ball games, as they had on all those days and evenings back in Brooklyn. From just behind the Dodger dugout, a man leaned forward, holding a baseball. "Hey, Jackie, Jackie! Would you sign this?" he called out, and then he tossed the ball in a gentle arc toward Robinson. "It hit him in the shoulder right up near his cheek," Claire recalls. "He couldn't see it, let alone catch it."

Immediately the group circled around to make sure Robinson was all right and then started pointing toward the stands. "Everyone was saying, 'Get that guy out of here! Get rid of him,'" Claire says. "But Jackie raised his hand and said, 'Calm down, calm down. Can some-one hand me the baseball?' He signed the ball and said, 'Please give this back to the gentleman.' And that was it. I was so impressed by how poised he was. His humility and his presence took over. But it was sad how he couldn't catch the ball."

Robinson's vulnerability that day was new to the many who had not seen him in some time, and it delivered a particular, sobering force given its contrast to the physical impression he had once made— the imprints that would always remain. "The greatest athlete I ever saw," Newcombe declared during the Old-Timers' Game weekend. (Robinson, it's worth remembering, was a man who had in his trophy room both a silver bat from Major League Baseball and a bronzed football cleat from UCLA.) In recent months, his physical decline had accelerated. Driving, as he had driven himself to Gil Hodges's funeral, was out of the question. He stepped uncertainly when not being guided. He moved stiffly through his arms and shoulders. At times, he drew short of breath. Recalling Robinson's condition about a week after the event in Los Angeles, Campanella wept. "Just goes to show, I guess, how the years can make a difference," said Campy, wiping his cheek.

The Dodgers drew 43,818 fans on that Sunday, June 4—the largest day-game crowd the team would attract all season. It was a bright, beautiful afternoon, and the great Bob Gibson was fixing to pitch for the visiting Cardinals. Along with Campanella, Koufax, and Robinson having their numbers retired, a host of stars had come for the game. DiMaggio, Mantle, manager Casey Stengel, who was being feted. Yet no one received greater applause or generated more discussion or warmth than Jackie Robinson, a repatriated son, as it were. In the lead-up to the number ceremony, he sat in the Dodger dugout, at the end of the bench near the bat rack, and players and staff approached him with greetings and thanks. "His signature was still fine, the lettering was strong," says Mike McDermott, the Dodgers batting practice pitcher who asked Robinson to sign a baseball for him that day.

For the ceremony itself, the three former Dodgers came out onto the infield, along with Peter O'Malley and commissioner Bowie Kuhn, and received framed replicas of their respective uniforms. An aide pushed Campanella in his wheelchair. Koufax, who had been named to the Hall of Fame just a few months before, told the crowd that the two players beside him had been heroes of his growing up in Brooklyn. He would never have imagined, Koufax said, that he would one day be standing on the field beside them on a day as remarkable as this. When Robinson stepped to the microphone, he said: "This is one of the truly great moments of my life. I'm grateful for everything that has happened." Campanella and Koufax wore their Dodger jerseys—Koufax in full uniform—but Robinson wore shirtsleeves and tie, and on his left wrist a watch he'd received from Bill "Bojangles" Robinson in 1947, twenty-five years before, the year he had broken into the major leagues.

Earlier during the Old-Timers' Game weekend, Robinson had met with Peter O'Malley at O'Malley's office at Dodger Stadium, to mend bridges and to talk about some issues that Robinson felt needed talking about: specifically the advancement of Black former players into baseball management. "I was very much impressed with

Peter's attitude," Robinson said afterward. "I don't know what he can do about it, but first of all there has to be sensitivity to it." All that weekend—around the field, at a luncheon for the honored guests—Robinson spoke so well of Peter O'Malley that a rumor, half baked and only half in jest, sprang up that he might take a job in the front office of the team. "Dear Pete," Jackie wrote shortly afterward from home in Stamford, "I also want you to know how pleased I was with our meeting at which was sensed a truer understanding of the nature of the things that evoked problems between baseball and me."

Rekindled now, they agreed to stay in touch, and in mid-June, Peter O'Malley wrote back to Robinson. "Dear Jackie: I am planning to be in Cooperstown on Monday, August 7, when the Dodgers will be playing the New York Yankees in an exhibition game and more important Sandy Koufax will be officially enshrined in the Hall of Fame. If possible I would like you and Rachel to be with me on that occasion." Robinson declined, with his regrets, but his openness to baseball remained.[31]

---

31. Robinson had not been to Cooperstown since his own induction, in the summer of 1962, when he became, inevitably, the first Black player to be enshrined in the Hall of Fame. He went in alongside Bob Feller, the great Cleveland Indians pitcher from Van Meter, Iowa, who had, after playing against Robinson in exhibition games in 1946, suggested that Robinson was too musclebound and broadly built to succeed in baseball. "If he were a white man, I doubt they would even consider him big league material," Feller said.

The comment followed Feller to Cooperstown, but the two men had long since covered it over between them—Robinson, eyes forward, tended to be forgiving of such things. At the induction they greeted one another and stood side by side with their plaques, out of the wind and heavy rain that fell on the day. "I only hope that I will be able to live up to this tremendously fine honor," said Robinson in his brief induction speech. "It's something that I think those of us who are fortunate, again, must use to help others."

Branch Rickey at eighty and less than hale, had come out to support Robinson and so had Mallie and, of course, Rachel and the kids. On the bus back to the hotel, Robinson sat by coincidence beside Claude Raymond, the young Braves pitcher who'd grown up in Saint-Jean-sur-Richelieu, south of Montreal, and had seen Robinson play as a Royal at Delorimier Stadium. They talked about the city and Jackie and Rachel asked after this person and that place and said how much they appreciated their year in Montreal. Jackie commented about the intertwined nature of the baseball world, and the circular

Those months of 1972, as spring moved into summer and summer into fall, Robinson continued to engage himself, going into the office at the construction company, attending events, advocating. He was feted, in July, with a luncheon at Mamma Leone's, by the government of the US Virgin Islands for his "unselfish efforts in developing opportunities for Black athletes." Robinson's brother Mack spoke at the luncheon, recalling Jackie's remarkable days on the football field and telling anecdotes that grew the legend.

One time Jackie came by the broad jump competition, still wearing his college baseball uniform after practice. "C'mon, try the broad jump!" Mack said. So Jackie tried it and won the event. Clyde Sukeforth, the Dodgers scout who in 1945 had gone at Branch Rickey's bidding to find Robinson playing ball for the Kansas City Monarchs, spoke next, and after Sukeforth, Ralph Branca stood up and told a few clubhouse stories. Another Dodgers teammate, Joe Black, had flown in for the luncheon from Arizona, where he worked as an executive at a bus company. "If anyone deserves the Nobel Peace Prize, it's Jack Robinson. He's done more to bring about racial harmony than anybody," Black said with full conviction. "A lot of doors opened up for me. If Jackie Robinson had failed, the doors would never have opened." Black pitched in parts of six seasons in the majors. He said that now, many years later, he looked around at his house and job in Phoenix and said to himself, "Thank God for Jackie Robinson."

The old Giant stake-driver Bobby Thomson attended the event at Mamma Leone's, as well as Buck Leonard of the 1940s Homestead Grays, and Jackie and Rachel sat together at a table off the dais. Reporters started calling the luncheon "This Is Your Life." Jackie

---

aspects of his baseball journey to be beside Raymond on the day he went into the Hall of Fame.

As a footnote to this footnote: Years later, at a 1969 gathering to honor baseball's greatest living players, Robinson and Feller sparred heatedly, in part over Feller's dismissal of Robinson's concern about the absence of Black front-office personnel in the game.

received a handsome plaque, lending even more of a valedictory feel to the afternoon.

The emcee at Mamma Leone's was Roger Kahn, the writer who'd grown up near Ebbets Field and covered the team in Brooklyn for a couple of years in the 1950s. Kahn had a clear and vulnerable appreciation of his relationship with his father. *The Boys of Summer* had come out a couple of months before, and already it was on its way to changing all those old Dodgers' lives. Jackie said that he hadn't been physically able to read the book, couldn't read anything anymore except if he held it very close up and even then, "the words all run together." But Robinson had no intention of missing *The Boys of Summer*. He'd asked Rachel to read it to him.

On the public stage, Robinson often met his physical condition with sangfroid, even optimism. "Well," he said in late summer, "I take the bitter with the sweet, you know. What are we going to do? We have some problems but if we sit and mope about them, we're not going to cure them." At other moments, he turned sober as lead. "There are times when I get tremendously depressed," he allowed. And added, "I'm only sorry I wasn't more careful treating my diabetes."

Ducks and geese landed and paddled in the pond out back on Cascade Road. When a hawk flew in, circling overhead, you could hear the honking and squawking from any room in the house. At dusk the fox might rouse the neighbor's dog. In August, the saw of crickets. Jackie's hair had gone white as the birches' bark, and there'd been a change in the set of his jaw. Fan letters came to the home, some of them with no street address, no zip code, no name of the town. Just: "The great Jackie Robinson, Connecticut." One woman, having read of his vision trouble, wrote to Robinson via a newspaper editor, offering to give him one of her eyes.

His doctors said to do less, but Robinson often did more. He traveled although it was advised against. He went to Chicago to support Jesse Jackson's Operation PUSH, which sought to build economic and social opportunities for Black Americans. He flew to Miami and gave a talk at the Everglades Hotel on behalf of minority business leaders. He went to a rally for voter registration in Harlem. In early September, wearing a symbolic hard hat, he planted a shovel in the earth, breaking ground on buildings to house more than four hundred low-income units in Bedford-Stuyvesant. He did a radio interview with Larry King. He worked, with the writer Alfred Duckett, on his autobiography, *I Never Had It Made*. Over the very last days of September, Robinson went to another PUSH event, the Expo at the Chicago International Amphitheater, and while there, attended a college football game at Soldier Field.

"The doctor told me that I could have ice cream once a week," he told a reporter who asked how he was holding up healthwise, "so just to prove a personal point to myself, I take ice cream twice a week." For a man in Robinson's condition, this was no venial sin. When the waiter came by with the house finisher at Mamma Leone's, Rachel waved him off for the both of them. "No. No spumoni here, thank you."[32]

And then, in mid-October, the Robinsons went to Cincinnati. David took his girlfriend, Tish. Sharon flew in from DC. The Reds were hosting the A's on a Sunday afternoon, Game Two of the World Series,

---

32. At the earlier PUSH event, labeled Jackie Robinson Day, Rachel herself was publicly honored. *To Rachel Robinson, who has given her life to healing, her man, her family and people*, read the citation from the newly founded Friendship Medical Center. The discussion around Rachel that day acknowledged her work in psychiatry, as well as her principles and the overall way that she, then nearly fifty, had chosen to live and to lead. From the earliest strides on Jackie's journey, and all along on his path toward effecting such enormous change, those close to the Robinsons understood that Rachel was not merely a source of support but a partner and a lodestar besides. She steadied the course. Jackie had come to refer to himself as *we* even if talking about a distinctly personal experience. "We had leakage in the blood vessel," he said about his eyes. Jackie had resisted—and how—Rachel's return to school, her commitment to work, her assertion of herself into a meaningful career. He resented the loss of any part of her. But he had come to regret his own resentment, and to admire her professionalism and her insistent pride. "I always knew I'd go back to work," said Rachel at PUSH. "It's an essential part of living."

and Robinson was to be recognized on the field. The idea had begun to formulate not long after Robinson's appearance at the Dodgers Old-Timers' Game. Peter O'Malley got hold of Bowie Kuhn. So did Villante. *Do something for Robinson at the World Series. It'll be good for the game. Good for everyone.* Fifteen years was a long time for baseball to be visibly estranged from its most influential player, and this was the milestone anniversary year of Robinson's debut.

The pregame event—and for Jackie and Rachel, this was the clincher, why they really wanted to come, as a family—focused on Jackie's work in raising awareness about drug use among young people. Along with the ceremony, donations would go to the Daytop rehabilitation center in Connecticut. For the Robinsons, neither a day nor an hour of the past fifteen months had gone by without thoughts of Jackie Jr., the ache at the center of their lives. "We have grown closer and closer through our tragedy," Jackie said. David had left school at Stanford and regularly drove Jackie to work. Sharon came home during breaks in her classes at Howard. Said Rachel: "When we lost Jackie, I found my strength in my husband, my children, and myself." The World Series event would be a day to connect with Jackie Jr. in a way still available to them. The family would stand together on the field. Kuhn would make a presentation. Robinson would have a turn at the microphone.

Before the game, in a small room at Riverfront Stadium, Robinson spoke with WCIN, a radio station geared to Black listeners. The baseball horizon, Robinson told his interviewer, was "bright because of the attitude of the players. It's great to see players of all races and creeds extend themselves. The handshaking, the involvement, extending themselves to see that things work out right. If it works well in athletics, it means it can work well in other areas. The leadership that the athlete is giving in terms of race relations is fantastic."

This was about an hour before the start of the game. "But beyond that," said Robinson, "I think it's a tragedy that the young Black can go out and give the better years of his life and once that's over, he is completely shut off from future involvement in the front office or in the managerial role."

Robinson left the interview room and rejoined the others. Sunshine covered most of the stadium, save for a portion of right field, and wind ruffled the flags and the fans' homemade banners. Already the stands were nearly full, and a steady hum came out of the crowd. "It was a World Series game in Cincinnati, so there was a great amount of excitement, and just streams and streams of people coming in," Jack Greiner recalls. He was at the game with his father, sitting high up in the red seats between first base and home. Greiner would turn fourteen a week later. For a gift, his parents gave him *The Boys of Summer*. "I remember seeing Robinson and all of them come onto the field from the third base side, all wearing coats and ties. On a day like that, we were pretty closely tuned in to everything that was going on."

Before stepping out, they had gathered at the mouth of a tunnel leading onto the field: the Robinsons, Kuhn, Peter O'Malley. Larry Doby had been invited and Joe Black. National League president Chub Feeney. Then, arriving to the group, came a familiar and welcome face. "Everyone began putting out their hand and greeting him, except for Jackie, who couldn't tell who the man was," says Fred Claire, who had come along with O'Malley. "Then someone whispered, 'Jackie, it's Pee Wee.' They had a good, solid embrace. It felt remarkable. And moving. Being in that setting, in that town with that history."

A quarter century had passed since Robinson and Reese and the 1947 Dodgers played their first series together in Cincinnati, a couple of games in May that were, as Robinson, recalled in 1972, marked by the death threats he received. There, at old Crosley Field, Reese made his noted public connection with Robinson—whether with an arm across the shoulder as legend describes it, or with a clasp of hands near home plate after Robinson came home to score, or by standing beside him to talk between innings. Reese's visible physical closeness with Robinson served to rebuke the hatred that spewed from the stands. Reese grew up on a farm in Kentucky, about 140 miles south of Crosley, and a lot of the crowd loved him as one of their own. Cincinnati was sometimes called the northernmost southern city in America.

The many-membered marching band paused in the outfield, and servicemen held large flags near second base, and the Robinsons and other guests stood in a row by the base of the pitcher's mound. The old Dodgers broadcaster Red Barber, now sixty-four and six years out of baseball, had been enlisted to do some pregame play-by-play. "This year," Barber began—*ye-ah* is how he said it, the syrupy accent intact—"marks the twenty-fifth anniversary of the entry of the Black athlete into Major League Baseball. Today we are about to honor the man who Branch Rickey selected to lead the way, who set a brilliant example for all to follow. He is Hall of Famer Jackie Robinson." The crowd broke into applause and air horns blew. Robinson nodded and raised his hand in acknowledgment.

One by one, Barber introduced the others who stood on the field, the three former players, the baseball officials, the family. Reese was about six months older than Robinson. He looked twenty years younger.

"Jackie Robinson is something special," said Bowie Kuhn, now stepping up to the mike. "Special as an athlete. Special as a husband and father. And special as a human being. Baseball is proud of Jackie Robinson, who has dedicated himself to help others in the crusade against drug abuse."

Kuhn then read aloud a long telegram to Robinson from President Nixon. The president cited the date of Robinson's Dodgers' debut, April 15, 1947, as the most significant and compelling "moment of greatness" in baseball history. He wrote how fitting it was to honor Robinson at the World Series, baseball's most exciting event. He thanked Robinson for his "vital contribution to the lives and future of our young people. It is through such dedication and determination today, just as it was a quarter of a century ago, that lives are enriched and strengthened and our country made a better place for all." Robinson stood listening with his head slightly bowed and his hands together in front of his waist.

Commissioner Kuhn finished reading the telegram and added some words of his own. Then Jackie stepped forward, with Rachel at his left elbow. Kuhn presented Jackie with a small trophy, and Jackie shook his hand and moved toward the microphone. The sun could not have been brighter, or the stadium much more full.

"Thank you very much, Commissioner." Robinson's voice was strong and high-pitched and very much his own.

> I would just like to say that I was really just a spoke in the wheel of the success that we had some twenty-five years ago. And I personally want to say thank you to a great captain, a guy who was the leader of our ball club and who really set the pace in many, many areas. Pee Wee, thanks so much for being here today. I would also like to say that it would be a real, real pleasure if Mr. Rickey could have been here with us today. But to the members of his family, my untiring love and gratitude for the things that he has done over the years.

The players on both teams had gone to the front of their dugouts and were leaning on one side of the railing or the other. Rachel wore a brightly colored dress, pinks and yellows, and Robinson held the trophy with both hands as he spoke.

"And I also want to say how pleased I am that my family could be here this afternoon. And to thank baseball for the tremendous opportunities that it has presented to me, and also for this thrilling afternoon. I'm extremely proud and pleased to be here this afternoon. But I must admit that I'm going to be tremendously more pleased and more proud when I look at that third base coaching line one day and see a Black face managing in baseball. Thank you very much."

They stayed on the field for the rest of the pregame ceremonies, right through the national anthem. Then they walked off, Rachel and Jackie with their arms around each other, Rachel holding the trophy now in her farther hand. As they neared the third base line, Dick Williams, the A's manager and the old Brooklyn Dodger part-timer, a teammate of Robinson's in the early 1950s, came up and shook Jackie's hand, and kissed Rachel's cheek. Red Barber was right there, watching the whole thing. Then Joe Morgan, the Reds second baseman who was three years old when Robinson started in Brooklyn, and who was one of more than a dozen Black players who would appear in that 1972 World Series, came over to thank Robinson for how he had inspired him, personally, and for what he had done for change. "I never forgot how he gripped my hand," Morgan would say four decades later. "For me it was a chance to express my gratitude to him, a hero of mine. I didn't know if I would ever get that chance again."

Jackie and Rachel made their way off the field and into the stands, and soon afterward, standing at his front-row seat, Robinson threw out a ceremonial first pitch to the glove of Johnny Bench. He watched the game beside Kuhn, with Doby and Black and Reese and the others around him. Later, at the airport heading back to Connecticut, Rachel noticed that Jackie seemed uncommonly tired.

On a couple of occasions in 1972—once when a magazine photographer gathered the family together for a portrait, and again during the visit to Cincinnati—Robinson said quietly, to whomever would hear, that he felt he was experiencing "the last hurrah."

RIVERSIDE

The Riverside Church rises off a crest of land on the far West Side of Manhattan, overlooking a spread of forested parkland, a wide commuter road, and beyond that road, the river. The church occupies a city block just a Furillo's throw from 125th Street, the Harlem thoroughfare home to the Apollo Theater and formerly, from 1964 to 1990, the Freedom National Bank. Built in the late 1920s, the church projects an air of classic grandeur, modeled as it is on the thirteenth-century cathedral at Chartres. The nave of Riverside Church spreads nearly ninety feet wide and extends more than two hundred feet from entranceway to altar. The ribbed ceiling reaches eight stories high at its vaulted peak, and the arched bays along the sidewalls curve around panes of stained glass. Colorful mosaics depict scenes both Christian and non-Christian, a spirit in confluence with the Riverside Church mission, articulated by its founding pastor, to be "interdenominational, interracial, international."

Martin Luther King Jr. addressed a congregation here—decades later, so did Nelson Mandela—and during the 1960s, the Riverside Church proved fertile ground for prayer, thought, and discussion around civil rights. In 1969, the activist James Forman interrupted a Sunday sermon by climbing the steps of the chancel and reading aloud the Black Manifesto. On important days, the church might fill to its official capacity of close to 2,500 people, although many more than that crowded in, and many, many more pressed along the neighboring streets and sidewalks, on the late morning and early afternoon of October 27, 1972, for the funeral of Jackie Robinson.

Five days had passed since the end of the World Series, and three days since Robinson's sudden collapse onto the floor of the home on Cascade Road in the early morning, with Rachel by his side. She had called the Stamford police and gone to the hospital and phoned Sharon in DC to tell her he was gone. Rachel helped to organize the days of public viewing and to set up the funeral, and she discussed the handling of the eulogy and specified who would be the pallbearers. When Rachel asked Bill Russell, the great and principled basketball star, to be among them, Russell broke into tears. "What an overwhelming honor," he said. Russell was in junior high school in West Oakland when Robinson started with the Dodgers.

The others who would carry Robinson's casket were the old teammates and peers: Newcombe, Gilliam, Branca—as well as Reese, Black, and Doby, three who had been on the ball field with Robinson in Cincinnati twelve days earlier. All through, the church was dotted with great athletes and notables: Joe Louis. Hank Greenberg. Willie Mays. Dick Gregory. Sargent Shriver off the campaign trail. A delegation of forty people sent by the president. Cab Calloway. Betty Shabazz. Ed Sullivan. Bayard Rustin. On and on. Beyond the famous people in attendance, and the grieving family, and the many who had known Robinson in his professional lives (less notable ballplayers, lawyers for the bank, an umpire, a construction foreman, volunteers from the Y, a government clerk), the strength of the assembly came as well from the many who had never met Robinson, but whose lives he had also changed. A high school teacher from New Jersey. Off-duty policemen. An administrator from the college nearby. A barber who'd shut down his shop through the middle of the day. Two schoolgirls in their late uncle's stead. Reporters would comment on the interracial makeup of the funeral gathering, calling it a melting pot.

Ira Glasser was thirty-four years old then and the executive director of the New York Civil Liberties Union, and he still had his Brooklyn boyhood running through him, never to leave. He'd come up to the funeral with an NYCLU lawyer, Alan Levine, who had been weaned on the same team and the same man. "I knew that I owed a lot of the way I approached the world—what to do with my sense of right and wrong—to having seen Jackie Robinson play," Glasser said. Fact is, the Riverside Church that day was lousy with Brooklyn Dodger fans.

A series of ministers bade Robinson farewell that afternoon— Wyatt Tee Walker read from Corinthians—and a sixty-voice choir delivered "Lift Every Voice and Sing," and the Reverend Jesse Jackson, who had been on the balcony of the Lorraine Motel on April 4,

1968, gave the formal eulogy. "Today we must balance the tears of sorrow with the tears of joy," Jackson began. "Mix the bitter with the sweet. Death and life."

The pews were overpacked. People stood in the outer aisles, in the hallways and in the open bays. You'd never have expected that with so many people, such silence, the silence of the transfixed, could fill the great church so powerfully as it did when Jackson paused between his opening phrases. "When Jackie took the field, something reminded us of our birthright to be free," Jackson said. And he added: "He didn't integrate baseball for himself. He infiltrated baseball for all of us, seeking and looking for more oxygen for Black survival, and looking for new possibility." By the end of the eulogy, a half hour long, the silence had yielded to responses from the crowd, cries of *Hallelujah! Amen!* and *You're right!* that echoed off the great stone walls. "Jackie's body," said Jackson, "was a temple of God, an instrument of peace."

The eulogy, with its rhythm and pitch, led into the larger voice of Roberta Flack filling the church with the spiritual "I Told Jesus." People wept, and Billy Loes, a New York kid who'd pitched in relief for the Dodgers in the 1950s, leaned over to Ralph Branca and whispered, *It's like a Hollywood production! It's like a Broadway show!*

Afterward, on the streets outside, crowds gathered around the ballplayers: Ernie Banks, Willie Stargell, Elston Howard, Monte Irvin, Vida Blue, Campy, and Erskine. Mays, a Met by then, drew the biggest crowd of all. Hank Aaron stood by himself for a while until some folks noticed he was there. Aaron was 41 home runs shy of Babe Ruth. "Most of the Black players from Jackie's day were at the funeral," Aaron would say. "But I was appalled by how few of the younger players showed up to pay him tribute."

For all the love and reverence at the funeral, you couldn't anticipate what the reception would be once the hearse and the trailing cars pulled away from the Riverside Church and began traveling through Harlem, and then through Bedford-Stuyvesant and to the cemetery in Brooklyn. Robinson had never found firm footing with the newer wave of the movement. He'd had the clash with Malcolm X and differed sharply with Adam Clayton Powell Jr., who was a beloved son in Harlem. Robinson once chastised Black protesters outside the Apollo Theater. More to the point, in recent years, Robinson's voice had not resonated so widely as it once had. "We knew Jackie Robinson wrote columns for the Black newspapers," says the scholar and historian Gerald Early, who was twenty years old in 1972. "But we didn't necessarily read them. He was my father's hero." So, when the funeral procession began to move through the streets, there was no telling just how the neighborhoods would respond.

People came out of their apartments. They came out of their shops and they came off the schoolyards. Cabdrivers stopped their rides in the middle of the fare. People stood in doorways and sat on rooftops and leaned out of windows. They gathered thick along the sidewalks and they jostled out onto the streets. Men and women. Old people and young. They wore dress suits and grocery store aprons, and uniforms from their school. Some along the route raised their fists in the Black Power salute as the cars rolled by. Others bowed their heads. Some called out Jackie's name and some stood silently, and some put a hand above their eyes like a visor and allowed tears to roll down their cheeks rather than interrupt the moment to wipe them away. The police estimated thirty thousand people along 125th Street, five thousand at the mouth of the Triboro Bridge, two thousand waiting at the graveyard. There was a time in many of these people's lives when Jackie Robinson carried the brightest light of hope.

From the pulpit, Jackson had described Robinson as "a rock in the water, hitting concentric circles and ripples of new possibility." An incoming rock disturbs the surface as well as the water below, and it rouses, too, the sediment on the water's floor. The smallest and most measurable indicators—the height and length of a rippling wave, say—can only suggest the larger impact. Before 1949, the year Jackie

Robinson hit .342 to lead all batters, no Black player—because of the history of exclusion—had finished among the top seven hitters in the National League. In 1972, the National League's top seven hitters were Billy Williams, Ralph Garr, Dusty Baker, César Cedeño, Bob Watson, Al Oliver, Lou Brock. You can look it up.

The condolence letters that arrived at Cascade Road were another measure, another small start. Wrote Ralph Abernathy: "Our nation in general and Black people in particular have lost a pioneer, a champion. . . . Jackie Robinson belonged not only to the Brooklyn Dodgers but to all Black and underprivileged people in America."

Ira Glasser began his letter, "Dear Mrs. Robinson: . . . I thought that perhaps you would like to know—insofar as I can explain—what it meant in the late forties and early fifties for a white boy to have a Black man as his hero," and he continued for pages on end. "We incorporated more than his style of play: to us, baseball was a metaphor of life, and there are many of us who have fought for what we believed the way he played baseball. Jackie Robinson gave us style, a stance with which to confront the world: recklessness when recklessness was least expected, intensity when others were beginning to relax, a sense of leadership and, perhaps most important and least appreciated, stamina to stay defeat and come back to win."

Aaron sent a telegram. This was one year, five months, and eleven days before he hit Al Downing's fastball over the left field wall in Atlanta. Aaron had gotten his start playing Negro league ball with the Indianapolis Clowns. "I share with you your grief upon the passing of a great American. Baseball and the Black athlete are the poorer because of his death. My own success in baseball has been in large measure because Jackie Robinson marked the trail well. May you and your family take consolation in knowing that he did so much for so many. —Henry Aaron."

At Cypress Hills Cemetery, six miles from the site of the first base bag at Ebbets Field, the teammates carried the casket from the hearse to the gravesite, and Robinson was lowered into the earth beside his son. Two burials in sixteen months. David stood beside the grave, and so did Robinson's siblings—Edgar, Mack, and Willa Mae all in from Pasadena. Neither Sharon nor Rachel got out of the car. This scene, Rachel knew, was more than she needed. She had held Jack as he lay in the hallway outside their room, and she had greeted mourners at the funeral home, and she had taken in the eulogy through her sense of disbelief. The many bells of the carillon rang and the voices of the choir sang as they'd left the Riverside Church.

She wanted to keep certain memories clear: Jack in his vibrancy, insistent, wry, purposeful. *My dearest Jack, my giant*, Rachel had thought on the morning he fell. Clouds had now moved in over Brooklyn—dark clouds in the reporter's words—and the larger group at the cemetery began to disperse and get into their cars. The loss, Rachel would say, felt unbearable, although she knew that she would bear it. She would allow herself to disappear for a time into grief and then she would emerge and she would go on. Lifted by her own implacable strength, buttressed as well by Jack's, she would begin to reassemble herself and build upon new notions and move forward with the rest of their lives.

APRIL 16, 2021

THE AFTERLIFE

Each January, at its airy, wood-floored main space in downtown Manhattan, the Jackie Robinson Foundation holds a drinks-and-canapés fundraising celebration pegged to Robinson's birthday. The ticketed event draws donors (actual and potential) as well as figures from the baseball and business and political worlds. Typically, the evening also honors a person with a connection to the foundation's principles. In 2012, the honoree, somewhat counterintuitively, was former Yankees owner George Steinbrenner, who posthumously received the foundation's Chairman Award for having "carried on the tradition of Jackie Robinson."

Although the Yankees were no friend to Robinson during his playing days, and Robinson had in the 1950s pointedly taken the Yankees to task for the team's galling reluctance to engage Black talent on the field or anywhere in its ranks, Steinbrenner had, over a thirty-seven-year ownership reign, beginning in 1973, been generous in charity and loyal to baseball people in need. The former Yankee Darryl Strawberry, an African American slugger whose career was derailed by drug use, was on hand that night in 2012 to express gratitude to "the Boss" for "sticking by me and pulling me up when no one else would."[33]

Several former ballplayers attended the event, including the Hall

---

33. A relevant note: In 1996, the Yankees' Bob Watson, a Steinbrenner hire, became the first African American general manager to win a World Series.

of Fame second baseman Joe Morgan, who had gripped Robinson's hand on the field in Cincinnati nine days before his death. Six-time big league All-Star Rusty Staub was on hand, as was the foundation's chair and former National League president Len Coleman. Yankees co-owner Hank Steinbrenner had come to accept the award on his father's behalf.

The light in the room, however, came from somewhere else: a woman in a black pantsuit, with shoulder-length gray hair and dangling earrings. She mingled unhurriedly, occasionally dispensing hugs to those she knew. Other guests kept looking toward her, angling to get close, to eavesdrop on her banter, to shake her hand, to take in her glow. She wore no name tag, for none was needed. To observe Rachel Robinson for any length of time that evening, and then to learn that she would soon turn ninety years old was akin to learning that, yes, in fact, cows can fly. She looked sixty-eight.

About an hour into the event, with patrons now seated at small tables or on leather chairs and divans arranged throughout, the conversation quieted and Morgan stepped to a lectern to emcee a short program. He noted that this was a year of significant milestones: sixty-five years since Jackie Robinson crossed the National League color line, fifty years since Robinson was inducted into the Baseball Hall of Fame, and forty years since his death. Coleman took a turn at the microphone and told of a trip he and Rachel had taken to Saratoga racetrack in the mid-2000s. Led by the trainer Nick Zito, Rachel walked along shed row, patting Thoroughbred noses along the way. When they reached the stall of Bellamy Rose, Zito's prized stallion who was owned by George Steinbrenner, the horse suddenly bucked forward and nipped at her. "Rachel did not miss a beat," said Coleman. "She pulled back her hand and said: 'Fifty years later, and the Yankees are still biting at me.'"

A few more people spoke—Strawberry as well as David Robinson, who had flown in from Tanzania, where he lived and ran a coffee farm—and then Morgan went up to the lectern once more. "Now," he said, "I have to formally introduce someone who is here tonight. You know that England has its queen, well . . . we have ours. The queen mother—Rachel Robinson."

At this, everyone in the room stood and applauded.

Rachel established the Jackie Robinson Foundation (JRF) in 1973, less than a year after Jackie's death, barely two years after Jackie Jr.'s fatal, single-car crash, and just months after the passing, at age seventy-nine, of her mother, Zellee. "My life, our family's life, was plunged into grief," Rachel said. "The foundation grew out of my mourning and my wish to hold on to [Jackie's] legacy, to continue our journey."

She laid the groundwork at the kitchen table of their home in Stamford. Morning light, and then afternoon light, reflected off the water at the base of the yard outside. Jackie's plaques still hung on the walls of the trophy room, his ties on a closet rack. Along with Rachel, the kitchen group included civil rights lawyer Franklin Williams, who had toured with Robinson doing NAACP work in the '50s; businessman Warren Jackson; and Marty Edelman, who had been Jackie's attorney. "The goal was to do something beyond a one-time event or monument," said Edelman, who remains on the foundation's board. "It needed to be something that could sustain itself and have a lasting impact."

"Jack and I were both very concerned about minority students getting higher education," said Rachel. "So that's where we wanted to steer it." The group decided to establish a scholarship program that would not only give money to help students attend college but also maintain a hands-on mentoring and leadership training program to help students through school once they got there. "What the Jackie Robinson Foundation became and what it is to this day," Edelman says, "is an outgrowth of the things we—and by 'we,' I really mean Rachel—were saying at that kitchen table."

The JRF awarded its first scholarship to Stamford high school student Debora Young, who would graduate from Boston College in 1978. "Rachel was right on top of me, being there to help, but getting tough to make sure I did what I had to do," says Young, who went on to a career in corporate public relations. "Over the years, we started calling her Mother Rachel."

Close to fifty years after its inception, the foundation has now provided for more than 1,900 students, including the roughly 220 JRF Scholars currently in school. Each receives yearly financial aid, as well as the mentoring. The foundation gets thousands of applications a year and accepts between fifty and seventy. Those selected are invariably from deeply disadvantaged backgrounds, and many are the first in their family to attend college. They follow a range of paths: a representative class could have students studying neurobiology at Harvard, film at Occidental, nuclear engineering at Texas A&M, economics at Yale. Dozens of companies provide sponsorship, among them Major League Baseball and individual teams. The most astonishing number is this: the foundation reports a graduation rate of roughly 98 percent.

"One big reason for that is the mentoring and the way the foundation supports you," says Reginald Livingston, who won a JRF scholarship in the 1990s, was a finance major at Georgetown, and became a commercial real estate agent in New York City. "In my years, we went to Rachel's house and sat with her and other members of the board. They listened to us, advised us, challenged us. The foundation opens you up to possibilities.

"But there's another reason why so many of us do well in school. When you apply for a scholarship, you make it your business to learn about Jackie Robinson. That leads you to learn about Rachel and the family. You understand what that family went through. Suddenly your problems in freshman econ don't seem as daunting."

Coleman, who chaired the foundation for nearly twenty years, added this: "Every kid in this program had the chance to meet and interact with Rachel. That may seem like a small piece, but it was not. They became part of the family. And then what are they going to do? No one wants to let down Rachel Robinson."

Through the decades after Jackie's death, Rachel achieved a singular balance, at once embracing the role of a great man's widow, guarding Robinson's legacy and gracefully expanding on it, while at the same time leading a self-directed and deeply impactful second journey centered on her work with the Jackie Robinson Foundation. Rachel's stature inside and outside of baseball—she dined with five presidents at the White House—stems from the significance of what she accomplished as well from her fine blend of diplomacy and moral conviction. At the foundation and in public life, she projects the traits that defined her when she was standing with Jackie, inspiring and often guiding him over their thirty-two years of courtship and marriage. This is the same woman who defied the WHITES ONLY sign above the airport water fountain during her first visit to the Jim Crow South in 1946, who steered the Robinsons through the cloaked and uncloaked prejudices of their suburban surroundings in the 1950s, who in the 1970s, when Yale recruited her to join its board, declined with conditions. "Not unless you hire another Black person or another woman," she said. "You won't get a twofer from me."

Rachel kept the foundation focused in a manner that her husband might not have. When it came to public and political matters, Jackie without question weighed in. He involved himself, dispatching his name, his thought, and his action to a range of issues around civil and human rights. Rachel, in the life afterward, less so.

Norman Siegel—a career civil rights lawyer and former head of the NYCLU who as a child in Brooklyn took the trolley to see Robinson play at Ebbets Field—has worked with the foundation since 1976. He recalls how over the years he often pushed to have the organization take on political and civil rights issues. Once he wanted to sue

Major League Baseball for its lack of minority representation in the front offices. Siegel believed he had a strong case and the JRF board was behind him. Rachel wasn't having it. "All along, I've wanted us to be focused—educating these young people to make a difference," she recalled. "I felt if we did one thing really well instead of spreading ourselves thin, that was our best chance at social change."

"Once the foundation was up and running, Rachel could have taken an honorary title, shown up a few times a year, and that might have been fine," said Siegel. "Instead she was the one who made things happen. She was so capable and intelligent, so diplomatic, that she commanded everyone's respect. We had a twelve-person board and everybody had a vote. But if the vote was eleven to one and that one was Rachel? Well, then it wasn't long before the voting quietly shifted her way. It wasn't that she forced her opinion on us, but more that we saw her view, and more often than not, we'd realize that Rachel, in her quiet, determined way, was right."[34]

Since 2004, the foundation, now with a full-time, twenty-person staff and scores of volunteers, has been led, and grown, by president

---

34. Siegel is another who has dedicated his professional life to civil rights in large part because of Robinson's impact. He recalls the thrill of sitting in the Ebbets Field bleachers, a place where shared joy and angst crossed racial bounds. The ballpark was far more integrated than his neighborhood in Borough Park. Along with Glasser and many others, Siegel cites Robinson's on-field excellence and approach as specific motivators. In 1951, after the Giants' Bobby Thomson hit the home run to beat the Dodgers for the National League pennant, Siegel noticed Robinson remained at his position and watched Thomson closely as he trotted around, making sure that he touched each base. "I saw that as an example of staying in it to the end. I tell my clients we'll be smart but we also have to have stamina, and I use that example." Siegel, whose numerous high-impact cases include work on behalf of families of those who died in the 9/11 attacks, attributes a defining realization to his connection to Robinson: "I saw that you can change the status quo," he says. "An individual can change the status quo." Siegel has photos of Robinson in action on the walls of his private law offices. Hanging at Siegel's home is a framed illustration of Robinson in the iconic sliding-into-home moment, right fist raised, Brooklyn cap flying off, dust circling the Dodgers logo across his chest. The face on the sliding body is not Robinson's, however, but Barack Obama's. The drawing, by Barry Blitt, first appeared in the *New Yorker* soon after the 2008 presidential election and is called "Safe at Home."

and CEO Della Britton. Yet well into the late 2010s—that is, into her nineties—Rachel went to the office regularly. She weighed in on major organizational decisions, answered some of the many letters that arrived expressly for her, and made fundraising calls. Photographs decorated her workspace: Rachel and Jackie on their wedding day; Rachel in the stands for Jackie's debut at Ebbets Field, infant Jackie Jr. bundled up on her lap; Jackie stealing home against the Yanks. The shelves held replicas of some of the hate mail and death threats that Jackie received, as well as pictures of him surrounded by throngs of white fans seeking his autograph. There were photos of the family together, the three children young; of Jackie picketing on behalf of the NAACP in the 1960s; of Jackie and Rachel with Martin Luther King Jr.; of Rachel, later on, dressed for an event alongside her grandchildren.

Rachel's favorite of the photographs shows her and Jackie in the late '60s at one of the great jazz concerts on the back lawn at Cascade Road. They are lying together, eyes half closed, smiling, blissful in each other's arms. Rachel continued to protect Jackie long after he was gone, determining the use of his name and likeness. It's why you've never seen an official Jackie Robinson bobblehead doll—despite suggestions by baseball and the Dodgers that they produce one. "If there's one thing that man always had, it was dignity," Rachel said not long after the foundation cocktail event in 2012. Then, smiling and jiggling her head in bobblehead fashion, she added, "I could not see Jack's head bouncing around like this."

Rachel felt determined that Jackie not be seen as a martyr, because for all the difficulty of their journey, theirs was finally a life of good fortune and welcome purpose. She tried to emphasize that message while advising on the Ken Burns's documentary *Jackie Robinson*, as well as on the 2013 feature film, *42*. "She did what she'd do whenever I'd give her a book I was writing," Sharon said, describing her mother's advisory approach. "She'd make a big pile of notes. She called them 'suggestions.'"

For many years, Rachel and Sharon were mainstays at Major League Baseball's annual Jackie Robinson Day, participating in ceremonies at a Mets or Dodgers game, fielding questions from reporters and fans. There was also a visit to Montreal in 1996, during which the Expos retired the number *20*, which Jackie had worn as a Royal fifty years before. The following year, fiftieth-anniversary events tied to 1947 abounded, and baseball retired Robinson's Dodgers *42* across the sport. When, in 2007, outfielder Ken Griffey Jr. appealed to then commissioner Bud Selig to be allowed to wear *42* as a one-day tribute on April 15—a notion that ultimately led to all major league players and coaches wearing the number on the historic date each year— Selig told Griffey he would get back to him. "Let me ask Rachel," Selig said.

For so many years, Rachel had remained extraordinarily hale. For her seventy-fifth birthday, in 1997, she and about a dozen family members—she has twelve grandchildren, two great-grandchildren, and three great-great-grandchildren—climbed to ten thousand feet on Mount Kilimanjaro. In 2010, at age eighty-eight, Rachel fell and broke her hip. She refused to do her walker-aided rehab in public, instead keeping near home. "If we had to go out in the wheelchair, she put on a scarf and sunglasses. She didn't want anyone to see her," says Sharon. Two months after the fall, Sharon coaxed Rachel to go to a restaurant in Connecticut. Sharon parked and went to the back of the car to get the wheelchair. "There was a walk and then a long ramp going up to the front door," Sharon recalls. "But she refused the chair. She hadn't walked anywhere yet. I said. 'Come on, Mom, there's no way you can walk.' She looked at me and said, 'I'm walking.' And she did."

"Two things she does not like," said Edelman a few years later. "She hates arrogance in anyone. And she can't stand weakness." Edelman, whom Rachel has called her best friend, remembered one day noticing that Rachel paid particular attention whenever an older person walked by with a stooped gait: "I asked what she was doing. She said she wanted to make sure she never walked that way. She said, 'It gives them a bad attitude. You've got to keep your back straight.'"

In March each year, the active Jackie Robinson Foundation scholars—upwards of two hundred—came to New York for a four-day mentoring and leadership conference. Of the qualities and prerequisites needed to win a JRF scholarship—high academic achievement, financial need, the potential to lead—the most important is a commitment to give back to the community. Students are awarded grants for programs they have developed. At a luncheon during the conference in that milestone year of 2012, students from Northwestern, UCLA, and Syracuse were given grants for starting, respectively, an inner-city baseball academy, a guardian program for foster children, and an action council to fight gang activity. Rachel often said that her hope was not simply for people to know Jackie Robinson but to find something in him to emulate and aspire to as well.

At that same conference luncheon, held in a hotel ballroom filled with some four hundred scholars and alumni, none of whom had been born the day that Jackie Robinson died, Rachel was again introduced from a dais. The young people, just like the men and women of other generations who had applauded at the foundation's fundraising event two months before, rose and cheered, whooped and stomped, rattled their chairs. Even when Rachel, beaming but demure, bade them to stop, they would not. They kept up the noise, a great crowd of students, all of them on their way to somewhere, thanking her, the queen mother, for all she had done.

IN PRESENT MEMORY

To coincide with Jackie Robinson Day in 2021, more than a dozen major league players wrote "letters" to Robinson, which ran on Major League Baseball's website. "Dear Jackie" or "Dear Mr. Robinson," the letters began. "I aspire to be like Number 42, to leave this game and society better than when I found it," wrote Triston McKenzie, a rookie pitcher for Cleveland. Said Seattle Mariners outfielder Taylor Trammell, also a rookie: "Jackie Robinson is more than my favorite player, he's one of my heroes. . . . For him to withstand all of the hate and to be able to perform at a Hall of Fame level day in and day out is truly astonishing."

"Thank you for persisting against all odds and all prejudice," wrote the Tampa Bay Rays' thirty-four-year-old right-hander Collin McHugh. "Thank you for carrying on the work of generations before you, and empowering every generation of players to come." Added Mariners shortstop J. P. Crawford: "Man, what has Jackie Robinson meant to me. . . . First off, without him I probably wouldn't even be born. My parents are biracial."

Recent years have witnessed a resurgence in the recognition and understanding of Robinson and his legacy. The perception of his story—influenced in part by the contained (and beautifully unspooled) film narrative of *42*—tends to emphasize Robinson's self-restraint during his early days in the National League, his largely nonreactive approach to hate and intimidation that runs in a continuum with the nonviolent methods of Martin Luther King Jr. That's a crucial, even indispensable, part of Robinson's path and lasting message, although his later on-field aggressiveness and his outspokenness are perhaps the clearer representation of the man and his approach.

As Crawford's letter implies, Robinson's impact, still now, seventy-five years later, slips well beyond the boundaries of the game. It has been increasingly so recognized. *United States History*, perhaps the best-regarded textbook for the Advanced Placement high school course on the subject, covers a timeline from 1491 to present day. A resource for tens of thousands of college-bound students each year, the book tends to boil things brightly to their essence. In its recent Third Edition, the section titled "The Civil Rights Movement" begins with a subsection, "Origins of the Movement," which in turn begins: "The baseball player Jackie Robinson had broken the color line in 1947 by being hired by the Brooklyn Dodgers as the first African American to play on a major league team since the 1880s." The integration of the armed forces and the introduction of civil rights legislation followed soon after Robinson, today's sixteen-year-olds learn. And then, the 1950s.

Robinson's critical importance links, of course, to race relations and Black Americans, specifically to the mid-twentieth-century battle for an end to legal segregation. The lessons from his work, however, like lessons from other pioneers and activists, extend naturally to other contexts and to other groups who have been discriminated against, brutalized, or not accepted. That reach explains the avid and still lasting connection between Jackie Robinson and certain precincts of the Jewish community in America. From the very start, Robinson's relationships with fellow superstar Hank Greenberg and with teammate Sandy Koufax, both of whom tasted the hard salt of bigotry through their careers, ran deeper than ballpark camaraderie. Robinson played his first game for the Montreal Royals less than a year after the last concentration camps in Europe were liberated.

In 1960, Carl Erskine's son Jimmy was born with Down syndrome. "There is no doubt in my mind that what Jackie did to break down barriers helped Jimmy to lead a better life," Erskine said in 2020. "It feeds into a larger theme of people looking past their ignorance and being open to those who are different than they are." As Erskine wrote in his 2005 book, *What I Learned from Jackie Robinson*: "Jackie changed the way people view each other." He added that, in the parallels between Jimmy and Jackie, "there is an exclusion aspect similar to both experiences. They were both excluded, left out of the mainstream and denied access to public places and opportunities."

After the NBA player Jason Collins came out as gay in 2013, *USA Today* published a column titled: "Jason Collins Walks in Robinson's

Path." Analogies between Robinson and LGBTQ pioneers have proved commonplace—an analogy imperfect in its details, but analogous nonetheless.

In the classic, autobiographical 1984 children's story, *In the Year of the Boar and Jackie Robinson,* the Chinese-born American writer Bette Bao Lord amplifies the similarities between the experiences of a newly arrived immigrant girl from China, and the girl's hero, Jackie Robinson. Inspired by Robinson, Lord's protagonist negotiates the challenges of fitting in with a new culture without letting go of her roots.

"There are social and economic aspects unique to each form of discrimination—whether it's denying rights for Black people, for immigrants, for women, for religious groups, for the disabled, for gay people," says Ira Glasser. "But at a certain base level, it's not that different. It's all the same awful shit."

Hundreds of major leaguers donated their 2021 Jackie Robinson Day salary to the Players Alliance, a nonprofit organization of current and former ballplayers, which aims to improve Black representation in baseball and to aid Black communities. In Los Angeles that day, more than seventy-five Dodgers personnel, including the players and coaches in their *42* uniforms, gathered around a seven-hundred-pound statue of Robinson, in mid-slide, which presides near the stadium's main entrance. "We all know Jackie Robinson the name, the *42* in every ballpark, but we were just trying to give context on his life," manager Dave Roberts, who addressed the team at the statue, later told reporters. "His legacy, and what he meant, not only to people of color, in baseball, outside of baseball. Being treated fairly, being respected, not always being liked, but being determined in doing and saying and fighting for what's right."

The roster of memorials and physical tributes to Robinson, long present, has swelled in recent years. UCLA's Jackie Robinson Stadium, which opened in 1981, was a site of controversy, and harsh irony, after police used it as a "field jail" to detain Black Lives Matter protesters in June of 2020. (The university publicly condemned the incident.) Since 1997, an oversized bust of Robinson (and of his brother Mack, an Olympian) has occupied a greenspace across from Pasadena City Hall. A larger-than-life statue of Robinson and Pee Wee Reese stands outside the Brooklyn Cyclones minor league ballpark in Coney Island. The twelve-acre Jackie Robinson Park in Harlem, an official New York City landmark, completed a $4.7 million renovation in 2020. A statue depicting a scene of Robinson handing a baseball to a child stands near Olympic Park in Montreal—a city that in 2011 authorized the affixing of a plaque to the outer wall of the apartment where Jackie and Rachel lived in 1946. For thirty years, a sculpture made from the same mold as the piece in Montreal has graced the entrance to Daytona Beach's Jackie Robinson Ballpark—known as City Island Park when Robinson played there—which is now the oldest extant stadium in the minor leagues. Grady County, Georgia, marks Robinson's birthplace with commemorative signage, and has named not only a high school ball field but also ten miles of Georgia Highway 93 in his honor. Jersey City. Stamford. Cooperstown. Robinson representation is everywhere, symbols of courage and arc-bending.

In 2021, League 42, an eight-year-old baseball organization for urban children aged five to fourteen, unveiled outside its home field in Wichita a bronze, life-size Jackie Robinson—bat on his right shoulder, left arm akimbo. At about the same time, the Double-A Tulsa Drillers revealed an enormous Robinson mural painted opposite their ballpark in North Tulsa's Greenwood District, the affluent Black community that was terrorized in the Tulsa Race Massacre of 1921. A monument depicting the April 18, 1946, home plate handshake between Robinson and teammate George Shuba went up in Youngstown, Ohio, in the summer of '21. Pennsylvania legislators Stephen Kinsey, a Democrat, and Greg Rothman, a Republican, included in a wider effort toward bipartisanship, a joint introduction of a resolution for the state to honor Robinson. The NAACP's Jackie Robinson Sports Award honors athletes who "promote social justice through creative endeavors" and in 2021 went to the Golden State Warriors' Stephen Curry and the WNBA Players Association. Jackie Robinson Day has been celebrated, with official government ceremonies and with youth baseball clinics, in Romania and Uganda.

Robinson's brothers, Edgar and Mack, lived to the ages of eighty-four and eighty-five respectively. Had Jackie achieved that longevity, he would have seen both progress and setbacks in the continued fight for civil rights. He would have seen a Black manager win the World Series. He would have seen Rodney King and Amadou Diallo. He would not have lived long enough to witness the election of Barack Obama or the killings of George Floyd and Breonna Taylor and the widespread protests and sustained outrage that followed. "People have asked me, 'What would Jackie say about all this and this period of time?'" said Yohuru Williams in the summer of 2020. Williams is the distinguished chair and professor at the University of St. Thomas and served as the Jackie Robinson Foundation's chief historian from 2012 to 2014. "Honestly, I don't know. You couldn't pin him down. I see that as a point of genius in his personality. He spoke out against police brutality, and there's no question he would have been with the overall Black Lives Matter movement. But would he have supported something like 'defund the police'? That's hard to say. Jackie was on his own journey to what he believed, an independent broker."

Williams's essay, "I've Got to Be Me," in which he explores Robinson's "twoness"—a phrase taken from W. E. B. Du Bois's observation of the sometimes "warring ideals" within someone driven by their perspective as both a Black person and an American—is among the highlights of the excellent 2020 essay collection, *42 Today*, edited by Michael G. Long. "What I do know is that Jack would have been saying something," Williams added. "He would have been speaking truth to power—he was never uncomfortable about that, and he was never uncomfortable about using his celebrity to influence political action."

Gerald Early makes the point that Robinson was "true to his own contradictions, which a lot of people are not. We all have contradictions. Very few of us fit into a neat box of ideas and values if we really challenge ourselves. But many people swallow those contradictions as a way to belong to a larger group. Robinson didn't necessarily do that. He wouldn't likely be doing that now."

"I think about Jackie Robinson and the Robinson family probably every single day," says Nichol Whiteman, CEO of the Dodgers Foundation, the team's nonprofit, focused on social justice. In 1994, Whiteman earned a scholarship from the Jackie Robinson Foundation. She went to Spelman, became her family's first college graduate, and later, as part of her career trajectory, oversaw the Los Angeles office of the JRF. "I think of Jackie in terms of pure perseverance and resilience, of being a leader who uses his voice for others," Whiteman continues. "That inspires me. He was not conventional, neither in thought nor in action. If you are thinking, 'What would Jackie do?' you don't think conventionally. He was prepared to react spontaneously—to make a move in much the same way that he played baseball. Think about what might make a difference and be willing to just go, to move with your gut."

The property has been long since divided and the house number changed, but the home on Cascade Road still stands, its foundation and central structure intact. The approach. The stone cellar. The forested edges of the sloping backyard. Fox. Deer. Wild turkey. "We see an eagle sometimes," says Viviani Kulig, who has lived there with her family since 2016. She and her husband call the island in the pond Jimmy's Island, because their son likes to paddle out to it and explore. An old willow leans near the pond's main shore at the base of the lawn, and each spring a local librarian comes to the home, with Kulig's blessing, and gathers a first-grade class beneath the tree and reads to them Sharon Robinson's *Testing the Ice*, about the time Jackie shook off his fear and went out onto the frozen pond for the kids. "It still freezes over sometimes," Kulig says. "But not as much." Soon after moving in, she learned of the jazz benefits the Robinsons used to host on the lawn. Keeping to that spirit, she and her husband have for a few years hosted a late-summer "garden party" with more than a hundred guests, raising money for the charity Fraternity Without Borders.

The Robinson family plot at Cypress Hills Cemetery is itself shaded by old trees, as well as a low, abutting pine. A heavy hedge runs alongside the plot, and two smaller hedges, too, and within the space a pair of simple stone benches, each with room for two or perhaps three people to sit. A German couple named Tonn rests in the adjacent gravesite, and near to that an Italian family, the Torchios. Next comes the Weiner tomb, impressed with a Star of David, and just across the path rise headstones of numerous Chinese families and individuals: Hong Zuo Mei, Wong. Examples of a multicultural Brooklyn. The larger roadway that many drivers travel to get to the cemetery—a road first cut in 1870 and for most of the twentieth century known as the Interboro—was renamed the Jackie Robinson Parkway in 1997.

At the Robinson gravesite, visitors come upon the individual footstones as well as a taller marker, engraved with Jackie's famous epitaph, A LIFE IS NOT IMPORTANT EXCEPT IN THE IMPACT IT HAS ON OTHER LIVES, and his signature. Bats lean against this larger stone, and a hill of baseballs crowd at its base. Ball caps. A few handwritten notes. A small American flag planted in the grass. Some of the tendered items show weathering—baseballs split at their seams, bats waterlogged and cracked. But new offerings regularly appear, especially around significant days. Arriving to the site on April 16, 2021, for example, one found fresh flowers, both potted and loose, as well as a baseball inscribed with *Thanks Jackie 4-14-21*. Also at the grave that day: a black leather catcher's mitt, still with the new-glove smell. A leather luggage tag hooked to the mitt contained a black-and-white photograph of a man wearing partial catcher's gear, standing with his right arm cocked, and looking straight into the camera. The stenciling on the back of the tag read: JACKIE ROBINSON. WE MET ON 6.16.47. I WAS A CATCHER REPRESENTING THE TY COBBS AT EBBETS FIELD. THAT WAS A DAY. MIKE DESOLA.

There are those who still remember Jackie Robinson in the prime and flush of his monumental life, the brilliant summers of the late 1940s and the early 1950s when Robinson was a Brooklyn Dodger, purposeful and magnificent on the diamond, a minor god descended, a hero to these young people through and through. They adopted his pigeon-toed gait and replicated his stance in the batter's box and jounced daringly off every base.

"On our youth team, the code to steal was 'Jackie Robinson,'" says Steve Reece, who grew up in Avondale, a neighborhood in Cincinnati. Reece's recollections of Robinson are different from some of the other accounts that have been passed down from that city. "When Brooklyn and Jackie Robinson came to Cincinnati, we were all Dodger fans. We would put on our good clothes and we would get ready. We'd pack a lunch, and then we were gone. We were on our way." Reece took the bus to Crosley Field with his father and brother, and sometimes a couple of other kids from the neighborhood. Mr. Reece worked as a mail handler at the post office, and all throughout the year, he would put away a little something here and there for exactly this day, to take his children to see Robinson: tickets, bus ride, maybe a souvenir. "We'd get to Crosley Field way before the game started, and it was like a holiday out there! We saw people walking along the road to get there, and then church buses full of folks pulling in." People traveled up from the South, too, on those days, from places like Memphis and Mobile, a day and a half by train.

The Reeces sat on the right field side at Crosley, about eight rows up from the grass, and the boys kept to their seats all game, well behaved and rapt. All the rows in the section leaned forward when Robinson came to bat. They watched him in the field. They watched him on the basepaths. "I can see him out there now," says Reece, his voice rising with the memory—in the way that Ivan Livingstone's and Mitzi Melnick's voices rose as they thought back to the times in Montreal; the way that Ronny Glassman would suddenly laugh while telling about Ebbets Field; the way a light would spring to Ira Glasser's eyes as he spoke.

"Jackie Robinson!" Reece continues. "It felt to us like he was in control of everything that was going on out there on the baseball field. You would leave the park that day and you couldn't wait to get to whatever was in your life. You felt like you could do anything you wanted to do, beat anyone. I don't know if I can properly explain what it was like to have Jackie Robinson at that time, how much it meant." Sometimes before the start of an inning, Robinson would jog over near that area of the Crosley Field stands and take off his hat and wave toward the crowd in greeting. In acknowledgment.

Reece built a business for himself, and a long career. He raised a strong family, three kids. He set up benefit concerts in the inner city. He worked for the mayor of Cincinnati. He served on the board of Rainbow/PUSH. He played some sports. Reece still watches baseball these days, a few games a week. He feels that he was lucky to have seen Jackie Robinson play as a young man, and he says he carries that feeling with him wherever he goes, as others do, and he knows that he always will.

"Jack is with me every day, of course. Always," said Rachel Robinson, standing in her office at the Jackie Robinson Foundation in 2016. "What sometimes amazes me is that I still get so many letters from people saying what he meant to them. Here we are, it's sixty years after Jack played his last baseball game. From the very beginning of our time, we understood we were part of something extraordinary and important. But to be getting letters now, some of them from parents and grandparents talking about what they are passing on to their children and grandchildren—I can't say we would have expected that."

ACKNOWLEDGMENTS

To Jackie Robinson's immediate family, Rachel Robinson, Sharon Robinson, and David Robinson. I'm indebted for the talks, exchanges, and time spent in various contexts at various points over the years. Those interactions, most extensively with Rachel, helped to inform the book throughout.

As relates to Montreal, I'm grateful for Dan Ziniuk—reporter, suggester, connector, even translator—for his invaluable work. Also in and around Montreal, enormous thanks to the remarkable Ivan Livingstone and the inspiring Mitzi Melnick, to Charles Este, Glenn Gunning, Arnie Lechter, and to Saint-Jean-sur-Richelieu's Claude Raymond, along with others, for their memories and stories from a time and a place. Thank you to my former colleague and continued friend Michael Farber for his pointing and smarts at the outset, and thanks as well to Jack Jedwab, Mitch Melnick, Marcel Dugas, Matthew Ross, Tim Burke, and Annakin Slayd (whose song, with Leesa Mackey, also provided a sweet soundtrack). I was lucky for the assistance of Scott Crawford at the Canadian Baseball Hall of Fame and Andrew North at the Centre for Canadian Baseball Research.

Among the ballplayers who shared insight valuable to various aspects of the book, special thanks to Bob Aspromonte, Ralph Branca, Lou Brock, Dom DiMaggio, Carl Erskine, Jerry Koosman, Joe Morgan, Darryl Strawberry, and Ralph Terry. Also from within the baseball world: Fred Claire, Leonard Coleman, Mike McDermott, and Branch Rickey III.

Anyone benefits from examining things with Ira Glasser. Thank you, Ira, for your thoughts and insights and time. Big thanks as well to Sol Gittleman, Ronald Glassman, Danny Greenberg, Alan Levine, Alice Miller, Art Ostrove, Mitchell Ostrove, and Larry Raphael. To Vivi Kulig and Barbara Smith in Stamford. And special appreciation to Norman Siegel and to Tom Villante.

For the later years, my thanks go out to Steve Reece and Jack Greiner as well as to John Erardi and Bob Crotty.

For generously devoting both time and thought in our discussions, many thanks to Gerald Early, Yohuru Williams, and Nicole Whiteman.

Thank you to NYU's Vince Gennaro, for his leadership and his baseball acumen. Also at NYU, I am grateful to Daniel G. Kelly and Bri Newland.

At the Jackie Robinson Foundation, big thanks to Damian Travier as well as to La'Tonya Johnson, Cecilia Marshall, Mireille Stephen, and the foundation's president, Della Britton.

No one researches alone. At the Baseball Hall of Fame, thank you to the master Bill Francis, and also to Jim Gates, Roger Lansing, and Cassidy Lent, as well as Tim Wiles. Also a hearty cap tip to the Dodgers' Joe Jareck, Mark Langill, and Jon Chapper, the Yankees' Michael Margolis, and the Mets' Jay Horwitz and Ethan Wilson. From the extraordinary team at MLB Network, special thanks to Micah Karg and Nate Purinton. Thank you to Donnali Fifield for the connection on Branch Rickey, and thanks to the team at the Larchmont Public Library, in particular Liam Hegerty.

A quiet and appreciative salute to those who spoke with me or helped steer me but asked not to be mentioned by name.

Thank you to my colleagues at Dotdash Meredith, in particular to Stephen Orr for his words of guidance and to Jeremy Biloon, who'll be a baseball GM someday.

In this book as my others, I am beyond grateful for the partnership and wisdom of my literary agent, Andrew Blauner. At St. Martin's Press, thank you to George Witte, a wonderful editor and superb reader. I, and this book, are lucky to have him. Thank you to the deeply helpful Kevin Reilly and Brigitte Dale, to Jen Enderlin for supporting the book, and to Athena Lark and Eliani Torres for making it better.

To Kathrin Perutz, the guiding light who took me to my first ballgame and first told me about Jackie Robinson, and to Michael Studdert-Kennedy for his clear eyes and warm counsel. I wish you both were here.

Amy, Sonya, Maya: My inspiration, my motivation, my everything.

SELECTED BIBLIOGRAPHY

BOOKS

Baldwin, James. *Collected Essays*. New York: Library of America, 1998.

Barber, Red, and Robert Creamer. *Rhubarb in the Catbird Seat*. Lincoln: University of Nebraska Press, 1968.

Black, Martha Jo, with Chuck Schoffner. *Joe Black*. Chicago: Academy Chicago, 2015.

Branca, Ralph, with David Ritz. *A Moment in Time*. New York: Scribner, 2011.

Branch, Taylor. *Parting the Waters*. New York: Simon & Schuster, 1988.

Brown, William. *Baseball's Fabulous Montreal Royals*. Montreal: Robert Davies, 1959.

Carrier, Roch, and Sheldon Cohen (illustrations). *The Hockey Sweater*. Toronto: Tundra Books, 1999

Carson, Clayborne, ed. *The Autobiography of Martin Luther King Jr.* New York: Grand Central, 1988.

Clavin, Tom, and Danny Peary. *Gil Hodges*. New York: New American Library, 2012.

Connor, Anthony J. *Baseball for the Love of It*. New York: Macmillan, 1982.

Elliot, Richard. *Clem Labine.* New York: Page Publishing, 2015.

Ellison, Ralph. *Invisible Man.* New York: Random House, 1952.

Erskine, Carl. *What I Learned from Jackie Robinson.* New York: McGraw-Hill, 2005.

Falkner, David. *Great Time Coming.* New York: Touchstone, 1996.

Fischler, Stan. *Confessions of a Trolley Dodger from Brooklyn.* Flushing, NY: H & M Productions, 1995.

Gates, Henry Louis, Jr. *Stony the Road.* New York: Penguin Books, 2020.

Goodman, Walter. *The Committee.* New York: Farrar, Straus and Giroux, 1964.

Golenbock, Peter. *Bums.* Mineola, New York: Dover Publications, 1984.

Gravenor, Kristian. *Montreal 375.* Montreal: Megaforcemedia, 2017.

Halberstam, David. *Summer of '49.* New York: HarperPerennial, 1989.

Halberstam, David. *The Fifties.* New York: Random House, 1993.

Harris, Middleton A., with the assistance of Morris Levitt, Roger Furman, and Ernest Smith. *The Black Book.* New York: Random House, 1974.

Henry, Ed. *42 Faith.* New York: HarperCollins, 2017.

James, Bill, and Rob Neyer. *The Neyer/James Guide to Pitchers.* New York: Fireside, 2004.

Jedwab, Jack. *Jackie Robinson's Unforgettable Summer of Baseball in Montreal.* Montreal: Editions Images, 1996.

Kahn, Roger. *The Boys of Summer.* New York: Harper & Row, 1972.

Kahn, Roger. *Rickey & Robinson.* New York: Rodale, 2014.

Kashatus, William C. *Jackie & Campy.* Lincoln: University of Nebraska Press, 2014.

King, Larry, with Marty Appel. *When You're from Brooklyn, Everything Else Is Tokyo.* New York: Little, Brown, 1992.

Lacoursiere, Jacques, and Robin Philpot. *A People's History of Quebec.* Montreal: Baraka Books, 2002.

Lamb, Chris. *Blackout.* Lincoln: University of Nebraska Press, 2004.

Lamb, Chris. *Conspiracy of Silence.* Lincoln: University of Nebraska Press, 2012.

Lanctot, Neil. *Negro League Baseball.* Philadelphia: University of Pennsylvania Press, 2004.

Langill, Mark. *Dodgertown.* Charleston, SC: Arcadia, 2004.

Levine, Marc V. *The Reconquest of Montreal: Language Policy and Social Change in a Bilingual City.* Philadelphia: Temple University Press, 1990.

Long, Michael G., ed. *First Class Citizenship.* New York: Henry Holt, 2007.

Long, Michael G., ed. *42 Today.* New York: New York University Press, 2021.

MacLennan, Hugh. *Two Solitudes.* Toronto: New Canadian Library, 2008.

Mailer, Norman. *Harlot's Ghost.* New York: Random House, 1991.

Mann, Arthur. *The Jackie Robinson Story.* New York: Grosset & Dunlap, 1950.

Malta, Vince. *Louisville Slugger: A Complete Reference Guide.* Concord, CA: Black Diamond Publications, 2007.

Margolian, Howard. *Unauthorized Entry: The Truth about Nazi War Criminals in Canada 1946–1956.* Toronto: University of Toronto Press, 2000.

Markson, David. *Reader's Block.* Dallas: Dalkey Archive, 1996.

McGee, Bob. *The Greatest Ballpark Ever.* New Brunswick, NJ: Rutgers University Press, 2005.

Myrdal, Gunnar. *An American Dilemma.* New Brunswick, NJ: Harper & Row, 1944.

Naze, David. *Reclaiming 42.* Lincoln: University of Nebraska Press, 2019.

Newman, John J., and John M. Schmallback. *United States History.* Logan, IA: Perfection Learning, 2019.

Paper, Lew. *Perfect.* New York: New American Library, 2009.

Peary, Daniel. *Jackie Robinson in Quotes.* Salem, MA: Page Street, 2016.

Posnanski, Joe. *The Soul of Baseball.* New York: William Morrow, 2007.

Purcell, Susan, and Brian McKenna. *Jean Drapeau.* Toronto: Clarek Irwin, 1980.

Rampersad, Arnold. *Jackie Robinson.* New York: Alfred A. Knopf, 1997.

Reed, Ted. *Carl Furillo.* Jefferson, NC: McFarland, 2011.

Reiser, Jim. *Black Writers/Black Baseball.* Jefferson, NC: McFarland, 2007.

Richler, Mordecai. *The Apprenticeship of Duddy Kravitz.* New York: Simon & Schuster, 1959.

Richler, Mordecai. *St. Urbain's Horsemen.* New York: Alfred A. Knopf, 1971.

Rigueur, Leah Wright. *The Loneliness of the Black Republican.* Princeton, NJ: Princeton University Press, 2014.

Robinson, Jackie. *My Own Story.* USA: Allegro Editions, 1948.

Robinson, Jackie. *Baseball Has Done It.* Brooklyn: IG, 1964.

Robinson, Jackie. *I Never Had It Made.* New York: HarperCollins, 1995 (1972).

Robinson, Rachel, with Lee Daniels. *Jackie Robinson: An Intimate Portrait.* New York: Harry N. Adams, 1996.

Robinson, Sharon. *Stealing Home.* New York: HarperPerennial, 1997.

Robinson, Sharon. *Promises to Keep.* New York: Scholastic, 2004.

Robinson, Sharon. *The Hero Two Doors Down.* New York: Scholastic, 2016.

Robinson, Sharon. *Child of the Dream.* New York: Scholastic, 2019.

Robinson, Sharon, and E. B. Lewis. *Jackie's Gift.* New York: Viking, 2010.

Robinson, Sharon, and Kadir Nelson. *Testing the Ice.* New York: Scholastic, 2009.

Rossi, John P. *Baseball and American Culture.* Lanham, MD: Rowman & Littlefield, 2018.

Rowan, Carl T., with Jackie Robinson. *Wait Till Next Year.* New York: Random House, 1960.

Schoor, Gene. *The Pee Wee Reese Story.* New York: Julian Messner, 1962.

Shakespeare, William. *King Lear.* New York: Penguin, 1958.

Shapiro, Michael. *The Last Good Season.* New York: Doubleday, 2003.

Shuba, George "Shotgun," as told to Greg Gulas. *My Memories as a Brooklyn Dodger.* USA: George Shuba Family Enterprises, 2007.

Snider, Duke, with Bill Gilbert. *The Duke of Flatbush.* New York: Kensington, 1988.

Spink, J. G. Taylor. *Baseball Official Guide, 1956.* St. Louis: Charles C. Spink & Son/ The Sporting News, 1956.

Terry, Ralph, with John Wooley. *Right Down the Middle.* Tulsa: Muellerhaus, 2016.

Theoharis, Jeanne. *The Rebellious Life of Mrs. Rosa Parks.* Boston: Beacon Press, 2013.

Tygiel, Jules. *Baseball's Great Experiment.* New York: Oxford University Press, 1983.

Tygiel, Jules. *Extra Bases.* Lincoln: University of Nebraska Press, 2002.

Virtue, John. *South of the Color Barrier.* Jefferson, NC: McFarland, 2008.

Weintraub, Robert. *The Victory Season.* Boston: Little, Brown, 2013.

Weintraub, William. *City Unique.* Toronto: Robin Brass Studio, 1996.

Wilson, August. *Fences.* New York: Plume, 1991.

Winks, Robin W. *The Blacks in Canada*. Montreal: McGill-Queen's University Press, 1997.

X, Malcolm, as told to Alex Haley. *The Autobiography of Malcolm X*. New York: Ballantine Books, 2015 (1964).

Zirin, Dave. *What's My Name, Fool?* Chicago: Haymarket Books, 2005.

AUDIO AND VIDEO

42. Director: Brian Helgeland. Producer: Thomas Tull. Warner Bros. Pictures, 2013.

Ghosts of Flatbush. Writers: Aaron Cohen, Charles Olivier. Producers: Ezra Edelman, Amani Martin. HBO, 2007.

Jackie Robinson. Directors: Ken Burns, Sarah Burns, David McMahon. Producers: Ken Burns, Sarah Burns, David McMahon. Florentine Films, 2016.

The Jackie Robinson Story. Director: Alfred E. Green. Producers: Mort Briskin, William J. Heineman. Eagle-Lion Films, 1950.

Radio Broadcasts: 1949 World Series Games 1–7; 1955 World Series Game 7; 1956 World Series Games 1–6.

Miscellaneous video/home movie clips: 1946, 1947 1949, 1956.

ARTICLES, PAPERS, AND PUBLICATIONS

Als, Hilton. "Toni Morrison and the Ghosts in the House." *New Yorker*, October 17, 2003.

"The Brooklyn Juggler." *Newsweek*, September 23, 1956.

Black, William R. "How Watermelons Became a Racist Trope." *Atlantic*, December 14, 2014.

Crichton, Kyle. "Hot Tamale Circuit." *Collier's*, June 22, 1946.

Curran, Peggy. "Life Beyond the Two Solitudes." *Montreal Gazette*, April 7, 2004.

Duckett, Alfred. "The Tragic and Triumphant Untold Story of the American Family Robinson." *Sepia*, January, 1973.

Fifield, June H. "Branch Rickey's Day of Decisions." *Whitman College FiftyPlus News*, Summer 2013.

Meany, Tom. "Jackie's One of the Gang." *Sport*, August, 1949.

"Mexican Baseball." *LIFE*, March 11, 1946.

Williams, Dorothy W. "The Jackie Robinson Myth: Social Mobility and Race in Montreal." A Thesis in the Department of History. Concordia University, 1999.

Additional magazine references: *Ebony, Look, Life, Jet, Newsweek, Sports Illustrated, The Sporting News, Time.*

NEWSPAPERS

Afro-American, Alabama Tribune, Atlanta Daily World, Baltimore Sun, Boston Globe, Brooklyn Eagle, Chicago Defender, Cincinnati Enquirer, (Louisville) *Courier-Journal,* (New York) *Daily News, Fort-Worth Star Telegram, Hartford Courant, Le Petit Journal, Los Angeles Times, Miami Herald, Montreal Gazette, New York Amsterdam News, New York Post, New York Times, Philadelphia Inquirer, Pittsburgh Courier, Pittsburgh Post-Gazette,* (Bergen County) *Record,* (Rochester) *Democrat and Chronicle, Scranton Tribune, Stamford Advocate,* (Syracuse) *Post-Standard, La Presse, Washington Post.*

INDEX